AF270309

The Anthropological Lens

The Anthropological Lens

Rethinking E. E. Evans-Pritchard

CHRISTOPHER MORTON

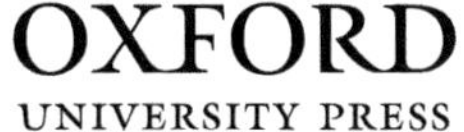

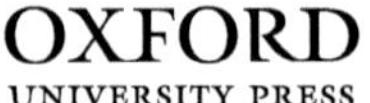

Great Clarendon Street, Oxford, OX2 6DP,
United Kingdom

Oxford University Press is a department of the University of Oxford.
It furthers the University's objective of excellence in research, scholarship,
and education by publishing worldwide. Oxford is a registered trade mark of
Oxford University Press in the UK and in certain other countries

Published in the United States of America by Oxford University Press
198 Madison Avenue, New York, NY 10016, United States of America

British Library Cataloguing in Publication Data
Data available

Library of Congress Control Number: 2019947000

ISBN 978–0–19–881291–3

Printed and bound by
CPI Group (UK) Ltd, Croydon, CR0 4YY

Acknowledgements

When I began research on E. E. Evans-Pritchard in 2003 as part of an Arts and Humanities Research Council-funded project on the Pitt Rivers Museum's South Sudan collections, I little imagined that I would write a book such as this. I owe its existence to the two colleagues who spearheaded that project, Jeremy Coote and Elizabeth Edwards, whose encouragement and support I will always be deeply grateful for. The research formed the basis of a subsequent postdoctoral fellowship at the University of Oxford funded by the Higher Education Funding Council for England, during which time some of the ideas I explore in this book were first published. A section of chapter 2 was published in the *History of Anthropology Newsletter* (2007); chapter 3 is based on an essay first published in a volume that I edited with Elizabeth Edwards, *Photography, Anthropology and History: Expanding the Frame* (2009); chapter 4 is a reworked version of some ideas first published in *Photography in Africa: Ethnographic Perspectives* (2012) edited by Richard Vokes; parts of chapter 5 are based on an article I published in the journal *Visual Anthropology* in 2005, and chapter 7 is based on another article published in *Visual Anthropology* in 2009. All of the photographs reproduced are from the collections of the Pitt Rivers Museum, University of Oxford, unless otherwise stated, and I am grateful to the museum for permission to reproduce them.

After a detour to work on other topics, this book began to take shape during a Leverhulme Fellowship in 2016, and I am very grateful to the Leverhulme Trust for their essential support. I am indebted to many friends and colleagues in Oxford and elsewhere for their help, encouragement, as well as critical feedback over the years, that have shaped the work in many ways, including Perez Achieng, Ahmed Al-Shahi, Angelo Beda, Dominic Byatt, Zoe Cormack, John Evans-Pritchard, Philip Grover, Wendy James, Jok Madut Jok, Douglas Johnson, Patti Langton, Alexander Maitland for permission to reproduce the contents of letters to Sir Wilfred Thesiger, Mike O'Hanlon, Gilbert Oteyo, Katherine Rose, Bruce Ross-Smith, David Shankland, André Singer, Richard Vokes. This book is for Catherine, Blake, and Conrad.

Table of contents

List of illustrations

1

Photographs are to think with

Historicizing anthropology

This book is a new perspective on probably the most important British anthropologist of the twentieth century; new because I take his photography as a starting point to rethink the way in which his fieldwork experiences and encounters shaped his work. I examine his photographs, but say little about him as a photographer; I discuss his collection of vernacular texts and other archival evidence, but I leave the comprehensive search for correspondence and other evidence of his personal thoughts and life to future biographers. The photographs allow us a new route into understanding the way in which Evans-Pritchard's fieldwork shaped his theoretical contributions, offering us an alternative analysis of the generation of anthropological knowledge and theory. Yet this is not a book that seeks to rediscover Evans-Pritchard as an overlooked photographer who deserves recognition as an artist of the medium—he wasn't. Whereas other significant anthropological figures of the twentieth century—such as Bronislaw Malinowski and Isaac Schapera—have both had their field photographs published in volumes with commentaries in recent years, I have not set out to add Evans-Pritchard to this canon, whose future membership the historian Elizabeth Edwards awaited 'with rueful curiosity'.[1]

Through an engagement with his photographic archive, and by thinking with it alongside his written ethnographies and other unpublished evidence, I offer a new insight into the way in which Evans-Pritchard's theoretical contributions to the discipline were shaped by the historical contexts of his fieldwork, its colonial and academic structures, the agency of his local collaborators, as well as his extensive visual and material interests that are only hinted at in his published works. This book fills what to my mind are the essential gaps found in the only available short introductions to Evans-Pritchard's theoretical contributions to date—Mary Douglas's *Evans-Pritchard* (1980) and John Burton's *An Introduction to Evans-Pritchard* (1992). While these books were intended to summarize his theoretical contribution to the discipline, with Douglas's in particular being a brilliant essay in this regard, they were written, it seems, entirely in the library, with only Evans-Pritchard the theorist in mind. My intention in this book is to rediscover

---

[1] E. Edwards. 2000. Review of *Malinowski's Kiriwina: Fieldwork Photography 1915–1918* by M. Young, *American Anthropologist*, New Series, 102(3), 602.

Evans-Pritchard the fieldworker, as well as the communities and individuals that shaped his fieldwork through their encounters with him and his camera, and also to suggest ways in which the archive can be used to rethink some key themes in the history of the discipline. In doing so, I think we get closer to how Evans-Pritchard saw himself and his own contribution. In a photograph of himself that he kept on his desk at the family home (Figure 1.1), in one half of a leather frame, his wife Ioma on the facing side, we see Evans-Pritchard at rest in Cairo around 1932,

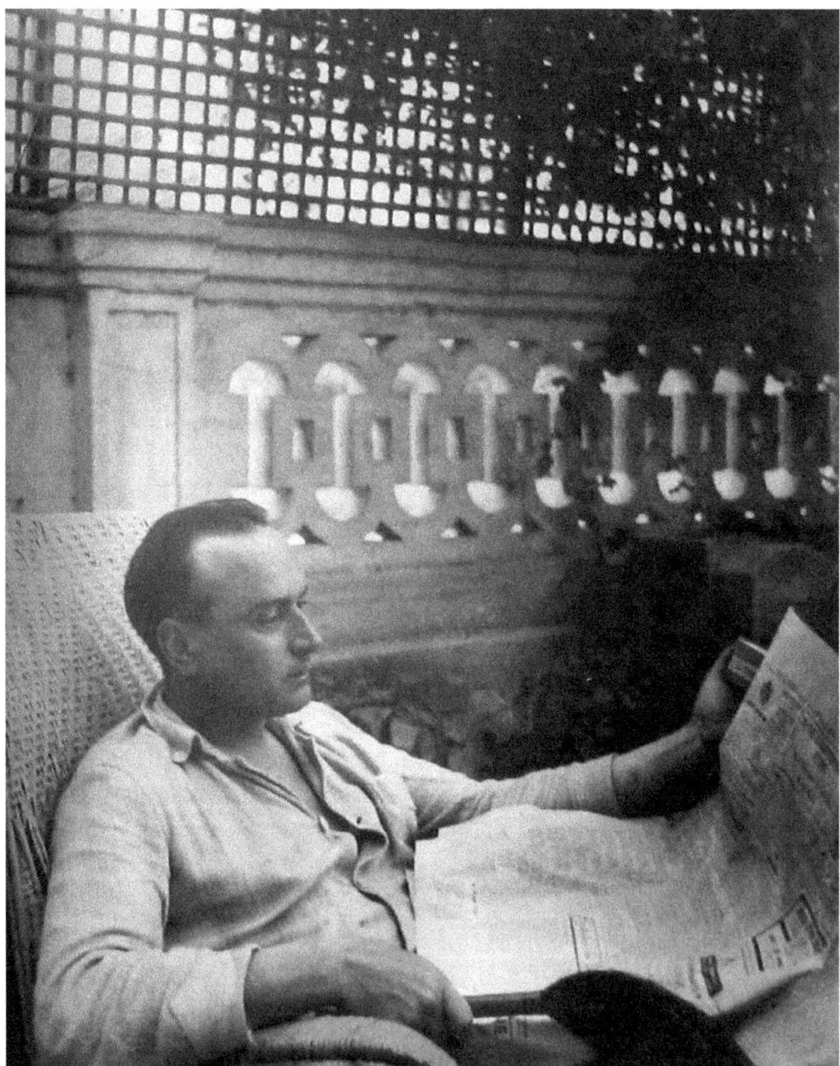

Figure 1.1 Portrait of E. E. Evans-Pritchard in Cairo, around 1932. Photographer unknown.

fly-whisk in one hand, English newspaper in the other; 'a sort of double marginal man, alienated from both worlds'—a phrase he would later use to describe his experience of being a fieldworker. By taking his field photographs as our starting point we move back towards the fieldwork experience and away from an intellectual biographical approach that might reveal more about our own intellectual debts or allegiances than anything else. This of course was the criticism levelled at Mary Douglas following the publication of her intellectual portrait of Evans-Pritchard. In getting back to fieldwork experience through photography we are exploring some aspect of lived reality so persuasively argued by the philosopher Georges Didi-Huberman in his moving exploration of four photographs known to have been taken by concentration camp inmates, where he argues for the recognition of historical reality as embodied and lived experience that underpins the photographic moment: 'images that were snatched, at incredible risk, from a Real that they certainly didn't have time to explore', he writes, 'yet which managed in a few minutes to capture incompletely, fugitively, some aspects of that Real'.[2]

This approach allows us to reconsider Evans-Pritchard's photographic archive as something that essentially connects the lived reality of both the anthropologist and those he encountered, and leaves us with vivid traces of the social encounter, as well as traces of their various presences. These presences we can engage with now, despite the distance of time. While the photographs I discuss in this book are history, they are history that is experienced by us right now; a sense of history, wrote the philosopher Eelco Runia, 'that can be 'visited' on the plane of the present'.[3] With this in mind, I set out to write a new history using photographs as objects connected to lived realities and having an archival life today. Every student of anthropology is taught about Zande ideas of misfortune and witchcraft, as well as the segmentary lineage system of the Nuer. But Evans-Pritchard's role as a prolific field photographer, collector of artefacts, creator of extensive vernacular texts in Zande, and pioneer sound recordist in the field, has been completely overlooked in the historiography of the discipline of anthropology, which has mostly limited itself to discussion of his theoretical contribution embedded in detailed ethnographic textual accounts. Yet Evans-Pritchard's fieldwork photographs provide direct evidence of his interactions with the communities with which he worked, revealing otherwise submerged details about his social interactions and levels of access, and how his published ethnographies and theoretical contributions were forged in the fieldwork encounter.

The book also sets Evans-Pritchard's fieldwork and published results in their historical context, examining many of the colonial and academic networks that

<hr>

[2] G. Didi-Huberman. 2008. *Images in Spite of All: Four Photographs from Auschwitz*. Chicago and London: University of Chicago Press, 60.

[3] E. Runia. 2006. 'Presence', *History and Theory*, 45(1), 1.

funded, facilitated, and collaborated with him. It discusses the extent to which Evans-Pritchard can be considered complicit in the attempt to expand colonial control over groups such as the Nuer or Anuak in South Sudan, or whether he is better understood as a 'frustrated radical'[4] within the colonial system who used colonial funding for anthropology to increase sympathy for indigenous peoples. I will argue that Evans-Pritchard's very significant theoretical contributions were developed within a particular methodological context forged in the crucible of the Malinowski seminar at the London School of Economics in the 1920s, but also equally influenced by his own method of responding to, and shaping, fieldwork events that would become key to the development of his published ideas. Many of these events were also photographed in part, and by comparing the visual and textual aspects of his fieldwork we gain a unique insight into the nature of these events and his positioning within them. These fieldwork practices involved capturing data photographically, textually, materially, and aurally in sound recordings. They were then reflected upon during gaps in fieldwork, shared with his supervisor, discussed, sold to museums, used for illustration, spread out on a table during the writing of articles and referred to in the text, translated, typed up. Despite this abundance, this wealth of traces of the field in Evans-Pritchard's archival collections, scholars have paid no attention to the visual and material dimensions of his research, and we have been left to imagine the anthropologist as alchemist, transmuting base fieldwork data into the gold of modern social anthropology via his genius alone. Yet the reality is much more messy and contingent, full of gaps and fragmentary narratives, the faces and voices of numerous contributors, both European and African, and is evidence of the way that historical circumstance plays a critical role in certain forms of knowledge creation. One aspect of this that is of real interest and worthy of much fuller treatment elsewhere is the question of gender. While recently rereading Evans-Pritchard's essay, 'The position of women in primitive societies and in our own', based on his 1955 Fawcett Lecture, some past student had marked in the margin as 'sexist' the passage where he questions the benefit of the changed position of women in England, when compared with the situation of women he had encountered in non-Western societies. No doubt this student was still fuming from his opening statement of 'never having properly understood the feminist movement'.[5] But for all its obvious flaws, the essay is of interest in the emphasis he seeks to place, not on gender per se, but on gender as a socio-economic category within industrial and pre-industrial societies. This is an insight that still resonates strongly today,

---

[4] W. James. 1973. 'The anthropologist as reluctant imperialist'. In *Anthropology and the Colonial Encounter*, edited by T. Asad. London: Ithaca Press, 50.

[5] E. E. Evans-Pritchard. 1965. *The Position of Women in Primitive Societies and Other Essays in Social Anthropology*. London: Faber and Faber, 38.

whether it be the exploitation of women workers in newly industrializing societies, or claims for equal pay in British supermarkets.

My emphasis upon the overall fieldwork archive allows for a new understanding of how emerging anthropological fieldwork methods in the generation after Malinowski were beginning to shape a new type of approach to the discipline. In the chapters on both his Zande and Nuer fieldwork, the evidence of the photographic archive is explored to shed new light upon Evans-Pritchard's role as both participant and observer in key ritual events that feature centrally in his published ethnography, such as the initiation of his servant Kamanga into the Zande corporation of witch doctors, and the Nuer rite of *gorot*. Scholars such as Clifford Geertz have focused upon Evans-Pritchard's evocative and pictorial writing style, arguing that 'his natural idiom is optical, his 'being there' signature passionately visual'.[6] That visibility and clarity were the keys to his writing power was a sense echoed by Mary Douglas in her comment that 'the lines of his thought were hard and clear, like late Rembrandt'.[7] My argument in this book is that we need to take Geertz's insight and understand it in the context of Evans-Pritchard's fieldwork methods, and in particular his photography and its importance in reassembling data visually when writing. Evans-Pritchard frequently refers to the visual evidence of his photographic archive to corroborate an ethnographic point on which his theory hangs, and yet this book is the first attempt to understand the role of the visual in both Evans-Pritchard's fieldwork and writing processes, and thereby his theoretical contribution. By rediscovering Evans-Pritchard as a fieldworker with strong visual and material interests, I intend in this book to transform our approach to his famous writings. When read again in this new light, and in the light of Geertz's insight, we understand Evans-Pritchard's work as suffused with the visual (as well as the other senses) and that his writings consistently visualize the field and the material realities of the people and events he describes. Although submerged by later abstractions of his key anthropological concepts, this book argues that it is time to revisit Evans-Pritchard through his anthropological lens on the field, and to revisit his brilliantly evocative anthropological writings in the process. This book contributes to a visual and material turn in history and anthropology more broadly by writing an anthropological history (or historical anthropology) using the visual in the form of the photographic record as the starting point for analysis, rather than as secondary to the textual evidence or as illustration of history. The photographs in this book are part of the argument, as much as they were for Evans-Pritchard, however little they have hitherto been considered. In Figure 1.2, I present a photographic argument on this theme; in a complex image, two Nuer warriors crouch in characteristic dance manner with spears in front of them, yet as Evans-Pritchard takes the photograph a man runs

[6] C. Geertz. 1988. *Works and Lives: The Anthropologist as Author*. Oxford: Polity Press, 65.
[7] Quoted in R. Fardon. 2002. *Mary Douglas: An Intellectual Biography*. London: Routledge, 29.

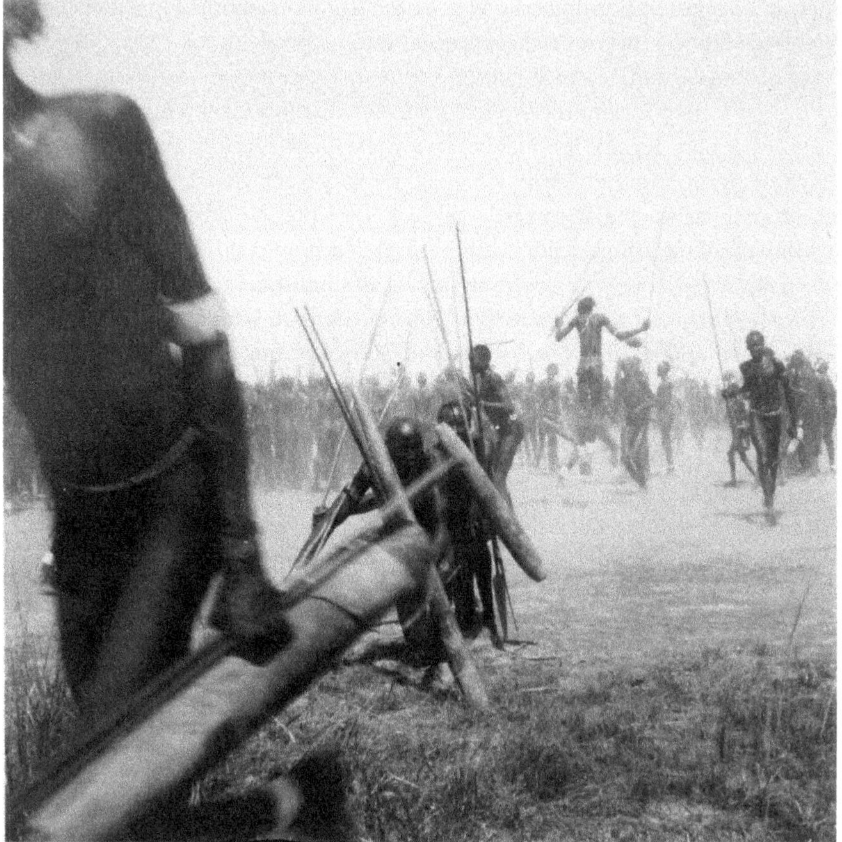

Figure 1.2 A Western Jikany Nuer dance. Photograph by E. E. Evans-Pritchard, 1936.

past, his parrying shield and spears in hand, and he is captured in the frame. Yet the man is not an 'intrusion' into a careful composition, he is part of the visual dynamic and confusion of a Nuer dance event in 1936; the man's movement through the image leads us visually and imaginatively beyond the photograph's frame and heightens our awareness of its partial nature and its unstable boundaries of meaning. Both the dance and the photograph are uncontainable within the frame of anthropological analysis, and as viewers of a fieldwork moment we are both there ourselves and feel the movement of the scene, and yet highly aware of our disconnection from it as a historical document at the same time; an illogical conjunction of the there-then and the here-now, in Barthes's memorable phrase.

But just what is it about thinking with photography that transforms our understanding of Evans-Pritchard? In essence, I explore the diverse archival deposits of Evans-Pritchard's fieldwork not merely as a source to be excavated, but as an analytical 'think-space'. I take inspiration here from the influential historian and photography theorist Elizabeth Edwards, upon whose office wall when I was a student and junior colleague was the slogan 'photographs are to think with'. This slogan has always remained with me, and remains at the core of Edwards's own intellectual manifesto and prodigious output. But what does it actually mean as a methodology? Well, a starting point could be said to be an understanding of the dominance that photography quickly achieved after its invention as the prime mediator of knowledge about the world, its places and peoples.[8] So profound has been photography's influence on modernity and our understanding of the temporal relations between past, present, and future that it frequently proves impossible to analytically isolate the work that photography does from its wider cultural embeddedness. One of the methodological implications of this for anthropologists and historians has been to think about how photographs as objects operate in particular social, cultural, and historical spaces, and how the social relations that they enfold and express can be seen afresh, not as illustrated by images, but connected within our image world. By taking the visual record of the anthropological 'field' as the starting point, and writing an anthropological history from the inside out, we get closer to understanding the way in which ethnographic knowledge is always and everywhere embedded in visual worlds, and that it is worth revisiting classic ethnographies afresh to reconsider the basis for their subsequent impact upon the discipline.

In two chapters in this book (chapters 3 and 7) I explore how Evans-Pritchard's embodied presence in the field as both participant and observer is revealed in the visual record, and show how the classic ethnographic accounts of Kamanga's initiation as a witch doctor, and the Nuer rite of *gorot*, both emerge out of events in which Evans-Pritchard was constantly but irregularly involved as photographer, discussant, note-taker, interviewer, participant, sponsor, community witness, and provocateur. In chapter 4 I consider the different ways in which local people shaped Evans-Pritchard's photographic engagement, an agency that exerts itself in markedly different ways between the groups he worked with, for very particular historical and cultural reasons. Indigenous agency rather than photographic intentionality then transforms how we read Evans-Pritchard's visual engagement with the field, and by doing so reinserts a sense of an ethnography shaped by local responses to what they understood the photographic act to be, and what it was for. Such local shaping of ethnographic knowledge is even more evident of course in the various narrations people spoke or sang into Evans-Pritchard's phonograph recorder, the objects they were willing to part with for his

---

[8] For one of the most nuanced studies of the relationship between photography and the historical imagination, see E. Edwards. 2012. *The Camera as Historian: Amateur Photographers and Historical Imagination, 1885–1918*. Durham, NC: Duke University Press.

collection, which stories they wanted to tell him or his Zande research assistants, and which questions they wished to answer.[9]

In the voluminous vernacular texts that Evans-Pritchard collected in Zandeland, the voices of Zande interlocutors and their cultural inheritances emerge mixed with the historical particularism of the moment in which they were spoken; colonial subjugation and control, missionization and cultural change are both the backdrop to, and also the precipitant of, the anthropological encounter from which the ethnography emerges. Engaging with the material evidence of fieldwork, almost as a form of 'excavation', allows us then to transform our understanding of Evans-Pritchard's ethnography as something more than a set of cognitive leaps by the anthropologist, from scientific observation to theoretical interpretation; it allows an alternative approach that has much in common with recent thinking in the social sciences on the important interaction between brain, body, and the environment (both physical and social) in the creation of knowledge and its communication to others. Whereas, for instance, Mary Douglas saw Evans-Pritchard as a 'master of modern thought' whose 'solitary confronting, in the 1930s, of intellectual dilemmas that are now crowding in heavily upon the social sciences',[10] my own approach is to understand his intellectual contribution as very far from being a solitary pursuit, and one that involved the contribution of numerous local African thinkers, asked by the anthropologist to reflect on their culture, kin relations, history, and society. His student Godfrey Lienhardt even went so far as to suggest that the success of this collaboration could partly be accounted for by a congruence between his character and that of the peoples with whom he worked in South Sudan, remarking that, 'His works are I think consistent with this character . . . In the Azande, he found lively humour, the quick mental reactions, the suspicion and even superstition which he would have admitted to be part of himself . . . they appealed to his sense of aristocracy . . . The Nuer appealed to his sense of personal independence, with their uncompromising and courageous forthrightness'.[11]

Anthropological fieldwork of course is grounded in numerous social, physical, and material interactions and communications between an ethnographer and members of a community, as well as other specialists both in the field (Figure 1.3) and at home, something that one may argue constitutes an 'extended mind'[12] that goes well beyond the ethnographer's own mental construction of the

---

[9] For an interesting think piece on anthropology's historical relationship to informants, see R. Sanjek. 1993. 'Anthropology's hidden colonialism: assistants and their ethnographers', *Anthropology Today*, 9(2), 13–18.

[10] M. Douglas. 1980. *Evans-Pritchard*. London: Fontana Paperbacks, 11.

[11] G. Lienhardt. 1974. 'E-P: a personal view: Sir Edward Evans-Pritchard, 1902–1973', *Man*, 9(2), 303.

[12] See A. Clark. 1997. *Being There: Putting Brain, Body, and World Together Again*. Cambridge, MA: MIT Press.

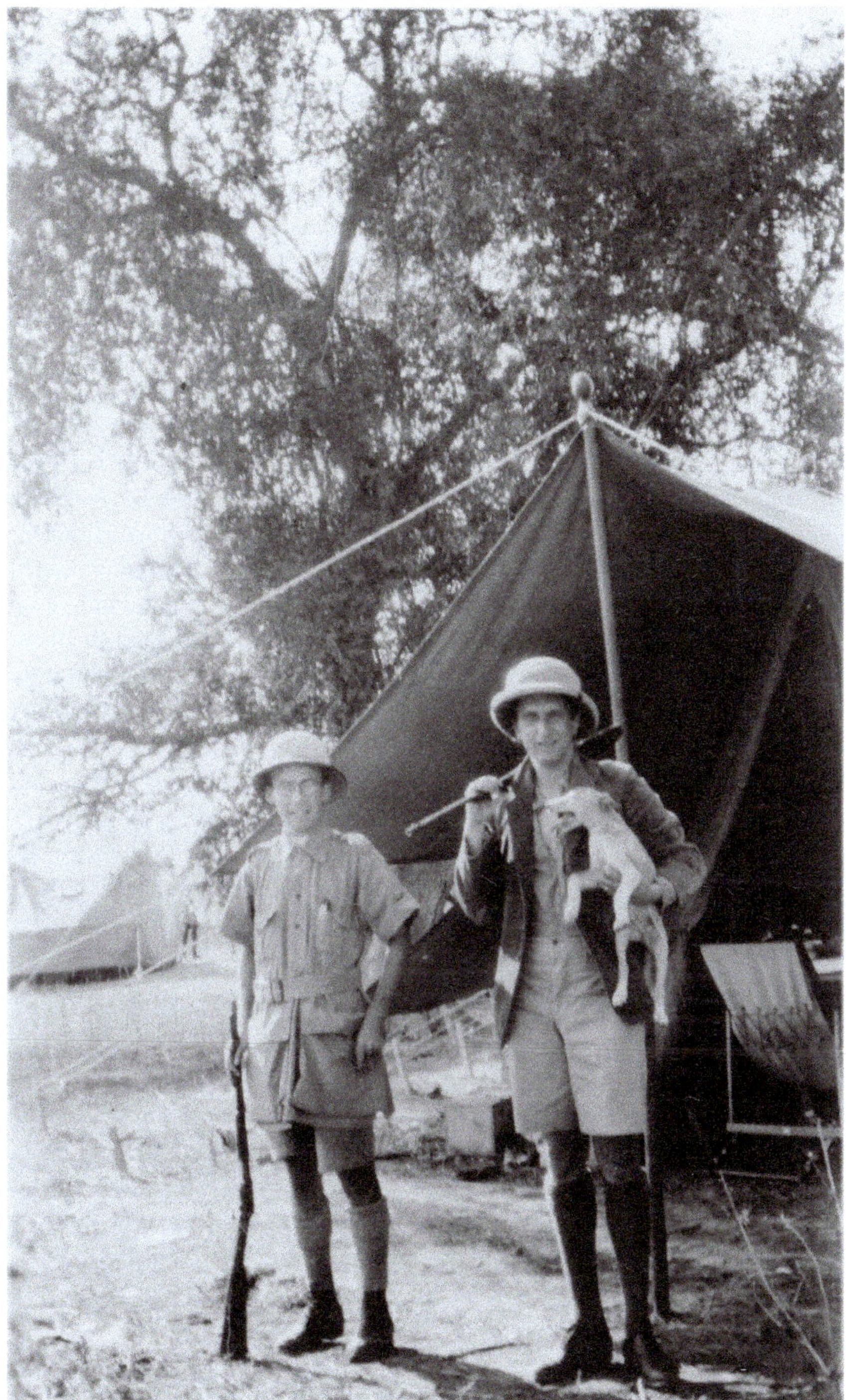

Figure 1.3 Evans-Pritchard with the linguist Archibald Norman Tucker, Nuerland, 1930. Photographer unknown.

field, and which contains knowledge that is held and expressed in 'fields of practice'[13] through embodied skill. More than this, the fieldwork archive has a grain along which, so Ann Laura Stoler shows us, we might consider what it is trying to tell us, in a sense. In the case of Evans-Pritchard's archive we gain a strong feeling that knowledge in the field is not an entity in itself to be found, recorded, extracted; instead the archive, in its repetitions, false starts, happenstance, fragments, sequences, multiple sets of orderings and numberings, as well as evidence of periods of engagement and non-engagement, are suggestive of the process of the ethnographer *becoming* knowledgeable over the course of several periods of fieldwork, and long afterwards. Key to this more processual understanding of knowledge is the idea of bodily movement through the social world, both physically and temporally, since it is through movement that the fieldworker arrives, participates, observes, communicates, collects, records, departs, reflects, and returns. Knowledge emerges from movement, and in the case of the fieldwork archive it was once an active agent in the construction of knowledge. Fieldwork photographs were printed, sorted, labelled, sleeved, captioned, and listed in Charles Seligman's office in London during gaps in fieldwork, before some were left behind and others taken back to the field to facilitate further communication and the creation of further ethnographic knowledge. Wax cylinders were tested on the boat during the long journey to Sudan, and earlier fieldwork notes reflected upon and written up for publication, with correspondence attached requesting their safe passage to journals.[14] Movement suffuses the archive and its traces of the field, as I discuss in detail in chapters 3 and 5 in relation to Evans-Pritchard's photography of ritual, and demonstrates how, as Ingold has argued, knowledge isn't built from static positions but grows and mutates with people (including anthropologists) as they journey.[15] The anthropologist Peter Pels has also sought to question the meaningfulness of the dichotomy between 'home' and 'field' in anthropology, arguing that it 'breaks down once one brings the physical work necessary to maintain these dichotomies into the analysis'.[16] The anthropologist makes a temporary home in the field, and the field is a mobile construction that is partly built through the work of engaging with its material residues: photographs, sounds, objects, drawings, maps, texts.

---

[13] See T. Ingold. 2001. 'From the transmission of representations to the education of attention'. In *The Debated Mind: Evolutionary Psychology Versus Ethnography*, edited by H. Whitehouse. London: Berg Publishers, 114.

[14] Letter dated 6 April 1928, written on board SS Amarapoora at Marseilles (Pitt Rivers Museum Manuscript Collections, Evans-Pritchard Papers, Section 3, Box 1, Item 13).

[15] T. Ingold. 2010. 'Footprints through the weather-world: walking, breathing, knowing', *Journal of the Royal Anthropological Institute*, 16, S121–39.

[16] P. Pels. 1997. 'The anthropology of colonialism: culture, history, and the emergence of western governmentality', *Annual Review of Anthropology*, 26, 169.

Frustrated radical?

While the material mobility of the field, as well as its metaphorical 'excavation' in the archive, are key concepts that run throughout the chapters of this book, it is also important to contextualize Evans-Pritchard's fieldwork historically, or rather to ask what an analysis of the various historical structures that afforded him access to the field might tell us about the development of his ethnography, and thereby his anthropological contribution. There is a well-known photograph from Evans-Pritchard's Zande fieldwork that acts as a useful gateway to approach this subject. The photograph (Figure 1.4) shows him smoking a pipe, seated in a camp chair, flanked by Zande boys (and a man) seated on the ground and standing behind. Two of the boys hold sticks in imitation of rifles over their left shoulders and salute the camera with their right hand, while the two to their left seem to participate in a much more uncertain manner, holding their right hands to their face and forehead, the other arm draped over the shoulders of the boy alongside, who holds a tin can to his mouth.

I have often wondered how we should read this much-reproduced photograph. It has no negative in the archive, possibly having been lent by Evans-Pritchard and never returned, and the print is torn in the lower right corner, evidence of its use and retrieval. On its reverse is just a pencil number, but in Evans-Pritchard's handlist it is captioned, 'Self and group of boys'. Although published widely to encapsulate Evans-Pritchard 'in the field', or even colonial anthropology more widely, no author has actually sought to understand this complex image. It is of course a highly constructed image, but probably not by Evans-Pritchard himself. The most likely candidate for the role of photographer is Major P. M. Larken, the District Commissioner for Zandeland, who was one of the few Europeans living nearby, and who Evans-Pritchard met 'for a few hours every new moon'.[17] If we accept this likelihood, then the photograph becomes more understandable: the group of boys has probably been posed around the anthropologist by Larken the colonial official, who has also orchestrated the boys' military style gesture. The image seems to sum up perfectly the awkward positioning of the anthropologist within the colonial situation: the anthropologist is identified closely with the community and yet hierarchically separated from them to an extent, while the wider sociopolitical context of colonial control is identified through the military gesture. The photograph also seems to illustrate the much-cited argument of the anthropologist Talal Asad, who suggested that 'the colonial power structure made the object of anthropological study accessible and safe—because of it sustained physical proximity between the observing European and the living non-European became a practical possibility. It made possible the kind of human intimacy on

---

[17] E. E. Evans-Pritchard. 1973. 'Some recollections on fieldwork in the twenties', *Anthropological Quarterly*, 46(4), 237.

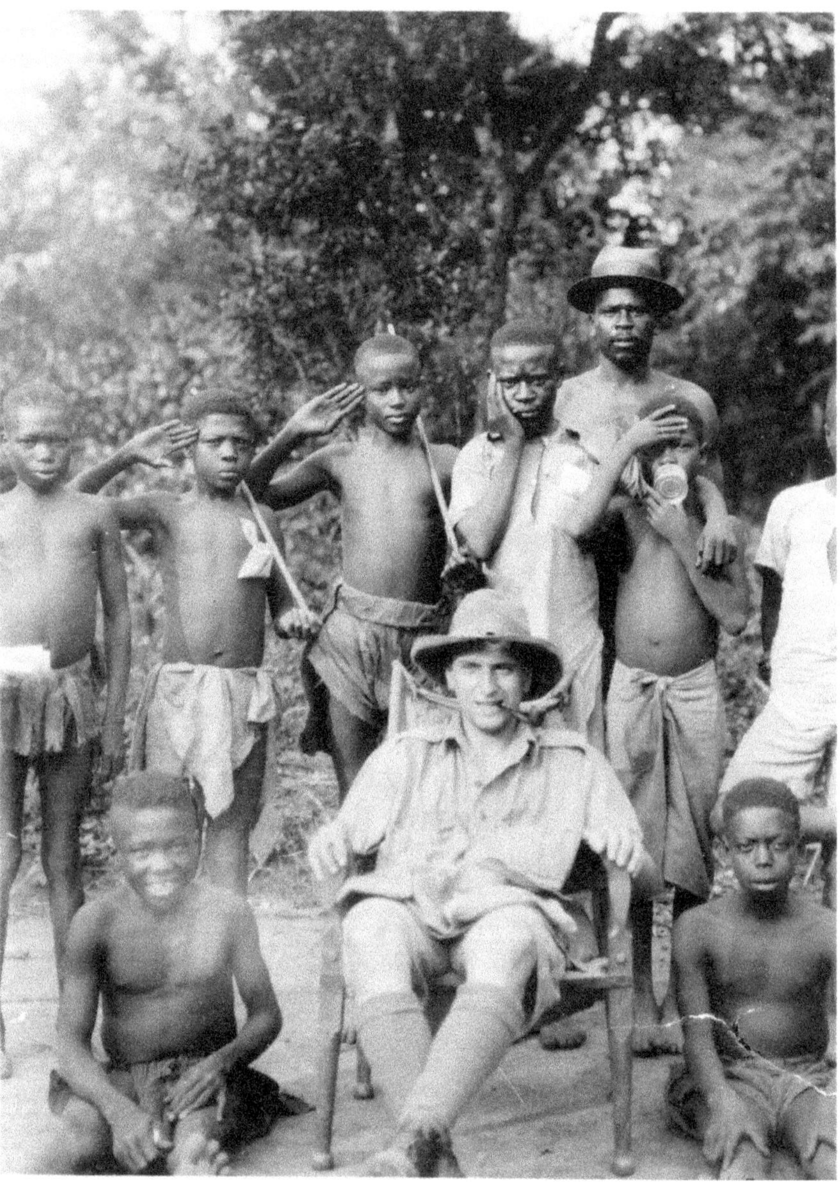

Figure 1.4 Evans-Pritchard with a group of Zande boys, 1927–30. Photographer unknown, possibly P. M. Larken.

which anthropological fieldwork is based, but ensured that that intimacy should be one-sided and provisional.'[18] According to this argument, anthropology did little to critique colonialism or its sociocultural assumptions, despite anthropologists occasionally having the reputation among administrators of being political radicals. For Asad, academics such as Evans-Pritchard were 'professionally at peace'[19] with the system they benefitted from, whatever their personal opinions of it. On the face of it, this is a characterization that appears to fit Evans-Pritchard, who has sometimes been caricatured (probably largely correctly) as an opportunist who used colonial funding to get into the field, but who then produced little of direct use to the colonial administration, despite quickly publishing pieces as promised in *Sudan Notes and Records*. In her nuanced discussion of Evans-Pritchard's relationship to colonial structures, Wendy James argued that although 'appearances of cooperation had to be kept up' to enable anthropologists to work, individuals such as Evans-Pritchard were critical of colonialism, and 'of the philosophy of Western superiority upon which it was based and in terms of which it was justified'.[20] She points in particular to Evans-Pritchard's argument for the rationality of Zande thought in relation to magic and witchcraft, which in the 1930s went against the grain of accepted colonial thinking that witchcraft was the product of an irrational primitive mentality, and that the most appropriate policy in development terms was to make it illegal. Evans-Pritchard's monograph *Witchcraft, Oracles and Magic Among the Azande* (1937) was designed, argued James, partly as a criticism of such policies and their assumptions, and partly as a direct challenge to administrative prejudices that fieldworkers such as himself had frequently come into contact with. A good example of Evans-Pritchard's ambition for his own academic influence on administrative thinking is summed up in his article on 'Sorcery and native opinion', in which he argues that:

It is important to understand native opinion about black magic, not only for the anthropologist but also for the colonial administrator and missionary, if they wish to show to the peoples whom they govern and teach that they understand their notions about right and wrong. The native does not so much distrust European justice and education as he despairs of the administrator and missionary ever understanding, or attempting to understand, his point of view as expressed in laws and public opinion. This despair springs largely from the handling by Europeans of such matters as sorcery, with which both missionaries and administrators frequently have to deal. The native becomes convinced finally that the European is quite incapable of seeing the difference between right and wrong, between the proper use of a cultural weapon fully sanctioned by public

---

[18] Asad, T. 1973. 'Introduction'. In *Anthropology and the Colonial Encounter*, edited by T. Asad. London: Ithaca Press, 17.

[19] Asad, 'Introduction', 18.   [20] James, 'The anthropologist as reluctant imperialist', 42.

opinion, such as white magic, and a heinous and cold blooded murder, such as the crime of black magic or sorcery.[21]

He goes on in this article to imply that without professional anthropologists acting as cultural translators, misunderstanding and maladministration are inevitable since 'it has often been shown that when two civilizations come into contact the lesser is always accused of sorcery by half-studied and ill-formed judgements of the greater.'[22] So, did colonial administrators heed such pleas to seek the advice of anthropologists on cultural problems? It appears not. 'During the fifteen years in which I worked on sociological problems in the same region' he wrote, 'I was never once asked my advice on any question at all.'[23] Although this may be true, it hides the fact that much of Evans-Pritchard's fieldwork and outputs were sponsored by the Sudanese government, often with the explicit intention that they would be of use to administration on particular problems, such as the control of the Nuer. Evans-Pritchard's earliest fieldwork, setting out in 1926, did benefit directly from colonial structures and funding. Since C. G. Seligman could no longer travel to Sudan to continue his survey work there (sponsored by the Sudanese government from 1910 onwards) due to health issues, he asked the government to allow his student Evans-Pritchard to collect data. As the historian Douglas Johnson describes, the Sudanese government in fact had no real project for him to undertake besides continuing a tribal survey of the Sudan–Ethiopian border, so he was allowed to roam freely southwards, collecting data on a number of small communities for Seligman's survey of 'pagan' tribes. However, in the wake of intractable Nuer resistance to colonial administration, from 1927, the relative importance of ethnographic information increased, partly since there seemed little in the way of traditional chiefdomship to exercise the usual British method of Indirect Rule through; all that seemed to exist were a loose collection of lineage heads and influential religious figures. Harold MacMichael, then Civil Secretary in the Sudanese government, acknowledged the difficulties in his letter setting out the rationale for spending further government money on helping solve the Nuer situation:

> grave errors have been all too often made through ignorance of local beliefs and habits and insufficient understanding of savage ways of thought, and there can be no doubt but that our troubles with the Nuer, e.g., have been intensified by our lack of knowledge of the social structure of this people and the relative status of the various kinds of chiefs... It is possible that Mr Evans-Pritchard himself is the right man, and might be willing to undertake the work. The period of his present

---

[21] E. E. Evans-Pritchard. 1931. 'Sorcery and native opinion', *Africa*, 4(1), 22.
[22] Evans-Pritchard, 'Sorcery and native opinion', 55.
[23] E. E. Evans-Pritchard. 1946. 'Applied anthropology', *Africa*, 16(2), 97.

engagement ends in April next year and he will then wish to spend some months in England collecting and preparing his material. If he does not wish to return upon our terms, I am certain that Prof Seligman, whom I consulted when last in England, could suggest a suitable alternative.

Evans-Pritchard did finally take up this challenge by the Sudanese government, but only after he had persuaded them to also allow him to return to Zandeland to finish his work there. Arriving in Nuerland in 1930 things got off to a rocky start, but he was soon joined by his trusted Zande assistants Mekana and Kamanga, who went with him and a Nuer youth called Nhial, who had agreed to work with him, to Muot dit (Figure 1.5). Although he later described his time attempting to get to know the Nuer at Muot dit as 'happy and remunerative', things quickly turned sour. Early one morning government soldiers surrounded the camp, searching for two Nuer prophets who were accused of revolt, and took some Nuer people hostage, threatening to take more if the prophets were not handed over. 'I felt that I was in an equivocal position', Evans-Pritchard wrote, 'and shortly after-wards returned to my home in Zandeland.' The experience left him with a sense of dismay, and sympathy over their 'deep resentment' towards the government. The equivocal position he found himself in was not only due to uncertainty about his personal safety, since he was looked upon 'not only as a stranger but as an enemy', but also, I believe, deep uncertainty about his complicity in the policy then being carried out by the Sudan administration.

The commissioning of Evans-Pritchard to go to Nuerland was, argues Johnson, 'the first time the Sudanese government employed an anthropologist to conduct research which was anticipated to have a direct benefit to administration'.[24] The direct benefit in this case is to be found in MacMichael's statement above that the government clearly had no idea of how the various Nuer groups interrelated and what, if any, structures of authority existed. This information was essential to the British model of Indirect Rule, in which colonial authority was exerted through existing power structures and hierarchies, their replacement, or imposition. Fred-erick Lugard first brought Indirect Rule to Africa in Nigeria, rolling out the same system in the south of the country after 1914 that had been successful in the north through organized emirates. However, while Lugard saw Indirect Rule as a hierarchical system whereby orders might flow from the top down through local authorities, those who came after him clearly interpreted it somewhat differently, as a system in which colonial governance was exercised through indigenous institutions.[25] The post-Lugard period of the 1920s thereby saw anthropology in

---

[24] D. H. Johnson. 2007. 'Political intelligence, colonial ethnography, and analytical anthropology in the Sudan'. In *Ordering Africa: Anthropology, European Imperialism, and the Politics of Knowledge*, edited by H. Tilley and R. J. Gordon. Manchester and New York: Manchester University Press, 322.

[25] H. Lackner. 1973. 'Colonial administration and social anthropology: eastern Nigeria 1920–40'. In *Anthropology and the Colonial Encounter*, edited by T. Asad. London: Ithaca Press, 124.

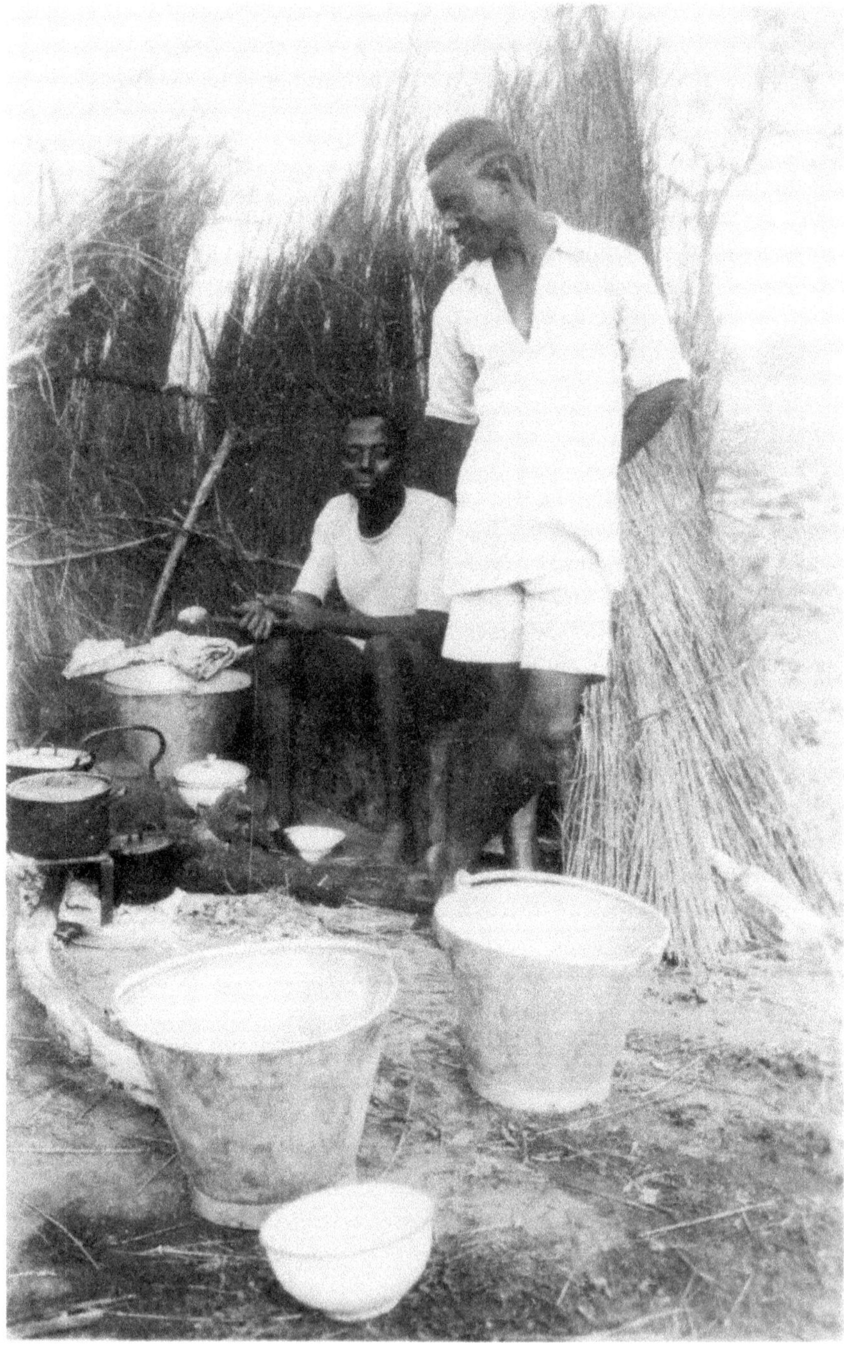

Figure 1.5 Evans-Pritchard's two Zande assistants Mekana and Kamanga at Muot dit in Nuerland, 1930. Photograph by E. E. Evans-Pritchard.

a much more positive light, informing administration about these indigenous institutions through which they were meant to be exerting control. As Feuchtwang has argued, 'Indirect rule in Africa was the mould of British social anthropology... [it] gave to anthropologists small-scale cultural formations as units of study to be treated as integrated and complete social systems.'[26] This isn't to say that British colonial administrations around the world were all rushing to grab anthropology graduates—they weren't; opinion was divided about the usefulness of what specialists like anthropologists might come up with, and so administrators frequently gained some anthropological training to suit their purposes. This mixed picture then characterizes the 1920s and 30s. Some anthropologists were commissioned to make major studies, such as Isaac Schapera in the High Commission Territories of South Africa, M. Read in Nyasaland, Audrey Richards in Northern Rhodesia, and P. J. Peristiany in Kenya, and probationary recruits for the Sudanese government were sent from 1908 to Oxford where they received eight special lectures each on the ethnology of the Sudan, on comparative technology, and primitive social institutions. In the 1920s, this training was moved to London University; but in the 1930s the Sudan recruits were sent to Oxford to attend the Tropical African Services Course set up for the Colonial Office.[27] The interactions between administration and academy were fragmentary at best, subject to the favour of particular colonial figures or situations, and suspicion about the benefits of the relationship remained on both sides. This then characterizes Evans-Pritchard's relationship to the colonial machine that he worked within and ostensibly often for; a relationship of convenience that was mostly disappointing on both sides. But of course, from the point of view of the South Sudanese whose villages he entered Evans-Pritchard was to all intents and purposes an agent of the colonial regime, no matter his explanations for why he wanted to know the name of their lineage: 'What will you do with it if I tell you?' one Nuer man memorably asked him: 'Will you take it to your country?'[28]

From natural science to history

In 1950, Evans-Pritchard was invited to give the Marett Lecture at Oxford, which remains the most distinguished event within the academic calendar of Oxford social anthropology. For him, it was a doubly important moment: not only was Marett his former 'friend and counsellor for over twenty years', but he was

---

[26] S. Feuchtwang. 1973. 'The discipline and its sponsors'. In *Anthropology and the Colonial Encounter*, edited by T. Asad. London: Ithaca Press, 99.

[27] Johnson, 'Political intelligence', 314–15.

[28] E. E. Evans-Pritchard. 1940. *The Nuer: A Description of the Modes of Livelihood and Political Institutions of a Nilotic People*. Oxford: Clarendon Press, 13.

delivering it at his old college, Exeter, 'in this familiar hall.'[29] If he had, only two years earlier in 1948 in his inaugural address on taking up his professorship, presented a manifesto of continuity from the work of his predecessor Radcliffe-Brown, he took the opportunity of this high-profile lecture to mark a complete break with functionalism and the natural sciences. His bold new manifesto was 'that social anthropology is a kind of historiography, and therefore ultimately of philosophy of art... that it studies societies as moral systems and not as natural systems, that it is interested in design rather than in process, and that it therefore seeks patterns and not scientific laws, and interprets rather than explains.'[30] This more humanistic approach, as he saw it, would do more than translate and make intelligible one society's culture to another; it would make it 'sociologically intelligible' by seeking the structural order of a society, 'the patterns which, once established, enable him to see it as a whole, as a set of interrelated abstractions'.[31] These social abstractions, he argued, were imaginative constructs on the part of the anthropologist, but if related to each other through logic would enable patterning sufficient to 'see' a society in both its parts and as a structural whole. He saw the social historian in this way as engaged in essentially the same pursuit as the anthropologist; one deals with mostly synchronic data and the other mostly diachronic, yet for him this was more a matter of emphasis rather than substance.

But what prompted this intellectual turn in Evans-Pritchard's own thinking, and why was it not even hinted at in his inaugural address two years earlier? An explanation came from Evans-Pritchard himself twenty years later in a letter to a journal, suggesting that he was overly cautious to present an academic viewpoint that chimed with his predecessor's and that of its adherents still in the department in Oxford. But he also relates that Radcliffe-Brown asked him to restate the theoretical position he gave in his own inaugural address, and then to destroy the manuscript. 'There is nothing to Radcliffe-Brown's discredit in this,' he wrote, 'only perhaps to mine. How could I have refused his request? But maybe I should have done so.'[32] Godfrey Lienhardt later argued, unconvincingly, that Evans-Pritchard's shift to a historiographical approach was a response to the intellectual environment he found in Oxford, that it 'was to some measure an attempt to restore its reputation among academics for whom Radcliffe-Brown's "scientific" principles cut no ice—quite the contrary, in some they produced glaciation.'[33] Although his early training in history is sometimes mentioned as a background to his later intellectual turn, what has been overlooked is that only the year before, in 1949, Evans-Pritchard published his monograph, *The Sanusi of Cyrenaica*, a mostly historical work based on secondary literature written 'in the light of my

[29] E. E. Evans-Pritchard. 1950. 'Social anthropology: past and present', *Man*, 50, 118.
[30] Evans-Pritchard, 'Social anthropology: past and present', 123.
[31] Evans-Pritchard, 'Social anthropology: past and present', 121.
[32] E. E. Evans-Pritchard. 1970. 'Social anthropology at Oxford', *Man*, 5(4), 704.
[33] Lienhardt, 'E-P: a personal view', 301.

own experience' with the Bedouin during the war, and which had occupied much of his thinking in the later 1940s.[34] Another important factor in Evans-Pritchard's turn to historiography, as I discuss in detail in chapter 3, is the value he placed on the collection of vernacular texts, a method that lay at the heart of his work with the Azande in particular.

The Zande texts that Evans-Pritchard collected were treated more like a body of literature on which he might draw for authenticating commentary and evidence, rather than as fieldwork notes or interview data, and were frequently quoted from in his ethnographies. His archive contains hundreds of these texts, some of which were collected for him during his absence from the field by assistants such as Reuben Rikita (Figure 1.6).[35] So extensively are they quoted from in his monograph

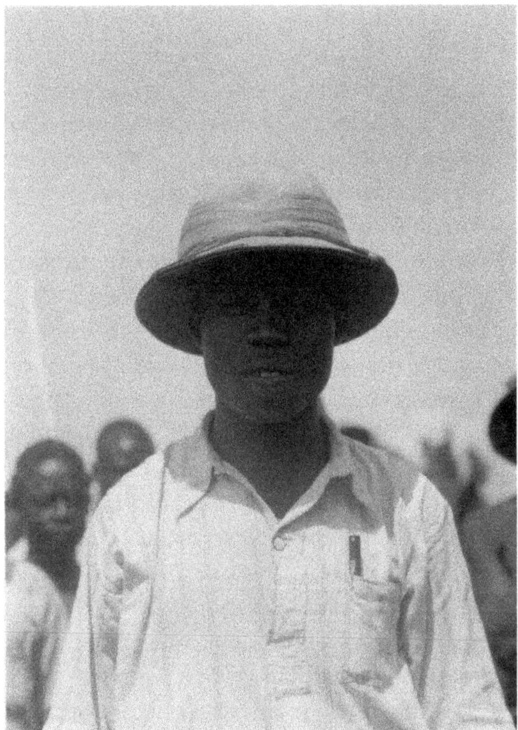

Figure 1.6 Portrait of Reuben wiri Rikita (a son of Prince Rikita), Evans-Pritchard's Zande clerk. Photograph by E. E. Evans-Pritchard, 1927–30.

---

[34] E. E. Evans-Pritchard. 1949. *The Sanusi of Cyrenaica*. Oxford: Clarendon Press, iii.

[35] In *The Azande: History and Political Institutions* (Oxford: Clarendon Press, 1971, 2, 11) Evans-Pritchard notes that 'I instructed my clerk Reuben Rikita, to take, during my absences in England in 1929 and 1930, as broad a census as he could of the adult males in the old kingdoms of Gbudwe,

Witchcraft, Oracles and Magic Among the Azande that he asked for a copy of the book with interleaved blank pages so that he could insert by hand the original texts in Zande alongside the published English translations (see Figure 3.11).

Evans-Pritchard also took the opportunity, when acting as external examiner at the University of Khartoum in the early 1960s, to collect many additional texts in the form of folk tales about the Zande folk hero Ture from a couple of Zande students studying there, Richard Mambia and Angelo Beda, some of whose versions appear in his 1967 volume *The Zande Trickster*. This volume, and his last major work *The Azande: History and Political Institutions*, published in 1971, were viewed, and still are by some social anthropologists, as 'almost perversely ethnohistorical and diffusionist'.[36] Yet to characterize this later work, as Adam Kuper does, as ethnographic (descriptive) rather than anthropological (analytical) is a misunderstanding of the important role that history and texts always played in Evans-Pritchard's anthropological works. To state that the real revolution in African ethnohistory occurred only in the decade after Evans-Pritchard's 1950 Marett lecture, when 'Jan Vansina and others showed how oral tradition could be tapped—something Evans-Pritchard never did to any great extent'[37] may be true as a disciplinary generalization, but does not account for the central role that vernacular texts played in Evans-Pritchard's field methodology and analysis. And it is precisely this fieldwork methodology, I would argue, that underpinned Evans-Pritchard's long-standing emphasis on historiography, rather than being some later theoretical turn made in response to the intellectual climate at Oxford, or in response to failings he perceived in Radcliffe-Brown's approach, although these were no doubt supporting factors. To go even further, as I argue in relation to the photographic record in chapter 4, the agency of the communities with whom Evans-Pritchard worked can also be understood to exert its own intellectual force. Kuper's criticism of Evans-Pritchard's last major work, *The Azande*, as 'perversely ethnohistorical' is a myopic judgement in anthropological terms, but more seriously it completely overlooks the agency of the many Azande who contributed to its content and whose deeply historical interests relating to the precolonial past are everywhere expressed in the numerous archival texts. A closer reading of the archive suggests that Evans-Pritchard's later historical and literary works eschew a more narrow concern with synchronic anthropological constructions in favour of indigenous preoccupations with myth, historical explanation, and belonging. In this sense, Evans-Pritchard's later literary works, such as *The Zande Trickster*, are both an attempt to preserve and give Zande oral literature wider attention, but

Ezo and Tembura... [p]erhaps also, my clerk, being himself a noble [i.e. Avongara], had a greater interest to record membership of his clan than of commoner clans.'

---

[36] A. Kuper. 1996. *Anthropology and Anthropologists: The Modern British School*. London: Routledge, 126.

[37] Kuper, *Anthropology and Anthropologists*, 126.

from an anthropological perspective can also be seen as a working through of earlier sociological problems, although he doesn't express it in these terms in the volume itself.

The adventures of the Zande trickster anti-hero Ture, as researched and compiled by Evans-Pritchard into the 1960s, thereby fits squarely within Douglas's argument about his overall theoretical contribution, that his 'method of tracing meanings through the process of fixing human accountability uncovers the fundamental system of hypotheses, both where the chain of reasoning stops and where its links are forged.'[38] Stories about Ture explore Zande notions of social accountability, morality, and reasoning, and it is clear that Evans-Pritchard began to collect such texts in the 1920s with these questions uppermost in his mind. Issues of temporality and historiography are also evident throughout his earliest anthropological writings, especially on the Azande, with frequent references to customs in the 'past', usually contrasted to differences observed in the ethnographic present of 'today'. It is clear from the context that in most of these instances what Zande meant by 'in the past' was precolonial times, under the rule of King Gbudwe, which ended in 1905, over twenty years before Evans-Pritchard's fieldwork. While Evans-Pritchard does acknowledge the question of social change as a result of colonial conquest in his writings, his attention remains firmly focused on those elements of cultural continuity that might allow the anthropologist room for sociological generalization. Yet at the same time we are led into frequent temporal entanglements: mythical time and 'the past' interweave with the present and protensions from an uncertain future, all of which register in different ways in the fieldwork archive. Take for instance the temporal tangles intentionally introduced by Evans-Pritchard in his use of a fieldwork photograph published in *The Zande Trickster* with the caption 'This could be Ture' (Figure 1.7).

This photograph, which he had donated to the Pitt Rivers Museum the year before the book was published in 1967, was originally captioned by Evans-Pritchard in his handlist for the collection as 'Man wearing hat', meaning that at the time he listed his photographs the man was not familiar to him by name (dozens of other portraits do include names). Evans-Pritchard took a number of Zande portraits of this type, with the subject close enough to allow them to be used flexibly in anthropological terms—cropped around the face by his supervisor Seligman for pseudo-scientific racial type characterization, or else in fuller frame like this to include information about dress, ornamentation, or physique in the way that most conventional honorific portraits did in the 1920s, and continue to do today. But Evans-Pritchard's use of this anonymous man's portrait in *The Zande Trickster*, some forty years after it was taken, leads us into a temporal and

---

[38] Douglas, *Evans-Pritchard*, 25.

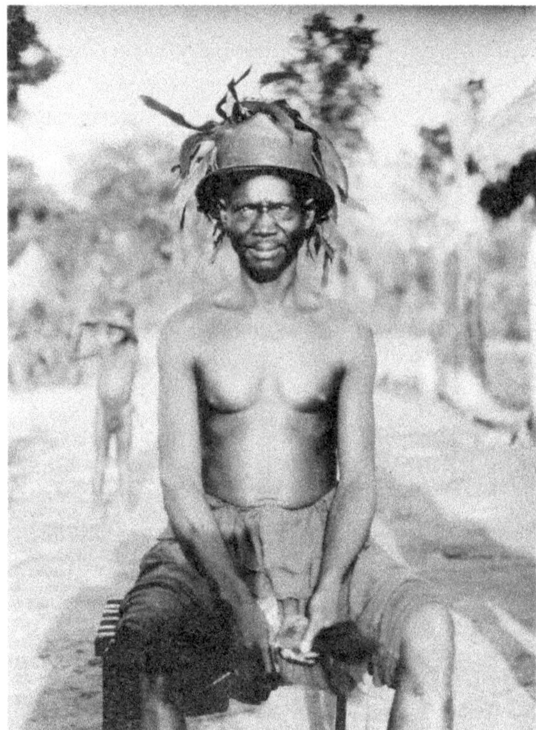

Figure 1.7 Portrait of an unidentified Zande man. Photograph by E. E. Evans-Pritchard, 1927–30.

anthropological conundrum which is entirely intentional on the author's part. This of course cannot be Ture, because Ture is a mythical folklore figure. A photograph has an indexical relationship to something once placed in front of a camera, and Ture the folkloric anti-hero cannot be photographed. And so using this syllogism we can deduce that this could not be Ture. Evans-Pritchard knows this, and so the caption sets up an internal contradiction about representation along the same lines as Magritte's 1928–9 painting *The Treachery of Images* that includes the famous text 'Ceci n'est pas une pipe'. Yet this tension between historical time (photography) and mythical time (Ture) is somehow resolved in Evans-Pritchard's caption that this *could* be Ture, in the sense that Ture is the Zande everyman in his unconscious desires, in which case his choice of portrait is arbitrary since all Zande men represent Ture. But this reading is unsatisfactory also. Evans-Pritchard doesn't use the illustration in the way that a physical anthropologist might to represent all Zande men; he uses it to introduce the idea that Ture has a reality in Zande thinking beyond that of an abstract folk character—that his appearance in culture is as real in some sense as something or someone that might be photographed. 'This could be Ture' becomes a statement about Zande rationality, which is consistent with his earlier writings on belief in witchcraft as an explanatory framework for misfortune, and the temporal entanglements that the use of a photograph to represent Ture involve only add to the anthropological point that Evans-Pritchard is attempting to make.

Photography and anthropological fieldwork in the 1920s and 1930s

One of the most significant wider contexts for any study of Evans-Pritchard as a fieldwork photographer, and his use of photography in subsequent published accounts, is how we might compare him with others in the period, how unusual or conventional was his photography, or other methods for that matter such as collecting objects, sound recordings, and vernacular texts. While his collection of over 2,500 photographs at the Pitt Rivers Museum suggests a prolific photographer, it is worth remembering that he spent more than three years in the field between 1926 and 1936. Nonetheless, his output is more than enough to make us question the occasional characterization of social anthropology in the period as less interested in photography and visual methods in general than the previous generation, with their physical anthropology, technology, and material culture interests. Whereas in the period 1870–1920, photography was a key tool for a generation of administrators, missionaries, and travellers to record other cultures, the general narrative goes that those being trained in UK universities had an increasingly ambivalent relationship to visual data gathering, seeing it as a tool of the 'old anthropology' including anthropometry (portraiture that includes a measuring device), general racial type description, recording items of material culture and technology, stages in the construction of art and craft objects, stages in ritual activity etc., all suggested as topics worthy of visual record in the guide *Notes and Queries on Anthropology*, published by a committee of the British Association for the Advancement of Science between 1874 and 1951. As Elizabeth Edwards wrote in her introduction to *Anthropology & Photography 1860–1920*, the new anthropological study of social institutions did not necessarily conceive of its subject matter as being visible in photographic terms. Photographs, Edwards argued, became specific to particular fieldwork engagements, and marginal to the process of explaining the general function of social institutions. As the anthropologist Anna Grimshaw has noted, there is a curious paradox in the 'centrality of vision to the kind of ethnographic fieldwork developed by Malinowski and his contemporaries, and yet the disappearance of explicit acknowledgement concerning the role of visual techniques and technologies, indeed vision itself, in the new fieldwork based monograph'.[39]

---

[39] A. Grimshaw. 2001. *The Ethnographer's Eye: Ways of Seeing in Modern Anthropology*. Cambridge: Cambridge University Press, 3.

But is this really true, or is it the result of a historiographical hall of mirrors in which our understanding of the period is constantly diverted by our reading of subsequent disciplinary histories of it? Did anthropology in the period really suffer from what Grimshaw terms 'iconophobia'? Well, the evidence I present throughout this book suggests that if we examine more closely the fieldwork, the archive, and the publication history of the period, we do reveal anthropology in the 1920s and 30s to be a highly visual practice, and occasionally we do even find explicit mention of fieldwork photography in the monographs of the period. In *Coral Gardens and Their Magic*, for instance, Malinowski states that he 'treated photography as a secondary occupation and a somewhat unimportant way of collecting evidence…I put photography on the same level as the collecting of curios – almost as an accessory relaxation of field-work.'[40] This statement is in an appendix; an almost throwaway comment, but one that shows just how radical was Malinowski's change of approach to that of the *Notes and Queries* generation of fieldworkers, assiduously recording culture with the camera. In this casual statement the new horizons of visual methods within academic anthropology in the UK, heralded by the Cambridge University expedition to the Torres Strait in 1898, took an enormous broadside hit: the most influential anthropologist of his generation only pulled out his camera for the 'dramatic, exceptional and sensational', and on the basis that something was picturesque and accessible. It could have been quite different. Malinowski in fact goes on to say how mistaken he was in his earlier attitude to photography during fieldwork, and that by giving it more attention later he was even able to check his field notes through reference to his photographs, which had led him to reformulate his statements on various points. But his most revealing comment by far is his criticism of his own aesthetic decision-making process that meant that he invariably didn't photograph socially meaningful or significant activities if they didn't look visually interesting. This, he said, was 'a deadly sin against the functional method, the main point of which is that form matters less than function'.[41] A gathering of Trobriand people talking about something important looked exactly the same as a gathering of people talking about something mundane, and so he didn't photograph it. This characterization of photography by Malinowski as a technology of limited use to anthropologists, since it couldn't distinguish subtleties of social context, was undoubtedly influential. His struggle with the possibility of the photographic image goes right to the heart of the matter, namely social anthropology's ambivalence about the sort of work the image can be expected to do, what evidence it

---

[40] B. Malinowski. 1935. *Coral Gardens and Their Magic: A Study of the Methods of Tilling the Soil and of Agriculture Rites in the Trobriand Islands. Vol 1: The Description of Gardening*. London: Allen & Unwin, 461.
[41] Malinowski, *Coral Gardens*, 462.

provides—is it data or merely illustration? And what is the importance and role of illustration in anthropology anyway?

While Malinowski's comments set the scene for British anthropology's uncertain intellectual relationship with photography from the 1920s, it is not the full picture by any means. Examining the fieldwork of a few near contemporaries in the period, the idea that photography was an ancillary activity does not square with the evidence of the archive, or in actual fact the original published article or monograph, and instead is probably more connected to the historiography of the discipline in the later twentieth century, and of the foundational history of functionalism and social anthropology in particular (in other words, a bias based on a strain of intellectual history writing). In addition to this, as I explore in detail in chapter 5 in relation to Evans-Pritchard's published imagery in *The Nuer*, historical shifts in the extent to which anthropology and photography came together as intellectual partners in the published account were crucially dependent on shifts in the economics of twentieth-century academic publishing. It is also worth reminding ourselves that the brand of social anthropology at the London School of Economics wasn't the only anthropology around in the interwar period: questions of race, the recording of material culture, technological practices, archaeology, architecture etc. were still of deep interest within universities up and down the UK, particularly in places like Oxford and Cambridge where the institutional organization of anthropology teaching was atomized in different departments and colleges, and photography continued to play a key role in research methods, as well as in the generation of archival and teaching resources.

Whereas in the analysis of race, cultural diffusion, and technology photography had a perceivedly (more than actually) data-collecting role, its social scientific role in the collecting of so-called 'social facts' such as, for instance, the morphology and function of magic (the title of Evans-Pritchard's first post-fieldwork research paper at the London School of Economics), was less clear. 'Social facts' gathered during fieldwork were obviously not so easy to corroborate with photographs. Nonetheless, the archive suggests that photography's descriptive power remained of crucial importance—its ability to describe and translate 'the field' in fact rose to the fore in social anthropology with the advent of more affordable cameras and film, becoming a ubiquitous visual notebook for anthropologists of the period, and, as I will argue in chapter 5, was of critical importance for Evans-Pritchard (as it was for Malinowski) in later cross-checking data in the writing process. Notebook. Pen. Pipe. Matches. Camera. You can almost hear Evans-Pritchard's morning mental checklist in the background detail captured in this image of a Zande potter's work (Figure 1.8); 'I attempted', he later wrote, 'without much success, to master the art under their guidance',[42] and it is in photographs such as

---

[42] Evans-Pritchard, *The Azande*, 95.

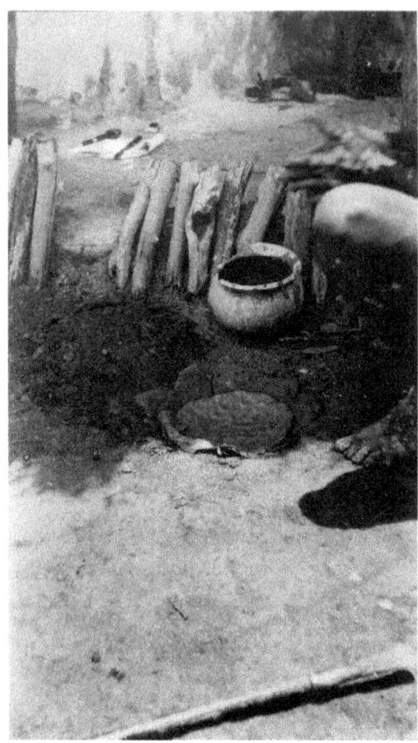

Figure 1.8 Iowa the Zande potter at work, with Evans-Pritchard's notebook, pen, pipe, and matches in the background. Photograph by E. E. Evans-Pritchard, 1927–30.

this that the ethnographer as participant shifts mode into observation, looking back on the scene of his participation and the tools of his observation.

The abundant evidence of visual interests in the archives of fieldworkers such as Evans-Pritchard goes against the grain of disciplinary histories of visual methods within anthropology in the 1920s and 1930s, which have suggested that the 'camera quickly disappeared from this model of ethnographic practice'.[43] Instead of image-based techniques, so the characterization goes, the Malinowskian revolution instead promoted the ethnographer's vision, their witness of a society at first-hand, as a central tenet, one that involves intuition and insight, rather than technology. If, in such a project, there was no place for the camera, then why do the archives of this period in anthropology show an explosion of photographic material generated by long-term field working anthropologists? My argument here is that this can't just be explained as being the result of technological developments that made cameras smaller and photography cheaper and easier to undertake in remote locations. We need a framework to reconcile this paradox, of the greater use of the camera (and other innovative audiovisual methods) in

---

[43] A. Grimshaw. 2008. 'Visual anthropology'. In *A New History of Anthropology*, edited by H. Kuklick. Oxford: Blackwell, 299.

fieldwork on the one hand, and intellectual histories of the discipline on the other, that see photography as being at best relegated to an illustrative function. While I return to this crucial theme in detail in chapter 5, where I compare the archival and publication contexts of Evans-Pritchard's photography, it is also a broad question that all the chapters in this book seek to address. For anthropology students in the 1920s more interested in functionalism than race, photography obviously held an uncertain position methodologically speaking, and it shifted frequently in the sorts of work it was put to. When looking across archives such as Evans-Pritchard's you can see a sort of visual identity crisis, but this doesn't seem to result in photographic paralysis—if anything, the prolific photographic output in the period suggests a representational freedom to explore anything and everything photographically. This is the snapshot generation after all, who had taken up photography as an informal social activity at home, and they brought similar practices to the field. I discuss in chapter 4 the way in which Evans-Pritchard's use of photography shifts in register within his fieldwork. His survey work among some of the smaller cultural groups in South Sudan, obtained for his teacher C. G. Seligman, tend to be dominated by physical anthropology, material culture, technology, and ritual classification images; he improvises by using a raincoat or cape hung up on a tree behind the subject so as to provide contrast against the features being recorded, as well as the figure being more or less carefully positioned to show the head and upper body only, as well as profile and back shots. Seligman was working on a large-scale survey of pagan (that is, non-Muslim) groups in the Sudan, and Evans-Pritchard's photographs left in Seligman's office at the London School of Economics were used liberally within the book. The photographs he took among the Azande contain some similar types of subject matter, but are quite different in general terms. In particular, while there are many portraits in his archive, there is very little concern with capturing the scientific reference of profile and full-face images in a shallow visual field. Instead, Evans-Pritchard's Zande portraits have a much more relaxed and individual style of representation, indexed in a less scrutinizing approach to the subject as a racial type, suggestive of closer social relationships developed during long-term fieldwork. Figure 1.9 shows a typical example, a portrait of Bangazegino, one of Prince Rikita's sons. Rather than the close observation of the physical type photograph, these portraits are at one remove, allowing space for personal expression and local meanings to crowd in. The subjects of these portraits bring possessions into the portrait with them, such as weapons or items of clothing, and although the portraits are often uniform in style, there is no feeling of an imposed or dominating scientific frame, but rather a given space within which aspects of Zande self-representation are allowed to be articulated.

These prints also show signs of having been placed in an album, and we know that Evans-Pritchard took photographs back to the field with him because he

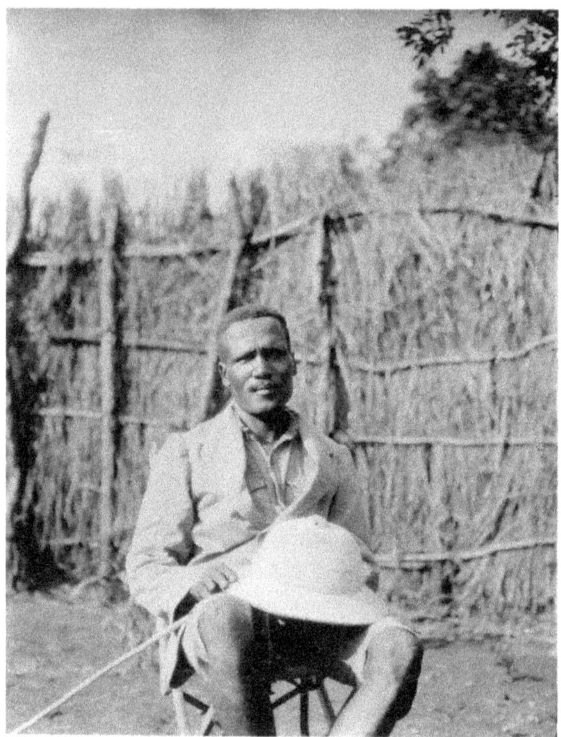

Figure 1.9 Bangazegino, a son of Prince Rikita. Photograph by E. E. Evans-Pritchard, 1927–30.

wrote a letter to Seligman on board a ship docked in Marseilles in early April 1928 on his way back to Sudan talking about the organization of his photo collection in Seligman's office during his break in fieldwork: 'I made a big effort to finish the work of cataloguing & arranging all my prints & negatives at the school, but I regret to say that the task was not completed.'[44] He then lists the locations for where his fieldwork photos should be kept, with his Ingessana and Moro prints at Seligman's house in Toot Baldon, and their matching negatives in his office at the London School of Economics; his Azande negatives were also to be kept at the London School of Economics, but his prints he was taking back to Sudan. Some of these prints are captioned in Zande rather than English, perhaps suggesting that he captioned them during fieldwork and using the language on a daily basis.[45] The relationship between photography and textuality in Evans-Pritchard's anthropology is something I return to in detail in chapter 3 in relation to his Zande

[44] Letter dated 6 April 1928, written on board SS Amarapoora at Marseilles (Pitt Rivers Museum Manuscript Collections, Evans-Pritchard Papers, Section 3, Box 1, Item 13).
[45] Written in pencil by Evans-Pritchard on the reverse of a print (Pitt Rivers Museum Photograph Collections, accession number 1998.341.681.2).

ethnography, and in particular his record of the initiation of his Zande assistant Kamanga as a *binza* or witch doctor. What the archive suggests to us is a complex relationship between observation and participation in which photography played a crucial role. While some have argued that British social anthropology came to see participant-observation as obviating the need for photography, I argue in chapter 7 that this is far from the case, and that if anything photography became even more essential to the participatory as well as the ongoing observational method in the discipline, with the anthropologist increasingly being found in the role of participant-photographer, rather than detached observer. In 1935 and 1936 for instance, Evans-Pritchard completed his final two short periods of fieldwork among the Nuer, of five weeks and seven weeks duration, taking over 400 photographs on each visit—roughly 10 per day on average. During his more extensive fieldwork of eight and a half months in Nuerland during 1930–1, he took on average just over one photograph per day. In chapter 7, I argue that the reason for his relative photographic inactivity in 1930–1 was the political situation prevailing in Nuerland at the time, a result of the mistrust caused by punitive strikes against Nuer herds by the colonial administration, meaning that he 'abstained from photographing a single cow'.[46]

The dramatic increase in his photographic activity in his later two short periods of Nuer fieldwork was due to several factors, including a slightly changed political context. More important was the decision to visit the home villages of two former Nuer assistants he had employed in his earlier fieldwork: in 1935 he went to Mancom at the mouth of the Nyanding River where his former assistant Tiop's family lived, and in 1936 he went to Nyueny, the home village of a youth called Nhial (Figure 1.10), 'as a friend of the family'.[47] The familiarity built up in this way by being introduced as a guest to a community by an existing contact is one that many anthropologists have experienced, and there is no doubt that Evans-Pritchard's photographs of 1935 and 1936 evidence an informality and level of access that was impossible in his earlier troubled fieldwork as an outsider to Nuer society. He even stated that to gain the acceptance (or at least the tolerance) of his Nuer hosts, he eventually acquired his own herd of cattle, which gave him a social existence, and then became a discussion point and opportunity to photograph activity in the cattle camp.[48] The acquisition of cattle as a direct result of fieldwork also resulted in a family dispute for one of Evans-Pritchard's Nuer field assistants, a youth called Wia (Figure 1.11). Wia had begun to work for Evans-Pritchard in 1930, and his willingness to come *rei Turuk* 'among the Turks', the generic name for government outsiders derived from the Turkish occupation in the nineteenth

---

[46] E. E. Evans-Pritchard. 1937. 'The economic life of the Nuer: cattle (part 1)', *Sudan Notes and Records*, 20(3), 242.

[47] E. E. Evans-Pritchard. 1956. *Nuer Religion*. Oxford: Clarendon Press, 35.

[48] E. E. Evans-Pritchard. 1973. 'Some reminiscences and reflections on fieldwork', *Journal of the Anthropological Society of Oxford*, 4(1), 2.

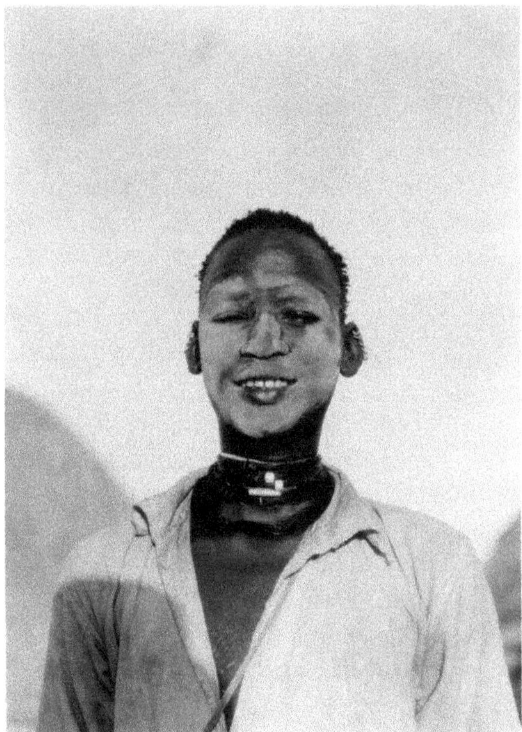

Figure 1.10 Evans-Pritchard's Lek Nuer assistant Nhial. Photograph by E. E. Evans-Pritchard, 1931.

century, was seemingly due to friction with his father, a man called Cam. After Evans-Pritchard finished fieldwork, Wia worked for the District Commissioner Frank Corfield in Nasir, and then again for Evans-Pritchard for a month in 1935 when he took the anthropologist to Cam's cattle camp at Yakwach. As a result of this employment he had bought cattle, which he kept at Nasir. A dispute then erupted between Wia and his father Cam, who argued that these cattle, earned as a result of working for Englishmen, should be used to pay bride-wealth for Wia's marriage. This Wia strongly rejected, arguing that it was his father's responsibility to provide the cattle from his own herd. 'There were lengthy and sometimes violent discussions on this theme', Evans-Pritchard noted, but Wia refused to give way, and Cam eventually did use his own cattle to provide the bride-wealth.[49] However, the rupture in relations between Wia and his father Cam brought about by his employment by Evans-Pritchard and Corfield seemed unhealable, and Wia

---

[49] E. E. Evans-Pritchard. 1945. *Some Aspects of Marriage and the Family Among the Nuer*. Rhodes-Livingstone Paper No. 11. Livingstone: The Rhodes-Livingstone Institute, 46.

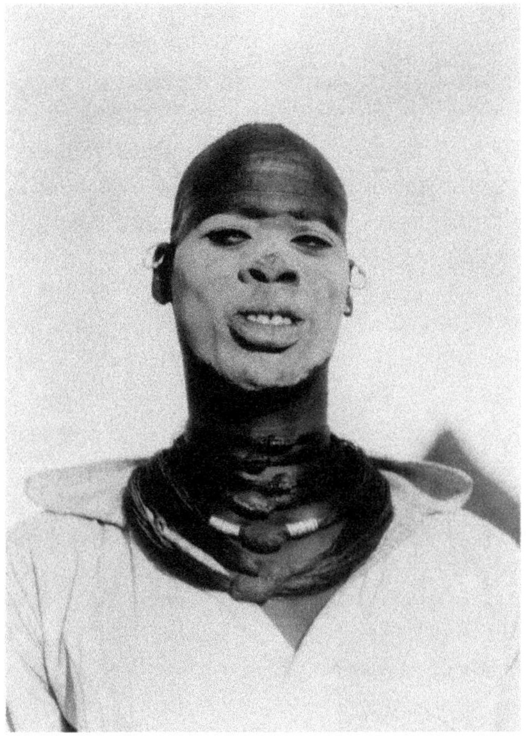

Figure 1.11 Evans-Pritchard's Lou Nuer assistant Wia. Photograph by E. E. Evans-Pritchard, 1931.

told Evans-Pritchard that he would almost certainly not settle in his father's camp again, but go and live with other relations elsewhere.

The ethnographic information that Wia's dispute brought to the surface was something that needed time and repeated visits to establish, and this shows just how important the two short visits he made to Nuerland in 1935 and 1936 were to the quality of data he eventually used to great effect in his published work. Evans-Pritchard's later Nuer fieldwork is also characterized by a completely new set of visual interests: the creation of photographic series and the desire to capture fleeting activity for later analysis, especially ritual activity, much of which was later to form the case studies in *Nuer Religion* (1956). Since he was invited to witness ritual activity as an accepted guest of the kin group he was living with, his ritual photographs are marked by their participatory and fragmentary nature; phases of photographic involvement around ritual activity are mixed with visual gaps that are often due his own involvement, gaps that are filled in with note-taking and subsequent narratives by participants. A close reading of the archive in conjunction with the published account therefore has the potential to turn on its head the dominant narrative of early British social anthropology as being uninterested in visual methods, which from a fieldwork, data-checking, and writing perspective is far from true. If we instead ask why anthropological publishers began to reduce the number of illustrations included in monographs as the twentieth century progressed, we uncover a new history of the discipline's relationship to the visual that has often been assumed to be the choice of its academic practitioners, but which was influenced much more by economic factors. Take for instance the collection of 1,900 field photographs taken in the early 1930s by another of Malinowski's students, Audrey Richards, which makes her almost as prolific a photographer as Evans-Pritchard who spent longer in the field. They are also very similar to Evans-Pritchard's, capturing everyday economic activities such as making pots, pounding grain, and gardening, as well as social activities such as dancing and children's play. Richards also took a number of photographs that require context, such as of men sitting on the ground next to a path, captioned 'Waiting for the blessing of nets'. This is the sort of photograph Malinowski didn't take because it was visually uninteresting, but which he later lamented, saying that such a gathering might look the same as a group of people come to gossip, but they were in fact as culturally dissimilar 'as a war canoe from a sago spoon'.[50] So why might Richards have taken the photograph which she later captioned 'Waiting for the blessing of nets'? We can only surmise that it was to record the socially significant stages of an ostensibly economic activity (hunting) that was interspersed with ritual activity (blessing). But the photograph doesn't show the blessing, it shows people waiting for the blessing, which is then echoed in the ethnographer's own waiting for socially significant activity to occur.

Audrey Richards published sixteen plates in the first 1939 edition of *Land, Labour and Diet in Northern Rhodesia*, including a classic frontispiece (after the manner of Malinowski's 'The ethnographer's tent on the beach of Nu'agasi') which she captions simply 'Bemba village – Nkula, 1930 (ethnographer's tent on left)'. Such photographs of course do multiple things—they help the reader visualize the field, but also situate and authenticate the ethnographer's experience and authority to write about the society with whom they lived. Most ethnographers have such images; Evans-Pritchard also published one in *The Nuer* that shows the pole and flaps of his tent (which I discuss in detail in chapter 5), and he took many more (see, for instance, Figure 4.5). Although sixteen plates were originally published, most copies of *Land, Labour and Diet* used by students over the last fifty years or so have been from the 1952, 1961, or (more likely) 1969 reprints, which reduced the plates to just four (two double-sided pages) besides the frontispiece. In the reprint, Richards tells the reader that 'since it has not been possible to reproduce all the illustrations used in the first edition of this book,

---

[50] Malinowski, *Coral Gardens*, 362.

references in the text to plate numbers of the original edition should be ignored'.[51] This is a common story; later reprints, especially after the Second World War, tended to cut the large number of illustrations drastically to save money. They were seen by editors as nice to have, but expendable in terms of the anthropological content. Despite authors occasionally raising a protest, they were often powerless since the rights to reprints and further editions were owned by the publisher. Of the four plates that did make the cut, the most interesting (Plate 4) again shows Richards's interest in photography and anticipation. The caption for the top image reads, 'Harvest ceremony. Bringing beer to the chiefs, Mpika District 1933. Note beer in gourd and man about to roll on his back to salute the dead chiefs.' Does she offer this note to explain his odd body posture? Did she take the image at this moment to capture his expected gesture to the dead chiefs? Whatever the answer, the explanatory note again asks the reader to think about what is about to happen in social life, as with the blessing of the nets, not beyond the photographic frame in a spatial sense, but in time.

In making a case for British social anthropology in the early to mid-twentieth century as anything but a non-photographic or non-visual practice, one other key piece of evidence is that the period was when the anthropological archive was essentially born, along with significant archives for other disciplines such as archaeology and art history. Aby Warburg's 'iconological' Mnemosyne Atlas of art historical photography came to London from Hamburg in 1933, and was reorganized in 1934, the same period in which archives at both the Pitt Rivers Museum in Oxford and in Cambridge were being assembled systematically for the first time. Henry Balfour's photographic archive project at the Pitt Rivers in 1931–2 was precipitated by about 2,000 photographs being made available from Beatrice Blackwood's Papua New Guinea fieldwork of 1929–30. So transformative was Blackwood's photographic material to the Pitt Rivers' existing collection that it precipitated a complete re-evaluation of the rationale for keeping photographs for comparative purposes, and led to the creation of an organized archive for exactly these purposes.[52] On Alfred Cort Haddon's eightieth birthday, in 1935 in Cambridge, he was presented with a collection of several thousand photographs mounted on card, arranged geographically in several wooden cabinets. These included copies of his own photographs, along with those of other Cambridge-connected scholars and their international networks. Haddon then donated these cabinets to the university's Museum of Archaeology and Anthropology to form the nucleus of a research collection. This was also a crucial period in the development of the Royal Anthropological Institute's (RAI) photographic archive, with

[51] A. Richards. 1969 [1939]. *Land, Labour and Diet in Northern Rhodesia: An Economic Study of the Bemba Tribe*. London: Published for the International Institute of African Languages and Cultures by the Oxford University Press, XIX.

[52] See C. Morton. 2012. 'Photography and the comparative method: the construction of an anthropological archive', *Journal of the Royal Anthropological Institute*, 18(2), 369–96.

new fieldwork collections being deposited by fellows to compliment the older research material that had gradually accumulated. A good example of its utility as an archive in the period is the heavy use made of it in general anthropological texts such as Jack Driberg's *At Home with the Savage* of 1932—nearly all plates having been sourced from the Royal Anthropological Institute's archive. The Royal Anthropological Institute had always collected photographic material via its members, exhibited it at meetings alongside correspondence and papers, and kept material for the research of fellows in its museum following meetings. In the 1920s and 30s, the academic role of the RAI archive continued, but shifted slightly from the keeping of visual evidence for consultation by members to a more general anthropological resource for its members to draw on for research, teaching, and illustration. Large teaching slide collections were built up in the period, copied from a wide range of sources. Increasingly, students began to learn about other cultures and societies in the lecture theatre through slides made from field photographs, rather than in the museum galleries looking at objects. Both field photography and its copying (rephotography) for pedagogical purposes is an important dimension of the visual history of the discipline that has been largely overlooked. The sharing and copying of fieldwork imagery among the first generation of fieldworking anthropologists was enormously important for teaching purposes, and the survival of one of Evans-Pritchard's sets of teaching slides allows us to see the selection he made from his own collection for teaching illustration (Figure 1.12). Anthropologists used professional networks to obtain valuable imagery for use in the classroom, building up comprehensive personal and institutional libraries of slides for general geography and anthropology teaching. While anthropologists could control the quantity and range of fieldwork material in their teaching collections of slides, the range of visual material in academic texts varied over time.

The 1930s saw a paperback revolution for popular reading, but the Great Depression led to high costs for lower volume academic works, with a resulting impact on any visual material included. Paper rationing from 1939 meant that editors needed to justify pages given over to images at the expense of text, and subsequent editions and paperbacks reduced the extent of visual material still further. What is more, their quality also gradually reduced due to the rephotography of plates. As I discuss in chapter 5, Evans-Pritchard's decision to reuse within *The Nuer* printing blocks from previously published journal articles was due to the increased cost of producing new blocks from original negatives at the onset of war.

As this book demonstrates, photography became an important aspect of the social interactions of fieldwork in the 1920s and 1930s, whether it was recording ethnographic information or taking informal portraits for local friends and informants, becoming the local photographer. This was not the case to the same extent in earlier survey anthropology without such nuanced social relationships nor having learned the local language. Anthropologists such as Evans-Pritchard

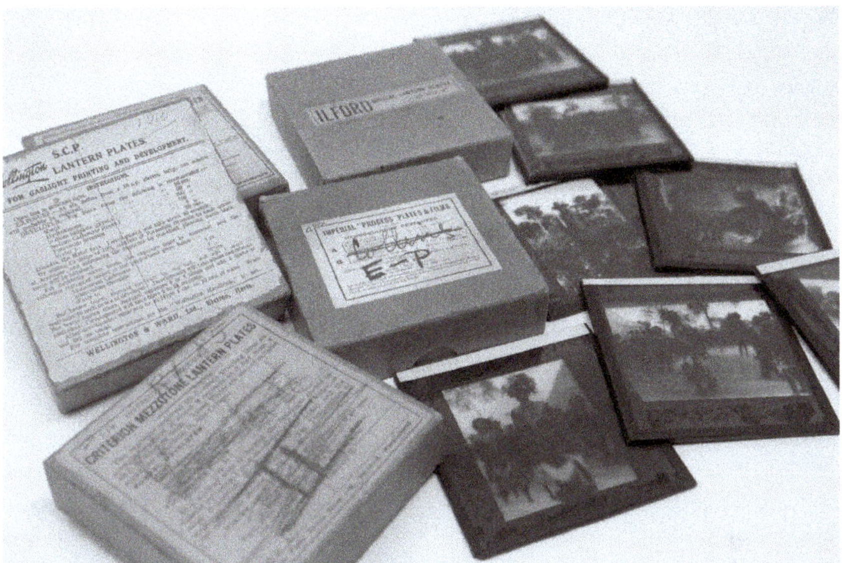

Figure 1.12 Evans-Pritchard's lantern slides, used for teaching until the 1960s. Photograph by the author, 2019.

lived in a much more visually mediated world than ever before; cinema and image-rich magazines and newspapers contributed towards the cultural dominance of the photographic image that continues to this day. We need then to reconcile on the one hand these facts: that anthropologists did move with these cultural shifts and did generate extensive collections of audiovisual material, that photography became a normalized part of the social interactions of long-term fieldwork, that teaching became even more dominated by field photography, and that monographs included many more fieldwork images (albeit with fluctuations dependent on the economy), with the fact that on the other hand British social anthropology has been generally understood as turning its back on visual methods in this period, with a perceived analytical movement towards the textual analysis of social institutions, with functionalism and structural-functionalism, and that images were good only for front covers and showing the ethnographer's tent. This book sets out to argue that this perception has partly been promoted over the years as a political move to characterize the foundational story of institutional British social anthropology as a move away from the atavistic values of racial and cultural enquiry seen in the nineteenth and early twentieth centuries. This is a historiographical matter as much as anything. But as most of the chapters in this book explore, we will only gain a deeper understanding of anthropology's relationship to the visual if we look beyond superficial histories of the discipline based only on its published form, and see beyond into its archival, material, and fieldwork realities.

2

Survivals, surveys, and struggles

First fieldwork

A life of adventure

Having enjoyed a privileged early education at preparatory and public school, Evans-Pritchard gained a scholarship in history at Exeter College, Oxford. Not thinking much of his history tutor there ('a complete philistine'), he found that Exeter College was in fact the 'home' of anthropology in Oxford, due to the presence of the ethnologist R. R. Marett, whom he later referred to as 'that genial boaster'.[1] Evans-Pritchard was, according to his contemporary Raymond Firth, 'an expert in the glancing blow'.[2] But Marett was not the only anthropologist at Exeter, with Henry Balfour (Curator of the Pitt Rivers Museum) and L. H. D. Buxton (a physical anthropologist) also members of the Common Room, as well as students such as Francis Turville-Petrie and colonial ethnographers such as R. S. Rattray passing through. It was the influence of these figures that Evans-Pritchard credits for establishing him during his undergraduate years as 'an anthropologist in embryo'. Although he had begun to vary his history reading with anthropological classics such as Tylor's *Primitive Culture* and Frazer's *The Golden Bough*, Evans-Pritchard wasn't attracted to the intellectualist tradition of studying the field reports of travellers—he wanted 'a life of adventure too'.[3] Seeing Oxford as firmly following Tylor's historical and comparative approach to culture, and that it would offer him little in the way of fieldwork training, in 1924 Evans-Pritchard enrolled at the London School of Economics to study with Charles Gabriel Seligman, who had been on the Cambridge expedition to the Torres Strait in 1898, and subsequently carried out fieldwork in New Guinea, India, and Sudan. Evans-Pritchard may well have first learned of the anthropological richness of the southern regions of Sudan in Charles Seligman's Lent (Spring) Term lectures at the LSE in 1925 on 'The Nile Valley and Its Peoples'. He subsequently formed a close bond with his teacher and wife Brenda, using his office between periods of fieldwork. He also stored there, and at

---

[1] E. E. Evans-Pritchard. 1973. 'Genesis of a social anthropologist', *New Diffusionist*, 3(10), 18.

[2] R. Firth. 2004. 'Bronislaw Malinowski'. In *Totems and Teachers: Key Figures in the History of Anthropology*, edited by S. Silverman. Walnut Creek, USA: Altamira Press, 89.

[3] Evans-Pritchard, 'Genesis of a social anthropologist', 18.

their home in Toot Baldon, Oxfordshire, photographs and objects brought back from the field.[4] For instance, in a letter to L. W. G. Malcolm of the Wellcome Historical Medical Museum, written on his return from fieldwork in 1930, he writes that he would be grateful if someone could collect the objects he was selling to them as soon as possible, since 'Professor Seligman is getting rather upset at their continued occupation of his room'.[5] Although he later described Seligman as not having a brilliant mind, but at least one of integrity, it is clear that Seligman's practical support of his young protégé was instrumental to his subsequent career. Circumstances helped the young scholar also. On his return from fieldwork in Sudan in 1922, supported by the Sudanese government, Seligman's health deteriorated to the point of ruling out further visits despite his large ethnographic survey project being only partially complete, and he persuaded the Civil Secretary Sir Harold MacMichael to take on his student instead; 'so all the rest follows', admitted Evans-Pritchard.[6]

Survival of a sun god?

With MacMichael saying he could go and study what he wished, since he chose the man but not the plan, Evans-Pritchard was soon attracted to working with the Azande. But as a dutiful student, he also agreed to assist Seligman in the collection of ethnographic data about a number of other 'pagan' (i.e. non-Arab) groups in Sudan during his travels to and from the region. The first of these visits was to the Ingessana, towards the end of 1926, as Evans-Pritchard made his way down the country towards Zandeland, a group that the Seligmans collected some information about on their first visit to Sudan and had long wished to follow up. Brenda Seligman states that all of her language information about the Ingessana living on Jebel Tabi was collected in 1909–10 at Jebel Gule, some distance away, over the course of almost a week. At Gule, the Seligmans investigated the ancestral cult of Queen Soba who was associated with a stone and two other rocks around the base of Jebel Gule (Figure 2.1). The information they gathered on the Tabi language was more sketchy, collected over a number of hours over three days from a sheikh and his people visiting Gule from Tabi. The people of Tabi are called Ingessana by the Arabs, but more recent ethnographers have preferred the term that the people call themselves—Gamk. Charles Seligman also talked to these visitors from Tabi, and later published a note in the colonial magazine *Sudan Notes and Records*. This note came out in 1924, at around the same time that Evans-Pritchard became

---

[4] Letter from Evans-Pritchard to Seligman, 6 April 1928 (Pitt Rivers Museum Manuscript Collections, Evans-Pritchard Papers, Section 3, Box 1, Item 3).

[5] Letter from Evans-Pritchard to L. W. G. Malcolm, 12 December 1930 (Pitt Rivers Museum, Related Documents File [1930.86.1–65]).

[6] Evans-Pritchard, 'Genesis of a social anthropologist', 19.

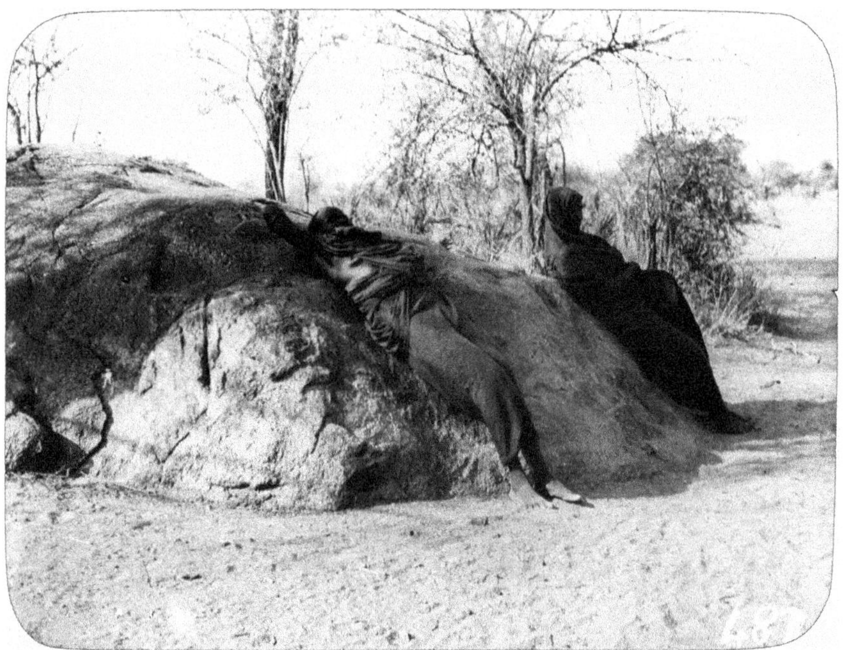

Figure 2.1 Tired women leaning against Soba rock. Lantern slide by C. G. or
B. Z. Seligman, Jebel Gule, Blue Nile, Sudan, 1910.

Seligman's pupil at the London School of Economics. In this article, Seligman
states that he offers his observations 'in the hopes that they may stimulate
others to investigate and publish accounts of the habits and customs of the
peoples of the anthropologically unknown area between the White and
Blue Niles'.[7] He may well have reiterated this hope in his lecture on the peoples
of the Nile the following Lent term, where Evans-Pritchard may have acquired
his first detailed introduction to the region from a man who had travelled there
several times. Seligman's hopes that others would continue anthropological
investigations in Dar Fung were motivated by more than a desire to collect
and collate information for his long-planned book, *Pagan Tribes of Nilotic
Sudan*, eventually published in 1932. After falling ill after his third trip to
Sudan in 1922, he did not fully recover for some time, and so it was likely
that when writing up his earlier notes he knew that future fieldwork in the
country would be impossible.[8]

A key reason that Seligman found the peoples of this region of especial interest
was 'the existence of a definite sun-cult' among them. The men from Tabi he met

---

[7] C. G. Seligman. 1924. 'Note on Jebel Tabi', *Sudan Notes and Records*, 7(2), 111.
[8] C. S. Myers. 1941. 'Charles Gabriel Seligman. 1873–1940', *Obituary Notices of Fellows of the Royal
Society*, 3(10), 635.

said that the sun was called Tel, and that 'the sun created all but who or what was first created was unknown'. According to his informants, a long time ago a shrine sacred to Tel had been built, before Islam had come to the region. People would gather there and pray to Tel before fighting, or offer sacrifices to heal the sick at sunrise.[9] Seligman compares his findings about sun worship to some notes published by J. P. Mostyn a few years earlier about the Burun to the south of the Ingessana of Jebel Tabi. Mostyn stated that in two locations he visited in 1915 'the sun is the big god' and that 'the rain and the sun are considered 'gods'. The sun being the bigger god of the two as he appears daily whilst the rain only comes in the rainy season'.[10] Mostyn doesn't give any further linguistic or cultural information about what his Burun informants were referring to, and considered his notes to be 'very possibly inaccurate'. Seligman also draws upon the archaeological evidence of a 'rock drawing' published four years earlier in the same journal by the Sudanese government's Director of Education John Winter Crowfoot. The rock drawing, covering the northern face of a detached rock at the south-east end of the main part of Jebel Qeili (or Geili), was described by Crowfoot as representing 'a Meroitic King, whose name was cut in an illegible cartouche above his head, worshipping a rayed solar divinity to whom he has apparently offered a number of captives'.[11] This rock drawing is now understood to be the only known monument to the late Meroitic King Sherkarer, in the form of a victory stele commemorating his triumph over some unknown enemies and receiving the blessing of the sun god.[12] Scholars have found the figure of the sun god in this monument something of a puzzle. Not being an obvious Egyptian deity, he features much less in Meroitic texts than the lion god. One suggestion is that this sun god is evidence of the spread of Persian influence through the Mithraic cult, which was popular throughout the Roman Empire at this time.[13] For Seligman, this evidence was tantalizing. 'Jebel Geili is only some 200 miles north of Jebel Tabi', he wrote with palpable excitement, 'so that it becomes a legitimate speculation to consider whether the sun-cult of the Fung region stands in direct continuity with that of Meroe and so with ancient Egypt.'[14] The cult of Queen Soba at Jebel Gule was also, for C. G. Seligman, a cause for reflection on ancient connections. Witnessing women speaking to Queen Soba at one of the rocks associated with her (Figure 2.1), he ponders whether the cult 'preserves the memory of such queens as that Candace who ruled the Sembritae of the Gezira in the third century BC, and of Soba, the great city which to the negroids of the Gezira no doubt appeared to dominate the north.'[15]

---

[9] Seligman, 'Note on Jebel Tabi', 111.

[10] J. P. Mostyn. 1921. 'Some notes on Burun customs and beliefs', *Sudan Notes and Records*, 4, 209.

[11] J. W. Crowfoot. 1920. 'Old sites in the Butana', *Sudan Notes and Records*, 3, 88.

[12] W. Y. Adams. 1977. *Nubia: Corridor to Africa*. London: Allen Lane, 312.

[13] Adams, *Nubia*, 327.   [14] Seligman, 'Note on Jebel Tabi', 111.

[15] C. G. Seligman and B. Z. Seligman. 1932. *Pagan Tribes of the Nilotic Sudan*. London: Routledge, 429.

C. G. Seligman, like many of his contemporaries, had a keen interest in the dissemination, adaptation, survival, and influence of cultural forms, especially Egyptian. In 1911 for instance, shortly after returning from his first trip to Sudan, Seligman co-authored a paper with his friend, the Egyptologist Margaret Murray, on the ancient Egyptian 'Sa' sign, which, they argued, was associated with the uterus.[16] A couple of years later, in 1913, he explored these ideas further in an essay on the survival of ancient Egyptian ideas and customs in modern Egypt. Rather than understanding any similarity between them as arising from 'instances of similar customs arising among cognate peoples', Seligman's line of argument in this essay was that 'it seems legitimate to regard them rather as direct survivals'.[17] The concept of 'survivals' in culture of course has a very specific meaning for anthropologists, arising from the work of Edward Burnett Tylor in his book *Primitive Culture* of 1871. 'When a custom, an art or an opinion', wrote Tylor, 'is fairly started in the world, disturbing influences may long affect it so slightly that it may keep its course from generation to generation'.[18] On the one hand then, Seligman's interest in the survival of a sun-cult in Dar Fung can be understood as being a fairly orthodox Tylorian exploration of the persistence or retention of a religious custom from Meroitic times to his own ethnological observations in 1910. As he himself acknowledged, this didn't necessarily mean that such survivals were unusual, it was just that given the relative richness of our knowledge of ancient Egyptian and Meroitic culture 'it is possible to adduce perfectly definite evidence of their direct continuity over a very much longer period of time.'[19]

Yet in making a direct and breathless connection across time between sun-cult customs in Dar Fung, Meroe, and Egypt in his 1924 journal article, Seligman was also reflecting a strong intellectual trend in the period. The year before, in 1923, William Perry had published his most significant work to date, *The Children of the Sun*, being the latest and most elaborate statement from what was known as the diffusionist school of anthropological thought. The main proponents of this school, Perry and Grafton Elliot Smith, Professor of Anatomy at University College London, had caught the imagination of their contemporaries in the midst of Egyptomania, with a bold new hypothesis that saw Egypt as the cradle of civilization, and that its cultural influence had diffused across the world over time. In *The Children of the Sun*, Perry argues that a great ruling caste arose in Egypt in the Fifth Dynasty (around 2750 BC) identified with Re, the sun god of

---

[16]   C. G. Seligman and M. Murray. 1911. 'Note on the "Sa" sign', *MAN*, 11, 113–17.

[17]   C. G. Seligman. 1913. 'Ancient Egyptian beliefs in modern Egypt'. In *Essays and Studies Presented to William Ridgeway on His Sixtieth Birthday*, edited by E. C. Quiggin. Cambridge: Cambridge University Press, 448.

[18]   E. B. Tylor. 1891 [1871]. *Primitive Culture: Researchers into the Development of Mythology, Philosophy, Religion, Language, Art, And Custom*. Vol. 1. London: John Murray (3rd edition), 70.

[19]   Seligman, 'Ancient Egyptian beliefs', 448.

Heliopolis. The influence of this powerful ruling caste, argued Perry, helped spread heliocentric culture to the east, and traces of their influence may be seen in many cultures, although degraded over time (Figure 2.2).[20] Although heavily criticized by many of their contemporaries, Seligman's relationship to diffusionism was more complex. In 1911, W. H. R. Rivers, one of Seligman's companions on the Cambridge Expedition to the Torres Strait in 1898, announced his 'conversion' to the new paradigm, interpreting certain cultural parallels between ancient Egypt and the Torres Strait Islands, most notably mummification.[21] In working through his own data from his 1909–10 and 1911–12 visits to Egypt and Sudan, Seligman likewise felt the allure of a diffusionist explanatory framework. In an extended journal article in 1913 on 'Some aspects of the Hamitic problem in Anglo-Egyptian Sudan', he wrote that by comparing his own data with that of ancient Egyptian records and medieval Arabic writers, 'comparison of this

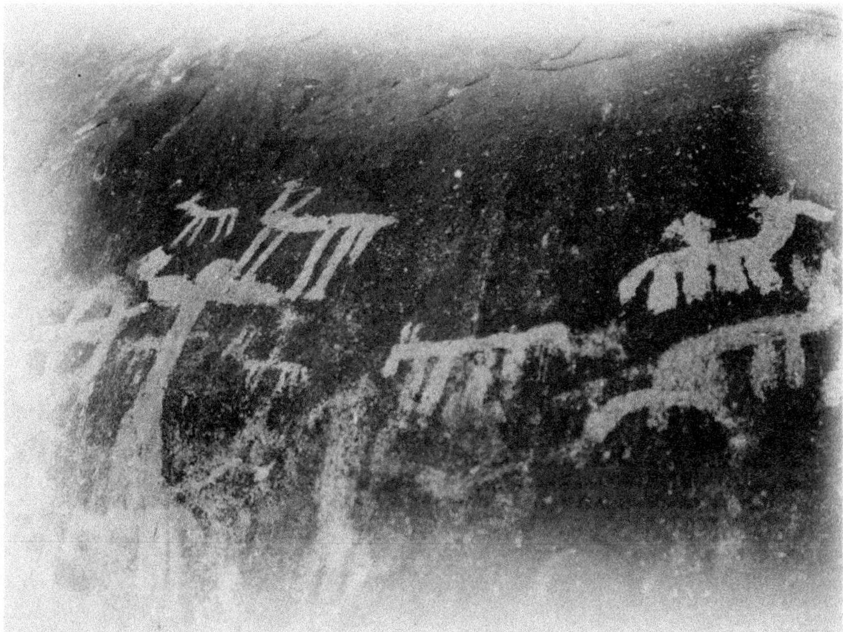

Figure 2.2 Animal designs painted on a rock face, possibly at Jebel Wadega (Jumjum people), Blue Nile, Sudan. Photograph by E. E. Evans-Pritchard, 1926.

---

[20] P. Crook. 2012. *Grafton Elliot Smith, Egyptology and the Diffusion of Culture*. Brighton: Sussex Academic Press, 57.

[21] F. Barth. 2014. 'Britain and the Commonwealth'. In *One Discipline, Four Ways: British, German, French, and American Anthropology*, edited by F. Barth, A. Gingrich, R. Parkin, and S. Silverman. Chicago: University of Chicago Press, 17.

material leads me to believe that among the culture strata lying buried beneath the present day cultures of North-Eastern and Eastern Africa there are remains of one which presents such substantial affinities with that of ancient Egypt that there can be no legitimate objection to speaking of it as Hamitic.'[22]

The Hamitic hypothesis had been discussed by anthropologists since the mid nineteenth century, essentially seeking an explanatory framework for elements of what were considered 'civilized' culture traits in sub-Saharan Africa. Seligman's contribution sought to bring a new scientific rigour to the old theory by exploring physical and linguistic data. Despite his great efforts in this direction, his conclusions sound today vague and conjectural in the extreme. The peoples of the region, he concludes, 'either represent the descendants of that stock which gave rise to the proto-Egyptians or have been permeated by its influence'.[23] In other words, their noted cultural and physical similarities can be explained either by the fact that they are related to them, or else have been the subject of cultural diffusion. What the argument did of course was firmly shut the lid on any idea of independent invention of ideas or customs by different peoples over time, an idea connected to Tylor's concept of the 'physic unity' of humankind and which had been a point of contention ever since, especially for diffusionists. In thrall to the allure of ancient Egypt, anthropologists such as Seligman could only really imagine cultural influence working in one direction. For instance, when comparing the Nuer custom of training the left horn of an ox to grow across its face with an ancient Egyptian depiction of an ox with an apparently trained left horn, Seligman concludes that, 'the fact that up to and including the Pyramid period Negroes are almost entirely absent from Egyptian representational art can but indicate that the spread was from Egypt up the Nile, and not in the reverse direction'.[24] The idea that cultural influences may have travelled down the Nile, or that such depictions were actually of highly prized oxen from Sudan, somehow did not fit the underlying story of Hamitic cultural influence.

The intellectual backdrop to Evans-Pritchard's first fieldwork trip to Sudan, and to Dar Fung in particular, was therefore one involving some of the grand anthropological debates of the preceding twenty years. But when it came to his own investigations in Dar Fung, beginning in early November 1926, Evans-Pritchard was not tempted to see the influence of ancient Egypt or Meroe. As for the Meroitic sun god identified by Seligman in his present form as *Tel* at Jebel Tabi, Evans-Pritchard was dismissive: 'Tel seems to be regarded as a beneficent but distant being. I think that in every-day talk the sun is regarded as a natural

<hr>

[22]   C. G. Seligman. 1913. 'Some aspects of the Hamitic problem in Anglo-Egyptian Sudan', *Journal of the Royal Anthropological Institute*, 43, 593.

[23]   Seligman, 'Some aspects of the Hamitic problem', 682.

[24]   Seligman and Seligman, *Pagan Tribes of the Nilotic Sudan*, 36.

feature rather than a deity.'[25] In this interpretation we find Evans-Pritchard echoing the words of Charles Elliot in his introduction to Hollis's account of the Nandi (whom Evans-Pritchard would later make a study of), when he notes that the Nandi sun god *Asis* was a 'benevolent and powerful, but somewhat vague deity'.[26] In heading to the Tabi Hills, it is already clear that it was the influence of Malinowski and a functional interpretation of religion that already held sway over the young anthropologist, rather than the diffusionist-inspired speculations of Seligman:

> The Ingassana appeal to *tel* when they want rain, they appeal to him when someone is ill, or when a woman is barren. When a man dies they say that *tel* has killed him. Thus it will be seen that they appeal to *tel* in the important emotional crises of life, such as in conception, in illness, at death, and when they are threatened with some natural calamity such as the absence of rain.[27]

This sort of formulation prefigures both Evans-Pritchard's literary style in his later monographs, but also his intellectual sympathy towards those he was to spend time with and study. His seemingly innocuous statement that Ingessana religion functions to help deal with the psychological stress of emotionally difficult life events prefigures his later formulations about the inherent rationality of Zande witchcraft belief as an alternative way of organizing social life. Evans-Pritchard's sympathetic psychological interpretation of the Ingessana's relationship to *tel* marks an important turning point in British social anthropology, one that signalled a definite break with the diffusionism, antiquarianism, and speculative racism that preoccupied much earlier anthropology. It was arguably the moment when Malinowski's influence and ideas met their match in an ethnographer.

It is curious then that, later in life, Evans-Pritchard was to become much more sympathetic to historicism and diffusionism in anthropology. Although, as a student at Exeter College, he was keen to get away from 'the tedium of the History School'[28] in anthropology represented by R. R. Marret and others, he was nonetheless drawn to both Elliot Smith and Perry at University College London during his London years. Indeed, Elliot Smith helped Evans-Pritchard get his first academic job, in the King Fuad I University of Cairo in 1932, and he was friends with two of Elliot Smith's sons.[29] Although not totally convinced by some of diffusionism's 'rather wild speculation' he nonetheless held that 'the point of view of Elliot Smith and the others

[25] E. E. Evans-Pritchard. 1927. 'A preliminary account of the Ingassana tribe in Fung province', *Sudan Notes and Records*, 10, 83.

[26] C. Eliot. 1909. 'Introduction'. In A. C. Hollis, *The Nandi: Their Language and Folklore*. Oxford: Clarendon Press, xix.

[27] Evans-Pritchard, 'A preliminary account of the Ingassana tribe', 83.

[28] Evans-Pritchard, 'Genesis of a social anthropologist', 18.

[29] E. E. Evans-Pritchard. 1971. 'Recollections and reflections', *New Diffusionist*, 2, 37.

(Hocart was more cautious) is entirely justified and should be restored to its place in anthropology'.[30] In the introduction to this book, I set out some of the contexts in which Evans-Pritchard's historical form of anthropology took shape. But here I want to explore further one particular dimension of Evans-Pritchard's intellectual move back towards history, and that was the tremendous personal, lifelong, competitive, animosity he enjoyed with Malinowski. Although heavily influenced by the new social anthropological approach in his break with the racial and cultural speculations of Seligman and others, his increasing turn back towards history was arguably as personal as it was intellectual. 'It has been a misfortune for anthropology', he wrote, 'that it lost its time perspective in this country, largely under the influence of Radcliffe-Brown and Malinowski, the first with no interest in particular events and the second having an interest in only one immediate set of them (the Trobriand Islanders).'[31] As we shall now see, his later statement that 'I never got on with Malinowski, and Seligman would not, or could not, stand up to him',[32] had its roots in a particular set of confrontations that were to arguably have deep consequences for the subsequent intellectual direction of British social anthropology.

Battles with Malinowski

Evans-Pritchard's arrival at the London School of Economics in the autumn of 1924 happened to coincide with Malinowski also joining the department as a tenured member of academic staff. Although Evans-Pritchard was to retain a lifelong intellectual respect for Malinowski, crediting him for impressing on him the importance of recording vernacular texts as well as the understanding that 'facts are in themselves meaningless' and that it is only through theoretical training that the anthropologist knows 'what and how to observe',[33] the relationship was explosive, and led to years of animosity. But what do we know exactly about the roots of this fractured relationship between teacher and pupil? Well, Malinowski's papers do reveal some of the circumstances, and are in fact a fascinating insight into both the highly personal nature of teacher–pupil relationships in the period, and the crucible of intellectual debate that characterized the anthropology department at the London School of Economics in the 1920s.

On 2 February 1928, soon after writing up a PhD thesis based on only six months' fieldwork among the Azande during 1927, Evans-Pritchard presented a paper on 'The Morphology and Function of Magic' at Malinowski's Thursday

---

[30] Evans-Pritchard, 'Recollections and reflections', 38.
[31] Evans-Pritchard, 'Recollections and reflections', 39.
[32] Evans-Pritchard, 'Genesis of a social anthropologist', 19.
[33] E. E. Evans-Pritchard. 1973. 'Some reminiscences and reflections on fieldwork', *Journal of the Anthropological Society of Oxford*, 4(1), 1.

seminar at the London School of Economics. A year later, in a letter to Elsie Masson, Malinowski remembers the event distinctly:

LSE. Sat. 19 January 1929

My own darling … I went to the School this morning and joined Yates who had to scrutinize Evans-Pritchard's article on Magic. You remember the paper he read to us last winter—you were present and then we all went to the flat and Evans-Pritchard got offended with me. Or was it in the autumn term? Somehow I think you were there. Anyhow, he gave me the paper, I commented on it, he has now just sent it back to me and asked me to pass it finally for press … we 'passed' it this morning, Cicely [Bevan, Bronio's Sec.] has taken it with her home to type it. I shall send it to Lowie to print in the American Anthropologist.[34]

To which Masson replied three days later from their home in Gries (a suburb of Bolzano (Bozen) in Italy): 'I was of course there when Evans-Pritchard was so beleidigt [offended]. That was a year ago exactly. That term was made rather ugly by Pritchard and Driberg quarrels.'[35] It is clear from this correspondence that, for it to be so bitterly remembered a year later, the 'offence' taken by Evans-Pritchard at Malinowski's basement flat in Doughty Street after the seminar must have been severe, and seems to be the first documented falling-out between the two, leading to an enduringly strained personal relationship. But, until recently, it had been entirely unclear just what happened at Malinowski's flat that Thursday afternoon in February 1928. Two letters from Evans-Pritchard to Malinowski however, in a folder marked 'Battles' among Malinowski's papers at the London School of Economics, are revealing. The first was evidently written the day after the Doughty Street incident, the second presumably a day or so after that. The first letter is typed, brief, and certainly offended, but not hastily written since it was composed the next day, 3 February 1928:

Dear Prof. Malinowski,

With reference to your statement last night that you believed that I had 'cooked' and 'faked' field-work material, I think that you owe me some kind of explanation. I have never been more deeply wounded in my life and you should have been the first to realize what bitterness such an insinuation must cause in a person engaged in & with a strong sentiment towards scientific work.
Yours, E. E. Evans-Pritchard[36]

---

[34] H. Wayne. 1995. *The Story of a Marriage: The letters of Bronislaw Malinowski and Elsie Masson. Volume 2 1920–1935.* London: Routledge, 132.

[35] Wayne, *Story of a Marriage*, 133.

[36] London School of Economics archive, Malinowski Papers, 37/21, letter dated 3 February 1928.

The second letter, handwritten and undated, shows signs of being much more hastily composed, and is contrite in the extreme:

Dear Dr Malinowski,

I unreservedly apologise for my letter. I was certainly under the impression you had made the statement I referred to & Schapera also was under this impression too.

However, I am very sorry indeed. I was angry not because it is by any means inconceivable that I should cook my facts but just because there is an incessant desire to do so which has to be rigourously [sic] repressed. I have to ask myself again & again everyday 'are you certain this is really so or are you simply selecting part of the facts to fit them in with your theory?' We are always angry when we think that we are accused of a line of conduct which we would like to take but have to repress—so please regard my letter in the light of Freud's teaching! I did not send you my M.S. to Italy partly because I did not think you would read it and partly because I did not think it was much good. I fully appreciate the compliment you paid me in coming to my lectures & was grateful for your praise. Your teaching was my great source of inspiration in the 'field'.

I consider my work to be deplorable, my material being inadequate, fragmentary, insufficiently checked–& I had hoped, & still keep on hoping, that you will help me reformulate the problems, gather up the uneven strands & make clear the objectives. Far from wishing to quarrel with you my desire is & has always been to learn from you & to be as friendly as possible. What infuriates me is that when I am anxious for your help about some problem you are completely inaccessible. However in future I shall take you at your word and bombard you with M.S. and hope for the best.

Yours, E. E. E-P.[37]

So the Doughty Street incident becomes a bit clearer. Even if Evans-Pritchard and Isaac Schapera did misconstrue a characteristically forthright remark by Malinowski as a personal attack on Evans-Pritchard's academic methods, it is evident that the criticism of 'cooking' data struck at the heart of the younger anthropologist's insecurity. The contrition of the second letter seems to address a number of rebuttals quickly made by Malinowski, presumably in an immediate reply. There are at least two other important contextual points to make about this incident. The first is a highly personal one for Malinowski. By the end of January 1928, Elsie Masson, whose health had deteriorated over recent years, had eventually received the diagnosis that they must have been dreading—multiple sclerosis.[38]

---

[37] London School of Economics archive, Malinowski Papers, 37/21, handwritten letter, no date.
[38] Wayne, *Story of a Marriage*, 110.

This recent hard news provides a highly emotional context to the meeting at their Doughty Street flat only a few days later.

In addition, and perhaps in combination, Evans-Pritchard's paper was a direct critique of Malinowski's work: 'I shall attempt to demonstrate in this paper', he wrote, 'that the principles of magic deduced from Melanesian data and formulated as general laws for all societies have, in view of a study of African peoples, to be reformulated and possibly modified. I shall show how this is so by a comparison between the magic of a Melanesian society described by Professor Malinowski and the magic of an African society investigated by myself.'[39] In other words, Evans-Pritchard's paper would generalize based on scientific comparison, whereas Malinowski's theoretical generalizations would be seen to have been drawn from only one example. No doubt Malinowski did feel, when listening to Evans-Pritchard's counterexamples of magical practice in Zandeland, that this student's six months' as opposed to his nearly two years' worth of fieldwork did not entitle him to 'reformulate' his own functional analysis of magic. There seems little doubt on the face of it that it was Evans-Pritchard's critique of Malinowski's theory of magic that prompted the Doughty Street incident. Malinowski's complaint that Evans-Pritchard hadn't passed him a copy of his paper before his presentation, which prompted the response that he didn't think Malinowski would read it, also suggests that relations between them were not particularly close or cordial.

Evans-Pritchard's second, apologetic, letter was possibly advised by Seligman, who understood how important a professional relationship with Malinowski would be to his future career. Indeed, this sort of ongoing mediation by Seligman between the two anthropologists was crucial in 1931 in gaining Evans-Pritchard his first teaching position in Cairo. Although Seligman was against him applying for the post at King Fuad I University, he knew full well that his student would need a reference from Malinowski to gain a position, and that the absence of one would look bad. In a letter to Malinowski in September 1931, Seligman writes that Evans-Pritchard 'feels you have so strong a feeling against him that it would not be fair' to ask Malinowski for a reference. Despite the bad blood between them, Seligman's insistence on a professional relationship based on academic ability, rather than personality, meant that Malinowski did indeed provide the crucial reference, despite Evans-Pritchard later claiming that he attempted to bar him and that Grafton Elliot Smith was more useful in getting him the position. In a response to Seligman's request in October 1931, Malinowski reiterated his own position:

> I perfectly well remember the gist of our conversation at the school and my promise to you to assist E-P in his career, and you will see from the enclosed

[39] E. E. Evans-Pritchard. 1929. 'The morphology and function of magic. A comparative study of Trobriand and Zande ritual and spells', *American Anthropologist*, New Series, 31(4), 619–20.

testimonial that I am redeeming my promise. You will remember also the two caveats I made: first that I could not very well co-operate with E-P in the same place, considering the bitter hostility which he has shown to me and is showing me, openly and above all underground…I naturally do not like motives of dishonesty being imputed to me and that is what he has been doing constantly.[40]

Although the strained relations between the two men did not end after Evans-Pritchard's departure for his new position in Cairo in 1932, their relationship did enter a new phase, partly characterized by an enduring mutual intellectual respect. The Doughty Street incident was arguably more than a clash of personalities—it was also a result of the new intellectual development of a discipline around a particular academic figure whose brilliance was undoubted, but who was also prone to feeling personal slights and bearing long grudges. This atmosphere was to produce some of the key figures in British social anthropology, including Isaac Schapera, Raymond Firth, Audrey Richards, and Jack Driberg, among others. The atmosphere was a critical one in the positive sense, and drove the discipline on to new standards of theory and methodology. But it was also a charged atmosphere, characterized by rivalry and competition over the future theoretical and institutional direction of the discipline, which is understandable given the very small number of jobs there were in anthropology in the period.

Surveying for Seligman

Setting out on fieldwork to the Sudan in 1926, Evans-Pritchard was still some months away from struggles with Malinowski, but he left London full of intellectual and methodological inspiration from him as a fieldworker. This was in stark contrast to the methods that his actual supervisor C. G. Seligman promoted and requested of him in the field: 'I have to confess', wrote Evans-Pritchard, in a short reflection on fieldwork written at the end of his life, 'to having on my first visits to the Sudan taken around with me callipers and a height-measuring rod. I did this to please my teacher Professor Seligman. I have always regarded, and still regard, such measurements as lacking scientific value, even being almost meaningless; but so it was at that time.'[41] Indeed he did more than take them around—he used them to collect physical data on a number of different groups for Seligman's ethnographic survey of South Sudan, on the way to, or on the way back from, his three phases of fieldwork in Zandeland between 1926 and 1930. These physical

[40] London School of Economics archive, Malinowski Papers, 27/4, Malinowski to Seligman, 4/10/1931.
[41] E. E. Evans-Pritchard. 1973. 'Some recollections on fieldwork in the twenties', *Anthropological Quarterly*, 46(4), 242.

measurements were combined with other notes on social and political organization, rainmaking, religion, and other practices, gathered in relatively short periods of time and subsequently published in *Sudan Notes and Records* before being summarized and combined with the Seligmans' own data in *Pagan Tribes of Nilotic Sudan* in 1932.

After completing the couple of months in Blue Nile in 1926, Evans-Pritchard conducted a brief survey of the Moro people in Amadi State (Equatoria) on his way down to Zandeland (where he finally arrived in March 1927). While collecting anthropological information later published by himself and the Seligmans on the non-Dinka people of this area, Evans-Pritchard was struck by the remarkable practice of megalithic grave monument construction which he identified with the Meza people in particular. Identifying two types of grave monument, pyramid, and dolmen, Evans-Pritchard compares them with other noted examples scattered in the Africanist literature before concluding that they 'are unique in Africa as contemporary structures', as opposed to ones left over from some historical period as in Ethiopia.[42] Given that this published note was prepared for publication in *Antiquity* by Seligman during Evans-Pritchard's absence on fieldwork among the Nuer, it is tempting to interpret Seligman's interest in his student's data as inspired by a vague diffusionist-inspired search for further evidence of the distribution and survival of ancient Egyptian culture among so-called 'savage' peoples, something that Evans-Pritchard was at pains to avoid speculating about in his published account. His photographs of the larger pyramid graves are of particular interest since he usually included African people who were accompanying him as scale. In one image (Figure 2.3), three men stand beside the approximately ten-foot tall grave of Chief Beliyiye, father of Chief Yilu, at Lui in Amadi District. Two of the men look as though they were in the employ of the Anglo-Egyptian Sudanese government, and possibly accompanying Evans-Pritchard on his tour; the other man is presumably a local guide. Apparently this tall megalithic grave once stood in the centre of the chief's homestead, but at the time of Evans-Pritchard's visit was in the bush, the homestead having moved.

The importance of photography to Evans-Pritchard's ethnographic survey method, and indeed as evidence in its own right, is indicated in his remark that 'most of my knowledge is contained in the photographs and I can add little by way of commentary'.[43] But what does Evans-Pritchard really mean here—that his knowledge is 'contained' in the photographs? In a number of his publications, Evans-Pritchard alludes to photographs speaking for themselves, saying as much as he can, illustrating clearly, making obvious, and needing no further comment. Most often these sorts of assertions are presented in the context of making

---

[42] E. E. Evans-Pritchard. 1935. 'Megalithic grave-monuments in the Anglo-Egyptian Sudan and other parts of Africa', *Antiquity*, 9(34) (June), 160.

[43] Evans-Pritchard, 'Megalithic grave-monuments', 152.

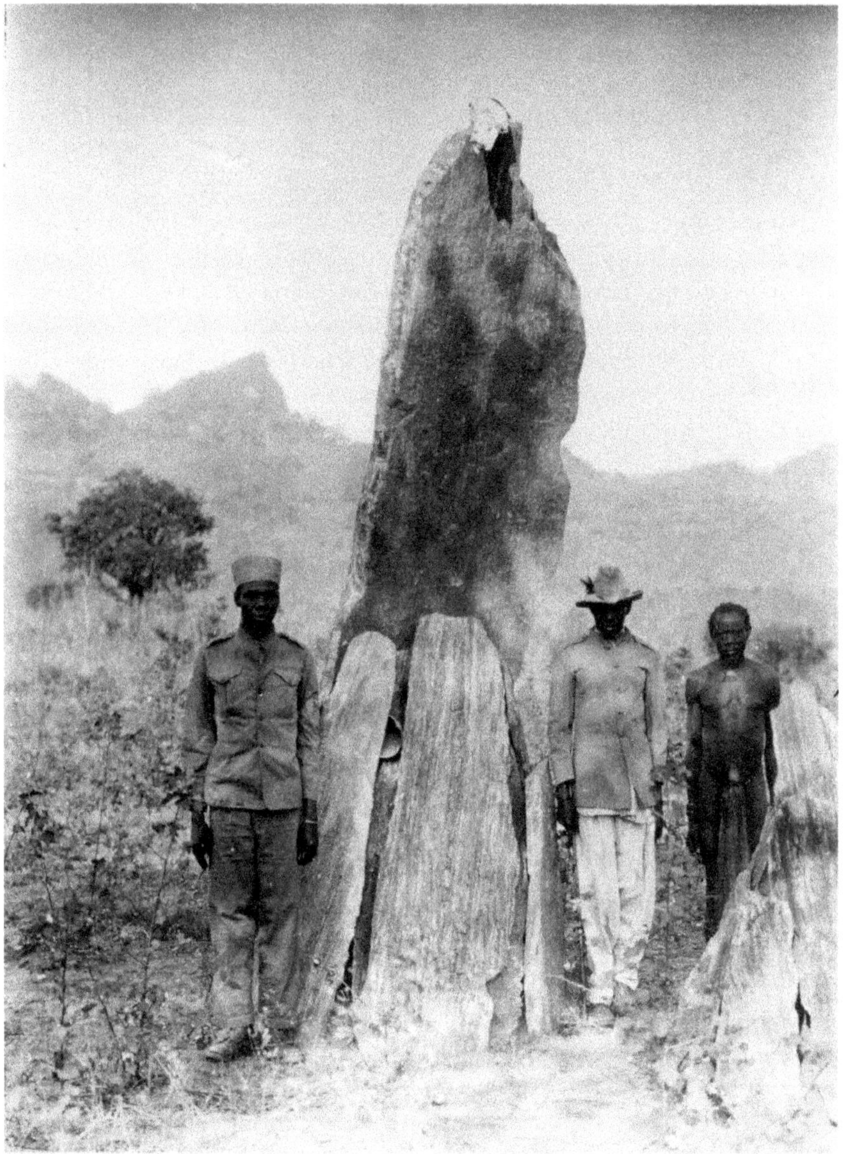

Figure 2.3 Megalithic grave marker for Chief Beliyiye, the father of Chief Yilu at Lui, Amadi District, Western Equatoria, South Sudan. Photograph by E. E. Evans-Pritchard, 1927.

description redundant since to do so would be to repeat visual information that is offered to the reader in an accompanying image. But in this case he goes further to offer that his knowledge of the megalithic graves goes little beyond what anyone might 'know' from a photograph, which sits awkwardly with his subsequent discussion of the orientation of such graves and their symbolism given to him by informants.

In many ways, Evans-Pritchard's formulation of photography as a form of knowledge in itself, rather than visual information requiring lengthy contextual interpretation, is an important starting point in gaining a better understanding of the complex relationship he had to the image in his work. It differs for instance from Isaac Schapera's approach, which was much more studied. Evans-Pritchard's photographs by comparison are like small scribbled notes, hastily gathered from the flow of fieldwork experience and without any ceremony. They are notes in the sense that he took photographs 'of' things, people, events, for later reference, evidence, or illustration. Yet his own disinclination to address the historical particularity of the photograph and its nature as a document, made at a certain place and time, also sits slightly uncomfortably with his approach to history in anthropology. Berger and Mohr give a particularly good insight into this relationship when they comment that 'photographs quote from appearances. The taking out of the quotation produces a discontinuity, meaning. All photographed events are ambiguous, except to those whose personal relation to the event is such that their own lives supply the missing continuity.'[44] This personal relation to the photographic event adequately describes the continuity that Evans-Pritchard allows the photographic image when he presents it to the reader as 'containing' knowledge.

To complement the collection of physical anthropology measurements of height, head, length, and breadth among the groups he briefly surveyed, Evans-Pritchard also took 'type' photographs, showing the (usually seated) subject in full face and profile, and sometimes from the rear. It is only during these brief survey visits in Dar Fung and among the Moro in Equatoria that Evans-Pritchard took such photographs, and it is likely that he was responding to Seligman's instructions to try and produce such images for comparative purposes.[45] To achieve the desired result of being able to visually trace the subject's facial features accurately, in the Blue Nile Evans-Pritchard used a raincape draped over a tree behind the sitter (Figure 2.4). The Seligmans used four heavily cropped versions of these Ingessana portraits, along with four taken by himself on Jebel Gule in 1910, to illustrate 'Darfung types', in their book *Pagan Tribes*.[46]

---

[44] J. Berger and J. Mohr. 1989 [1982]. *Another Way of Telling*. London: Granta, 128.

[45] Although a search for profile portraits among Evans-Pritchard's Zande photograph archive returns a few examples, principally of his two closest Zande servants, there was never any systematic attempt to produce type photographs.

[46] Plate XLIII (facing page 420). The plate is credited to E. P. Pratt, although it is composed of cropped versions of the Seligmans' and Evans-Pritchard's photographs.

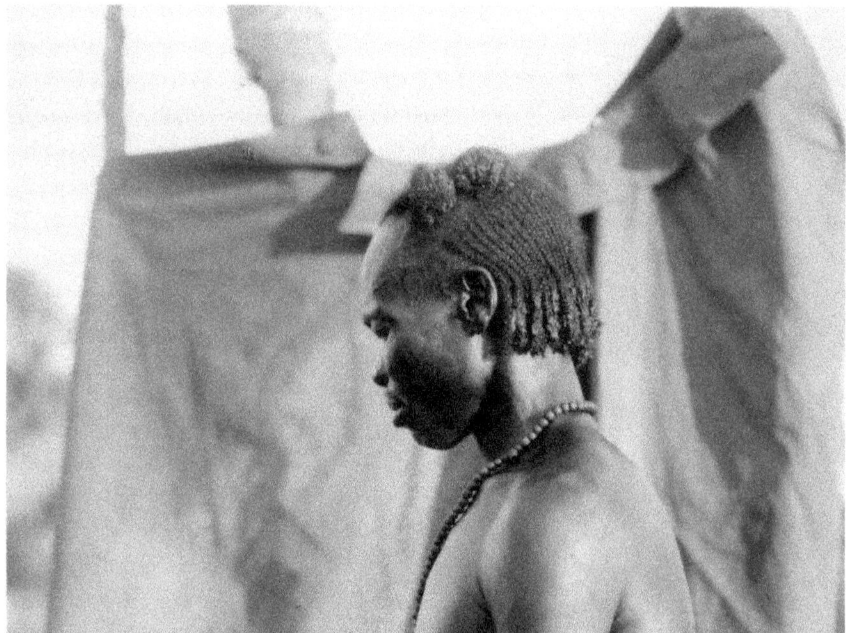

Figure 2.4 Physical type portrait of Dal, Evans-Pritchard's chief informant among the Ingessana, wearing the necklace he gave him. Photograph by E. E. Evans-Pritchard, 1926.

This sort of anthropological illustration, where a number of subjects were brought together for the comparison of racial features, has strong resonances with the collection and dissemination of racial type photography from the 1870s onwards. General Pitt-Rivers, for instance, collected hundreds of cartes-de-visite format photographs of local people when visiting towns in Germany and Scandinavia in 1879, displaying them alongside his collection of artefacts in London as part of a series to demonstrate, through multiple examples, regional racial types.[47] What becomes immediately apparent in the illustration reproduced in the Seligmans' book, however, is that four individuals have been selected out of Evans-Pritchard's portraits that represent particularly well characteristics noted as frequently being absent among Ingessana people, yet noted by Seligman further north—'typical negroid faces, with thick lips, marked prognathism'.[48] Despite noting in the text a large variation in people's features in this region, the compilation of portraits is suggestive of a marked difference in racial 'type' between Jebel Gule and Jebel Tabi.

---

[47] See C. Morton. 2015. 'Collecting portraits, exhibiting race: Augustus Pitt-Rivers's cartes-de-visite at the South Kensington Museum'. In *Photographs, Museums, Collections: Between Art and Information*, edited by E. Edwards and C. Morton. London: Bloomsbury, 101–18.

[48] Seligman and Seligman, *Pagan Tribes*, 419.

The attempt to interpret underlying racial types was one of the most important quests of nineteenth-century anthropology. As Edwards points out, the 'type' was a complex concept, with roots in the identification of type specimens in eighteenth-century natural science. By the mid nineteenth century, the notion of a 'racial type' representing the general characteristics of a community was generally accepted orthodoxy. Although variation existed within groups, the 'type' set the parameters of such variation.[49] For Evans-Pritchard, both the collection of physical measurements and physical type portraits did not sit comfortably with his anthropological instincts or developing interests in psychology and social phenomena. However, they were part of the established set of ethnographic fieldwork methods, even if rapidly going out of vogue, and desired by his supervisor.

The advice on photography given to travellers and student anthropologists in the pages of the British Association's *Notes and Queries on Anthropology* at this time was that 'the most important anthropological pictures will be portraits... the best background is the open doorway or artificial background'.[50] Although he read this standard guidance on field methods, Evans-Pritchard himself 'never found Notes and Queries the help it was supposed to be. It was written for the nineteenth century travellers, administrative officers and missionaries and not for anthropology students.'[51] Despite this statement, his photographic archive shows that he had absorbed much of its advice on photography. For instance, the advice on bracketing exposures, taking more than one photograph of the same scene using different F-stops: 'Unless the photographer is particularly unlucky one of the three should be a first-class negative.'[52] Such bracketing of negatives by taking two or three exposures of something which he felt might be particularly useful to publish one day is certainly evident in Evans-Pritchard's Zande archive. Reflecting on his use of the camera in the field at the end of his life, Evans-Pritchard felt that he 'had never been much good' with them:

> To make up for my fumbling I tried to take two or three photos of whatever it was I was taking a picture of, varying the time exposure or stop, so one of them was certain to be reproducible. But I had misfortunes. An Arab merchant's lorry, with, as I afterwards realized, faulty brakes went over the ferry into the Wau river at its period of flood and I lost my camera and collection of Zande negatives, and almost my life too. Then in Nuerland I had a new, never used very expensive camera which I smashed to pieces when running and tripping over harsh ground.[53]

[49] E. Edwards. 1990. 'Photographic "types": the pursuit of method', *Visual Anthropology*, 3(2–3), 240.

[50] British Association for the Advancement of Science. 1929. *Notes and Queries on Anthropology*. (5th edition). London: Royal Anthropological Institute, 376.

[51] Evans-Pritchard, 'Some recollections on fieldwork', 241.

[52] British Association for the Advancement of Science, *Notes and Queries*, 377.

[53] Evans-Pritchard, 'Some recollections on fieldwork', 241.

Another piece of fieldwork orthodoxy that Evans-Pritchard followed when it came to photography was that of recording sequences, for instance of manufacture or ritual, although he was not particularly systematic in this respect in comparison with some of his contemporaries with a more technological interest (such as Beatrice Blackwood). *Notes and Queries* advised that 'successive pictures in the stages of manufacture of an object or a ceremony are of the greatest value and can be taken rapidly with the reflex, or the vest pocket camera.'[54] Among the Ingessana, Evans-Pritchard took several photographs after this manner of men mixing earth with grass to form walling material, then carrying it, before applying it to the wattle walls of a hut. He also took several photographs of a man cutting fibre from a baobab (or tebeldi) tree before making a length of cord by weaving together the strands of fibre from a bundle at his feet, drawing the fibre between his toes. Another sequence shows two medicine men, or *kaik* (sing. *kai*), operating to cure the disease of a patient by drawing out the 'ghost-seed' which the spirits implant in the patient's body, and which the *kai* then extracts with his fingers and casts aside (Figure 2.5).

Another distinctive feature of Evans-Pritchard's survey photography is the focus on religious and ritual objects, shrines, sites of offering, and so forth. Having been given particular instructions by Seligman to record information about rainmaking rituals and the work of special ritual experts, a number of his photographs record scenes associated with this activity. For example, one photograph (Figure 2.6) looks across the compound of Totio the Beli rainmaker in Bahr el Ghazal region of South Sudan. Next to a hut on the right is a forked branch with several special horns (including buffalo) known as *bila* hanging from it that were said to have belonged to Gurutobo the ancestral rainmaker. These horns were blown by Totio and his relations in the event of the failure of his rainstones to cause rain. Arriving at Totio's compound on a fine day during the dry season in April 1929, there seemed little prospect to Evans-Pritchard that the rainmaker might be able to summon rain at his request. Yet much to his surprise, after a demonstration of the horns by Totio, rain fell heavily within half an hour.[55]

For the most part, Evans-Pritchard's photographs and their associated documentation are the only raw fieldwork data collected by him that remains, aside from his wax cylinder recordings.[56] It is generally considered that he destroyed notes upon publication, and towards the end of his life he destroyed many more in a series of fires, perhaps wishing his published record to stand on its own. The most extensive archive that remains (at the Pitt Rivers Museum) consists of

---

[54] British Association for the Advancement of Science, *Notes and Queries*, 377.

[55] Seligman and Seligman, *Pagan Tribes*, 477.

[56] These are held by the University of Oxford's Pitt Rivers Museum and consist of eighty-six wax cylinder song and voice recordings made in Zandeland.

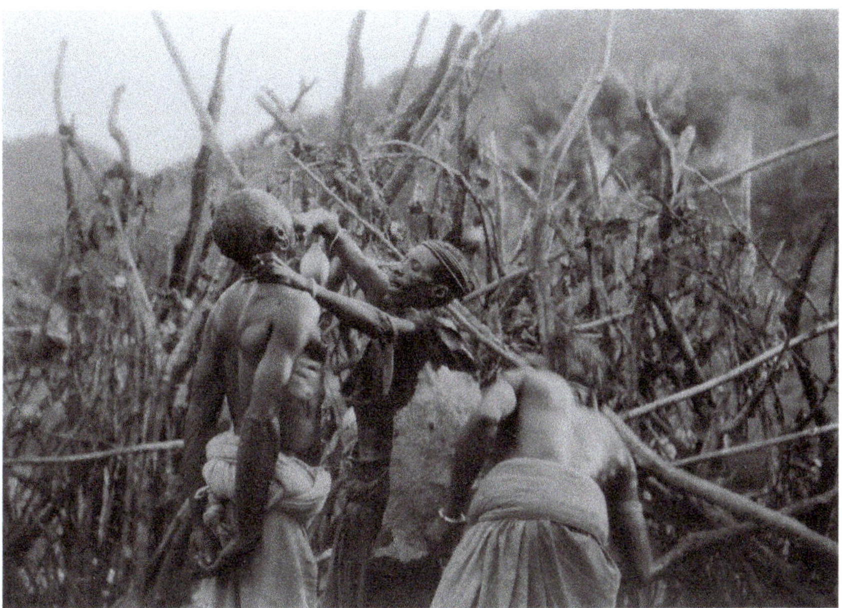

Figure 2.5 Two Ingessana *kaik* or medicine men drawing out the 'ghost-seed' from a patient. Photograph by E. E. Evans-Pritchard, 1926.

numerous Zande texts that he collected in the 1960s and published in *The Zande Trickster* in 1967, as well as a few sets of unpublished notes. As historical records of his fieldwork, one of their most significant and interesting aspects is how they shed new light on Evans-Pritchard's celebrated published ethnographies. This is particularly marked in the case of his survey fieldwork for Seligman in Dar Fung and other areas, where his photographs reveal a keen interest in a number of features of social and cultural phenomena that his cursory published notes gloss over, or which were not included by the Seligmans in their later publication. A good example are the Gamk 'dream players' known as *caalk* (published by Evans-Pritchard as *chalk*, and in his photographic documentation as *tsalk*) who he encountered and photographed in the Ingessana hills in 1926. In his survey publication, the *caalk* get a brief, encyclopaedic, entry:

> *chalk.* These are players who function at marriage, the birth of twins and the illness of children. The head of these players possesses a wooden figure of a man or of a woman, or both, and also a wooden phallus with which he plays. The office is generally hereditary, but anyone who learns the dances may play.

As a recent ethnographer of the Gamk has pointed out, Evans-Pritchard's definition missed the crucial fact that the word *caalk* means 'dreams' as well as 'ribald performers', and he did not offer any interpretation of their curious

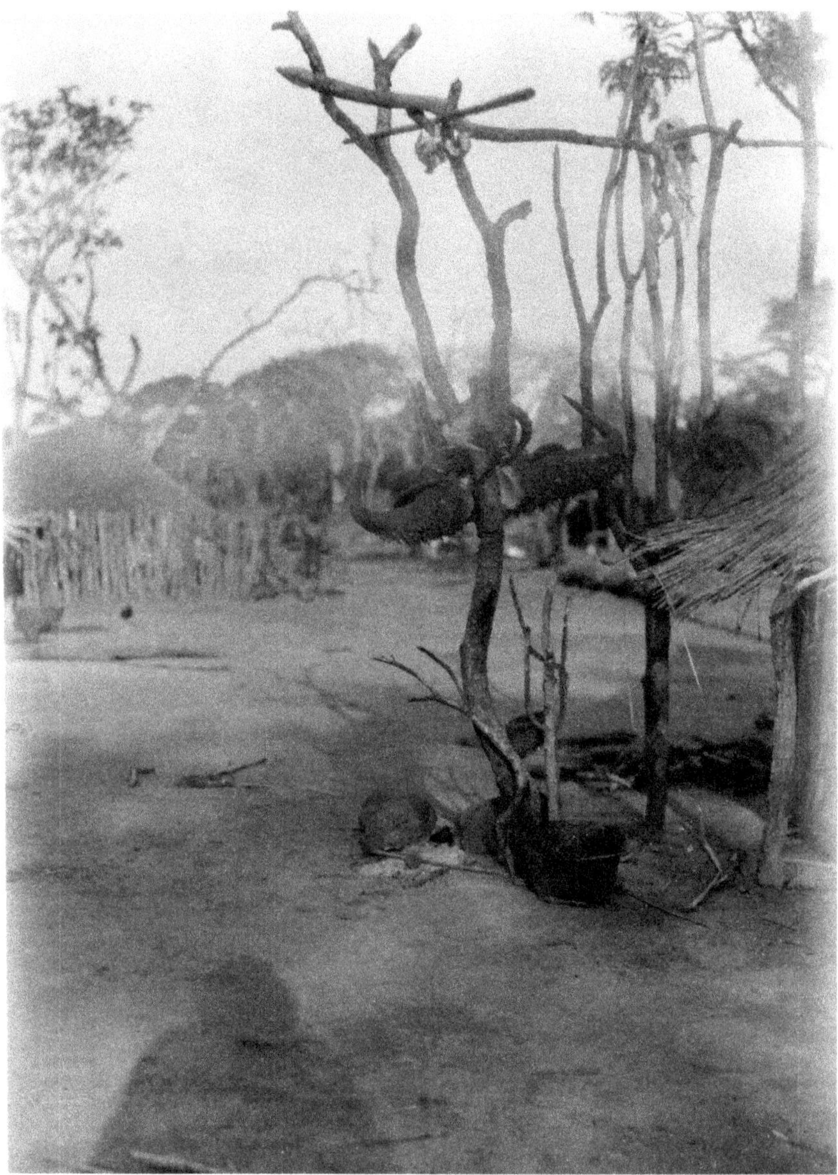

Figure 2.6 The compound of Totio the Beli rainmaker, with special buffalo horns (*bila*) used in rainmaking. Photograph by E. E. Evans-Pritchard, 4 April 1929, Toinya, Lakes State, Bahr el Ghazal, South Sudan.

actions, which are intended to heal sick children, reuniting a body with its shadow (soul), and by creating a happy state (*kund cuun* which literally means 'the bosom is sweet').[57] The Gamk word for shadow (*kuuth*) is used as a metaphor to mean the invisible or hidden aspect of a person or thing, as in the 'people in shadow' meaning deceased ancestors. Although Evans-Pritchard did not write further about his investigations into the *caalk*, apart from a brief mention later in life in his article on collective expressions of obscenity in Africa, it is clear from his photographs and their documentation that he did in fact recognize the social and ritual significance of the *caalk*, although having little time to study it in detail. So, for instance, we read on the reverse of one photograph showing two *caalk* performers, one playing a lyre and the other running with arm aloft holding a wooden switch, 'tsalk dance (exhibition near my home)'.[58]

Another photograph one frame later in the sequence (Figure 2.7) shows the two men much closer, with Evans-Pritchard having walked towards them and slightly to the right so as to get a better view of their dance together.[59] Although he mentions only in passing that a function of the *caalk* was to help heal sick children, as though it had cropped up in an interview, it is clear from his photographs that he witnessed at least one *caalk* ritual of this type. A note on the reverse of one print (Figure 2.8) reads, 'The tsalk playing at the home of an ill boy child',[60] one of three photographs that Evans-Pritchard took of the group. In the photograph, a group of *caalk* performers can be seen dancing in a circle holding thin sticks, in the homestead where the sick child lived, with the intention of restoring the boy's soul (*kuuth*) to his body. Such dances, led by an area's female ritual expert (*taun*), preceded the ritual treatment of the child, and were followed by animal sacrifice and more dancing.

As another subsequent ethnographer of the Ingessana, Charles Jedrej, has pointed out, the Gamk word *caalk* also means 'testicles', and their activities are not necessarily connected with all illness but with a shock or frightening experience suffered by a child, which may have separated body and shadow, as well as for twins.[61] The male performers sometimes brandish large wooden phalli or tie them to their waists, mimicking copulation with the female performers. Evans-Pritchard took a number of photographs of such phalli leaning against a hut wall,

---

[57] A. Okazaki. 2015. 'Recapturing the shadow: dream consciousness, healing and civil war in the borderlands between northern and southern Sudan', くにたち人類学研究 (*Kunitachi Anthropology Research*), 10, 44.

[58] Pencil note by Evans-Pritchard on the reverse of a print (1998.344.87.2), Pitt Rivers Museum, University of Oxford.

[59] The two photographs are identified as film numbers BB8 and BB9, making them sequential exposures.

[60] Pencil note by Evans-Pritchard on the reverse of a print (1998.344.68.2), Pitt Rivers Museum, University of Oxford.

[61] M. C. Jędrej. 1988. 'Twins, dreams, and testicles: an Ingessana ritual institution for the promotion of life', *Sociologus*, 38(1), 19–34.

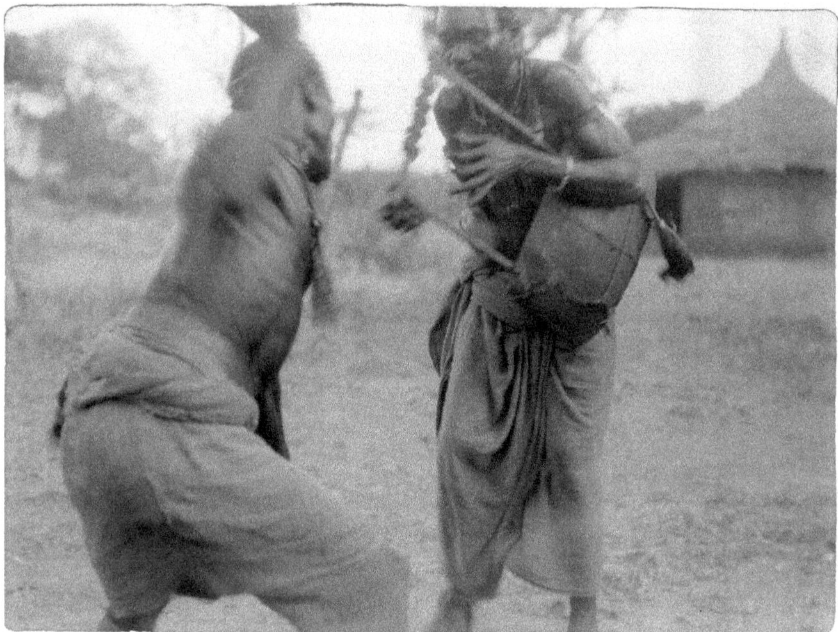

Figure 2.7 Two Ingessana *caalk* performers enacting a dance for Evans-Pritchard near his hut at Soda, Tabi Hills, Blue Nile, Sudan. Photograph by E. E. Evans-Pritchard, 1926.

as well as carved figures associated with the *caalk*, which he documents as *kai i calk*, a term that Jedrej has suggested might mean the diviner for the *caalk* group (Figure 2.9).[62]

Evans-Pritchard's use of demonstration, re-enactment, performance, and posing as a means to gather ethnographic information is a consistent feature in his fieldwork. In chapter 3, I discuss the tangled relationship between his photography and his commissioning of a Zande ritual outside his home. In the case of the *caalk*, it is possible that Evans-Pritchard asked the men to demonstrate their ceremonial dance outside his home so as to make notes about its nature. After all, he was to soon afterwards publish an article on Zande dance and was interested in its social function.[63] It is interesting to speculate that it was his encounter with the *caalk*, and understanding their ritual and social function for the Ingessana, that led him to investigate the social aspects of dance when reaching the Zande. Evans-Pritchard published four photographs to accompany his article on the Zande dance, three of which were chosen to show the social nature of the dance, with

---

[62] Personal communication, 9 February 2004.
[63] E. E. Evans-Pritchard. 1928. 'The dance', *Africa*, 1, 446–64.

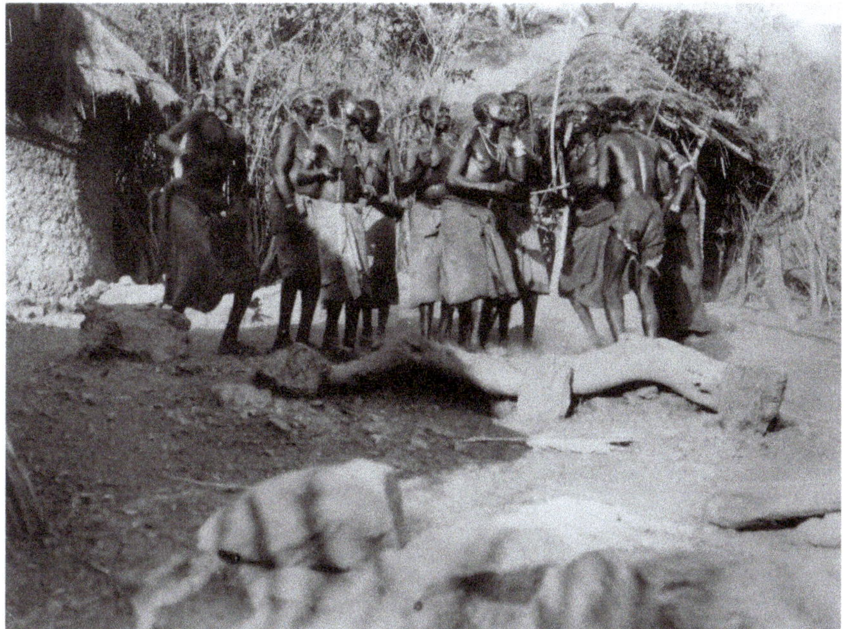

Figure 2.8 Group of Ingessana *caalk* performers at the home of a sick child, Tabi Hills, Blue Nile, Sudan. Photograph by E. E. Evans-Pritchard, 1926.

crowds socializing and dancers moving in close proximity in circles around a drum and wooden gong (Figure 2.10).

These images form part of a longer sequence of exposures in the archive taken during the event, most showing the tight formation of the dancers as they move slowly, circling the drum and gong at the centre of the dance ground. The photographs are crucial to the overall argument, which examines the relationship between individual bodies, collective movement, and social cohesion, as well as the wider social context and setting. The importance of the visual record to this broad analysis is acknowledged by Evans-Pritchard, stating that 'we have mentioned a few of the points on which more observation is desired. All these details are important. We want cinematographic pictures of dances in their full social setting.'[64]

As this chapter has argued, the relationship between photography and ethnographic survey was far more important to Evans-Pritchard than he ever acknowledged. Although he was highly sceptical of its scientific usefulness, his survey work in the 1920s did include measuring individuals for physical anthropology purposes, as well as type portraiture, although his discomfort with this area of

---

[64] Evans-Pritchard, 'The dance', 460.

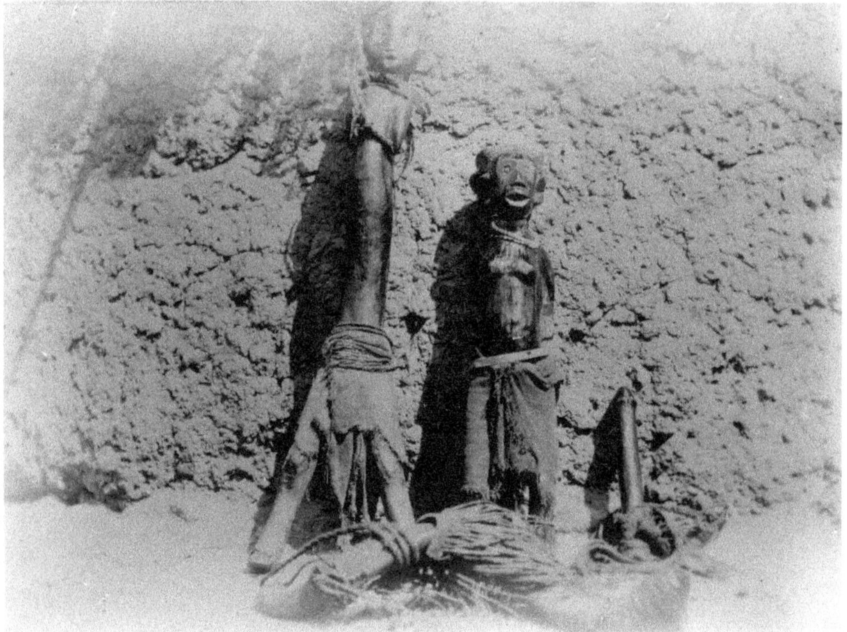

Figure 2.9 Two carved Ingessana figures (*kai i caalk*) and a phallus used in *caalk* performances. Photograph by E. E. Evans-Pritchard, 1926.

anthropology evidently held him back from systematizing such work with measuring devices and using identifying numbers in the images themselves. His comments about fieldwork photographs containing self-evident information and knowledge is suggestive of a motivation for photographing in the field that goes well beyond seeking potential illustrations for books and articles. There was no attempt by Evans-Pritchard to create a pictorial record in the way that Malinowski was at such pains to do in the Trobriand Islands, no aesthetic nod to a long visual tradition of placing the native in their landscape setting. Instead, as I have discussed, his survey photography is an extension of note-taking, of gathering data, and as I will argue later in this book, a site of potential reflection and rethinking the complexity of fieldwork. Although, therefore, some of his photographs, such as of Moro megaliths, are represented to the reader as visual descriptions taking the place of textual ones, some are recreations of cultural activity performed for the camera, such as the images of *caalk* dancers outside of Evans-Pritchard's own hut, or the activities of the *kaik* (medicine men) removing the 'ghost seed' (Figure 2.5). We can see in this mixture of photographic modes how his fieldwork not only integrated photography as a descriptive corollary, but how some fieldwork was essentially done for photographic purposes, rather than

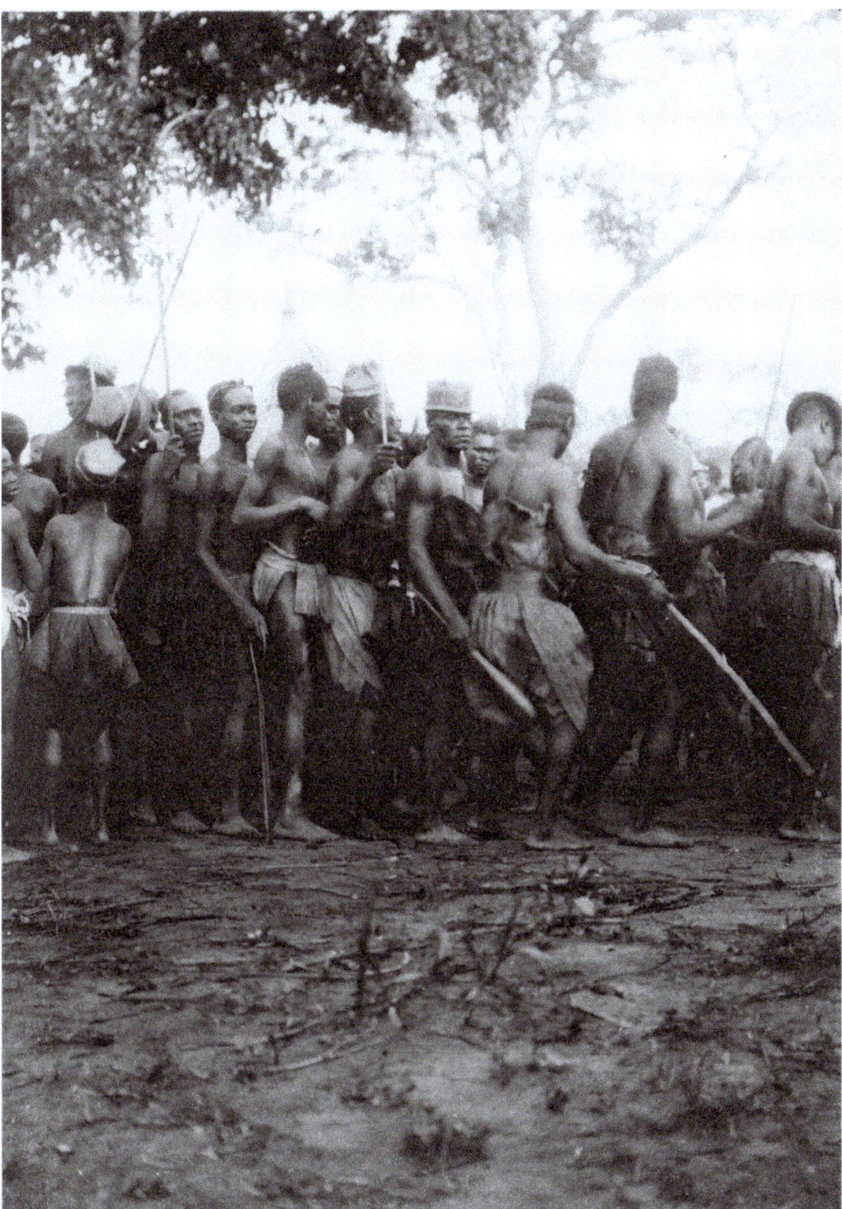

Figure 2.10 Zande men dancing in a circle at a feast held by Prince Rikita. Photograph by E. E. Evans-Pritchard, 1927.

to elicit textual data. So although Evans-Pritchard generally destroyed his ethnographic notes, we must now remind ourselves that photographs were not only an essential and integral aspect of his fieldwork data—they contain routes for us back into the fieldwork experience, of its historical contexts and local relationships, that textual notes are often silent about.

3

Visuality and textuality

Encountering Zande ritual

It is sometimes argued that photography was of less relevance to the sort of social anthropology promoted by Malinowski at the London School of Economics from the 1920s.[1] With a new focus upon social institutions, visual methods were considered as being a tool of the 'old anthropology' where surface appearance was presumed to be privileged over social depth, form over function, whereas the new anthropology sought to uncover the hidden rules behind human social organization, something not necessarily conceived of as being photographable. One scholar characterized this as a 'particular way of seeing animating the Malinowskian project which renders the camera, and other scientific instrumentation obsolete'.[2] Not quite obsolete of course, since Malinowski spent many hours taking and developing photographs in the field, and Evans-Pritchard took around 2,600 photographs during his fieldwork, a considerable number even today. Although photography remained a regular fieldwork tool for both Malinowski and Evans-Pritchard (as well as other Malinowski-influenced students, such as Raymond Firth), it is probably true to say that its evidential and scientific value had been challenged significantly within the discipline; certainly it no longer had the data-gathering utility that it had for the physical anthropologists, such as C. G. Seligman, Malinowski's colleague at the London School of Economics. In this chapter I seek to challenge this characterization of post-Malinowskian indifference to visual methods, and look in detail at the series of photographs that Evans-Pritchard took, probably in 1927, of the ritual initiation of his servant Kamanga into the Zande corporation of witch doctors. I do so in order to ask a series of questions about the relationship between his photography and fieldwork practice, as well as his use of the visual alongside his interest in vernacular texts. This is a theme that I return to in chapter 7 in relation to Nuer ritual, where the notion of Evans-Pritchard as participant-photographer is explored.

Six photographs taken by Evans-Pritchard at Kamanga's initiation were published in a two-part article in the *Journal of the Royal Anthropological Institute*

---

[1] E. Edwards. 2001. *Raw Histories: Photographs, Anthropology and Museums*. Oxford: Berg, 161.
[2] A. Grimshaw. 2001. *The Ethnographer's Eye: Ways of Seeing in Modern Anthropology*. Cambridge: Cambridge University Press, 54.

(JRAI),[3] and three of these plates were then reused in his subsequent monograph, *Witchcraft, Oracles and Magic Among the Azande*.[4] But when researching and cataloguing his archive I was able to reassociate a total of twelve photographs of this event, a complete pack of mechanically numbered quarter-plate film negatives (see Figures 3.1, 3.2, 3.4 to 3.10 and 3.12 to 3.14).[5] It was an innocuous, almost throwaway, comment in Evans-Pritchard's *JRAI* article that prompted me to consider these particular photographs in a new way. He stated that while he had witnessed the ritual burial of a *binza* (witch doctor) initiate on two occasions during his three fieldwork trips between 1926 and 1930, he had had his camera

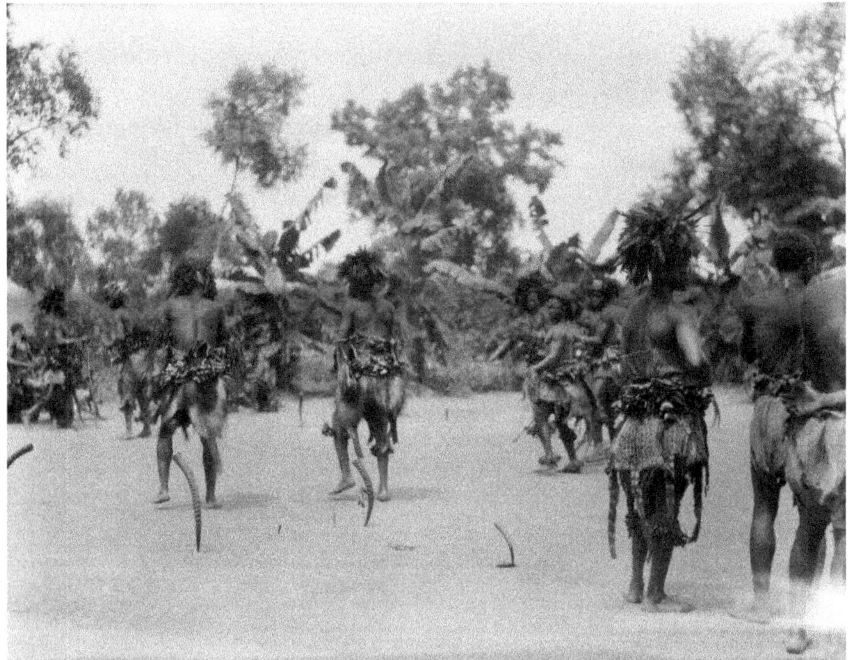

Figure 3.1 Frame 1 from the initiation of Kamanga sequence. Photograph by E. E. Evans-Pritchard, 1928–9.

[3] E. E. Evans-Pritchard. 1932. 'The Zande corporation of witchdoctors (part one)', *Journal of the Royal Anthropological Institute*, 62(2) (July–Dec.), 291–336, and E. E. Evans-Pritchard. 1933. 'The Zande corporation of witchdoctors (part two)', *Journal of the Royal Anthropological Institute*, 63(1) (Jan.–June), 63–100.

[4] *Witchcraft, Oracles and Magic Among the Azande* (1937) was published by Clarendon Press in Oxford as a 'CP Commission' book. This meant that Evans-Pritchard would have paid for the initial print run of 750 copies, receiving in return a portion of sales revenue.

[5] Probably a glass-plate camera adapted for film pack usage. Colin Harding (National Media Museum, UK), personal communication, 24 June 2005.

with him only on the second occasion, that of Kamanga's initiation.[6] In the preamble to his description of the event, he notes that he had 'kept a very inadequate record of the occasion',[7] and that his analysis thereby relied mostly on vernacular texts written down afterwards, based on discussions with Kamanga himself, his servant Mekana, and his clerk Reuben Rikita. This almost apologetic remark was removed when he was preparing the text for *Witchcraft, Oracles and Magic*.[8] To me, it seemed interesting to explore the notion that there was some relationship, suggested by this remark, between his being photographically engaged with the second ritual event, his lack of note-taking at the time, and his subsequent recording of texts about it. In particular, it seemed to suggest that Evans-Pritchard's field photography interrelated with his core methodological concern with vernacular texts in an important way, since both were intended to provide a record that could be interrogated beyond the fieldwork encounter, both by Evans-Pritchard himself as well as others, and both were held to provide an evidential basis for the analysis of Zande witchcraft.

There are two related but differing perspectives from which I explore this series of photographs. The first is to approach the images as a product of a specific fieldwork encounter which offers fragmentary evidence about Evans-Pritchard's fieldwork proxemics,[9] his participation in the ritual as sponsor of the initiate Kamanga, and his photographic choices. This approach to the series is also concerned with an understanding of the embodied presence of the ethnographer in the photographic record. The second perspective is the relationship between photographs and vernacular texts within Evans-Pritchard's fieldwork methodology, as well as in his published ethnography. Both vernacular texts and photographs occasionally bring to the fore historical contexts of fieldwork that are only sometimes acknowledged within the mostly detemporalized ethnography, such as local experiences of colonialism and resettlement, social trauma and upheaval, and changing indigenous forms of authority. And then there are the performances, selections, and visual discourses within the anthropological monograph itself. Close attention to the seriality of the archive offers us a fragmentary new narrative of a classic event in the ethnographic literature— one that seems to both diverge and converge with the anthropological analysis that Evans-Pritchard presents.

In his introduction to *Witchcraft, Oracles and Magic*, Evans-Pritchard makes it clear that, although he relies heavily on Zande texts throughout the book, he did not treat such evidence as 'sacred', and gave them equal analytical weight to his own observations. Part of his reason for quoting Azande so frequently was his

---

[6] Evans-Pritchard, 'Zande corporation of witchdoctors (part two)', 86.
[7] Evans-Pritchard, 'Zande corporation of witchdoctors (part two)', 86.
[8] See E. E. Evans-Pritchard. 1937. *Witchcraft, Oracles and Magic Among the Azande*. Oxford: Clarendon Press, 239.
[9] See E. T. Hall. 1968. 'Proxemics', *Current Anthropology*, 9(2/3), 83–108.

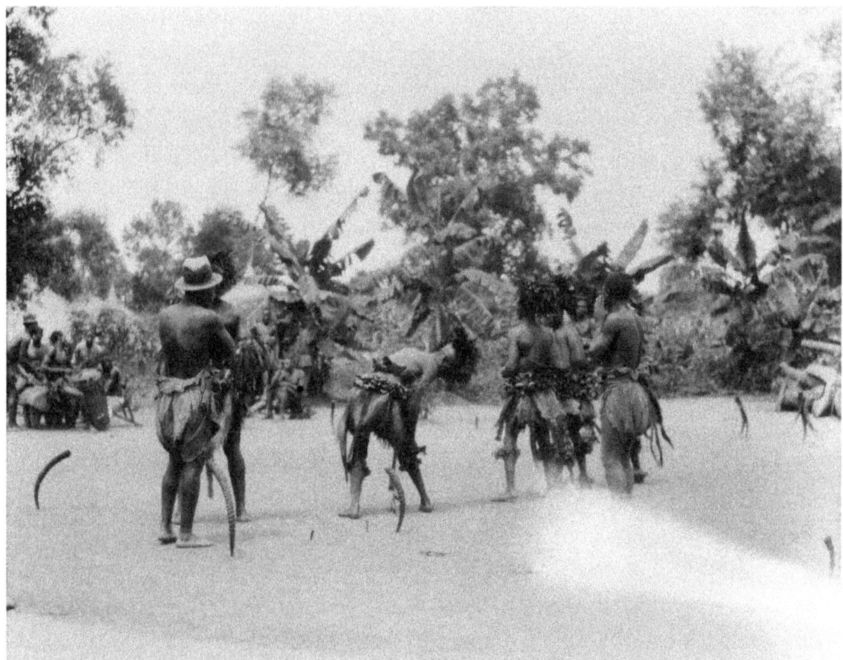

Figure 3.2 Frame 2 from the initiation of Kamanga sequence. Photograph by E. E. Evans-Pritchard, 1928–9.

assertion that an understanding of idiomatic expression was one way of exploring the Zande 'ideational system'. 'Is Zande thought so different from ours', he writes, 'that we can only describe their speech and actions without comprehending them, or is it essentially like our own though expressed in an idiom to which we are unaccustomed?'[10] Although it is of real interest, I do not delve directly in this book into Evans-Pritchard's contribution to debates about 'primitive thought'. Although it was the intellectual engine of his Zande thesis, I keep the focus here on methodology, however this is theoretically informed. Evans-Pritchard also excludes extended theoretical discussion about rationality from *Witchcraft, Oracles and Magic*, preferring to direct readers to articles elsewhere,[11] and throughout the book he prefers instead to raise general or theoretical points in conjunction with the vivid ethnographic descriptions that translate them

<hr>

[10] Evans-Pritchard, *Witchcraft, Oracles and Magic*, 4.

[11] These articles, published in the *Bulletin of the Faculty of Arts* (Cairo University), are difficult to get hold of, but two of them were later republished: 'Lévy-Bruhl's theory of primitive mentality', *Journal of the Anthropological Society of Oxford*, 1(2), 1970 [1934], 39–57 and 'The intellectualist (English) interpretation of magic', *Journal of the Anthropological Society of Oxford*, 4(3), 1973 [1933], 123–42. Evans-Pritchard sent a copy of his 1934 article (Evans-Pritchard, 'Lévy-Bruhl's theory') to Lévy-Bruhl, whose letter in response was also later published as L. Lévy-Bruhl. 1952. 'A letter to E. E. Evans-Pritchard', *The British Journal of Sociology*, 3(2), 117–23.

culturally for us. The evocative and highly visual quality of Evans-Pritchard's writings, his 'African transparencies' in Clifford Geertz's phrase, is certainly an important factor in his continued popularity in the discipline—one has only to consider how impossible it would be to teach key areas of anthropology without describing the collapse of a Zande granary and its meaning for those suffering the misfortune of having been beneath it.

Evans-Pritchard's analysis of Zande witchcraft has frequently been cited as a watershed in anthropology since he sought to understand it on its own terms as a social system that regulated everyday life in a highly effective manner, rather than as a flawed, if understandable, attempt to explain natural phenomena, as developed by Tylor and Frazer. He has thereby occasionally been placed in the vanguard of cultural relativists (such as Boas) by some commentators, but it is clear in many passages of the book that his own position was ultimately that of an absolutist,[12] seeking to translate and communicate Zande beliefs to a Western audience, sure of its grasp of objective (scientifically based) reality. Throughout the book he frequently compares ideas that would occur 'to our minds' to ones representative of Zande logic. Although critical of Lévy-Bruhl's use of terms and methods, he also credits him with the essentially sociological insight that 'primitive thought' 'is unscientific because it is mystical and not mystical because of an inherent incapacity to reason logically'.[13] In the case of the training of Kamanga for the Zande corporation of witch doctors, Evans-Pritchard takes his method of unveiling the ultimate falsehood of Zande witchcraft beliefs one step further by entrapping Kamanga's teacher Bögwözu into revealing his sleight-of-hand method of removing objects of witchcraft from a patient's body: 'The effect of these disclosures on Kamanga was devastating', he wrote. 'When he had recovered from his astonishment he was in serious doubt whether he ought to continue his initiation … it is remarkable that Kamanga, who, like other Azande, knew cheating to be possible, was so amazed when he discovered that witch-doctors do, in fact, cheat.'[14]

'The Training of a Novice', the chapter in which the initiation photographs appear, amounts to a remarkable and reflexive methodological statement. Tired 'of Badobo's chicanery and Bögwözu's bluff', Evans-Pritchard constructs a narrative of hard-won ethnography and the anthropologist as cunning hero.[15] Kamanga's ritual burial, the main subject of the photographs, was the final stage of his

---

[12] See Peter Winch's interesting discussion of Evans-Pritchard's approach to Zande rationality (P. Winch. 1964. 'Understanding a primitive society', *American Philosophical Quarterly*, 1(4), 307–24), as well as Segal's summary (R. A. Segal. 1987. 'Relativism and rationality in the social sciences (review article)', *The Journal of Religion*, 67(3), 353–62). Both authors make the important point that E-P's position shifts more towards relativism in *Nuer Religion* (1956).

[13] Evans-Pritchard, 'Lévy–Bruhl's theory', 57.

[14] Evans-Pritchard, *Witchcraft, Oracles and Magic*, 231–2.

[15] Evans-Pritchard, *Witchcraft, Oracles and Magic*, 230.

initiation into the corporation of witch doctors, an initiation process that, it can be argued, also reveals anthropology's continuing concern with making visible, dramatizing, and re-enacting tradition, both through the lens and on the page.

Ritual sequence, photographic seriality

When we consider the sets of relationships between Evans-Pritchard's Zande photographs and vernacular texts, we raise points of connection concerning their narrativity and seriality. The narrative relationship between both the texts and images of Kamanga's initiation is ultimately rooted in a sequential or linear understanding of ritual, which in anthropological literature can be traced back to the principal role given to the 'rite' in Robertson Smith's work on Semitic religious practice.[16] It has sometimes been noted how the sequential representation of ritual activity offers a false concreteness of cultural events, something that is too often done retrospectively after analysis rather than reflecting the messiness of actual ritual processes. This idea is given another twist in the case of the witch doctor initiation since it was the second such event attended by Evans-Pritchard, and its linear progression was possibly being anticipated by him photographically. The visualization of ritual as a narrative sequence was later to reach its zenith within Evans-Pritchard's work in his 1956 book *Nuer Religion*, where four photographs are presented with the titles 'Consecration', 'Invocation', 'Immolation' and 'Death'. But as I have just suggested, the textual influence of ritual interpretation extends beyond published contexts, and into patterns of visualization represented across a photographic series. As such a series, we are offered glimpses of both what Evans-Pritchard decided was meaningful action, and how this interrelates with established ways of representing such action visually.

It is clear from both the organization and documentation of Evans-Pritchard's Zande photographs, that although he systematically recorded film numbers on the backs of his working prints they were never kept or subsequently organized according to them, and that as they were used over the years confusions occa-sionally arose. As I discuss in chapter 7, although at some point, probably shortly before they were deposited in 1966, an attempt had been made to order the twelve photographs by numbering them on the print reverse, the resulting sequence is visually inconsistent with the known events. One problem with establishing the sequence seems to be that with his film-pack adapted quarter-plate camera, Evans-Pritchard often relied on the mechanical numbers recorded on the film-pack negatives for noting sequences; but in the case of the pack relating to Kamanga's initiation, many of the numbers are either missing or clipped. Careful

---

[16] W. Robertson-Smith. 1899. *Lectures on the Religion of the Semites*. Edinburgh: Adam and Charles Black.

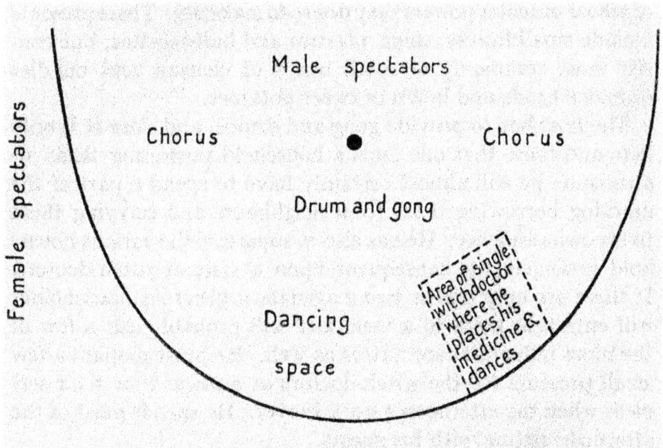

Figure 3.3 Diagram of the witch doctor dance ground. From E. E. Evans-Pritchard, *Witchcraft, Oracles and Magic Among the Azande.* Oxford: Oxford University Press, 1937.

analysis of the negatives, however, shows that seven have in fact good evidence of their original frame numbers, and only five out of the twelve negatives have no such evidence: frames 4 and 5, and the final three. The sequence as I have presented it in this chapter shows the sequence as I have reconstructed it, either using the original frame numbers, or else on the basis of the visual progression of the event as a whole, and by comparison with the published account.

There are a number of ways in which the understanding of this newly established photographic sequence provides an alternative perspective and narrative about a classic event in the ethnographic literature. The first is the realization that when Evans-Pritchard mentions in the text that the images were 'taken outside my hut', we should read *from outside my hut.*[17] Another photograph, labelled 'my hut' shows what appears to be the same structure seen in the background of the final frame, and was an open-sided meeting shelter where Evans-Pritchard would talk to visitors. This photograph appears to have been taken on a subsequent phase of fieldwork when a new rectilinear house was built just the other side of the fence beyond to the left. Another photograph, labelled 'Mekana in service dress standing outside my hut' shows this new structure from the other side, complete with hardcore walkways, and also shows the sort of status that Evans-Pritchard was unable to avoid during his fieldwork when staying in the homestead of a local leader.

Evans-Pritchard's own published diagrammatic representation of the spatial organization of a Zande witch doctor dance area (Figure 3.3) indicates that the position from where most of the photographs were taken, outside the open-sided

---

[17] Evans-Pritchard, *Witchcraft, Oracles and Magic*, 239.

shelter, is not with the other male spectators, but on the opposite side, so that the drummers appear in the background as the *abinza* address their audience. It seems likely that he moved from the area where the spectators were gathered to his shelter behind to take the photographs, and then remained there during the ritual burial phase of the event. Perhaps this movement around the space explains the glances back towards him by several of the *abinza* in some of the images. As the ritual hole is dug towards the right side of the dance-ground and the dancers dance around it, Evans-Pritchard appears to move towards Kamanga in the hole, and then to the right side to get a better view. He is here standing at the very edge of the area demarcated by horns as the area in which uninitiated *abinza* may not enter, and the sense of the embodied ethnographer is at its most insistent. At this point Evans-Pritchard himself becomes a social actor once more in the proceedings. 'While Kamanga was in the hole', he wrote, 'his wives, one of his brothers, his brother-in-law, two of his cousins, one or two friends, and I advanced to the edge of the hole and there threw down spears, knives, rings, bracelets, leglets, old tins, Belgian Congo coins, and Egyptian piastre and half-piastre pieces.'[18] When the gathered witch doctors considered the gifts sufficient, Kamanga was allowed to get out, and the proceedings were completed with some blowing of medicines up the nostrils and more dancing. It is during this last dance phase that the final two photographs were taken, the final frame possibly a portrait of Badobo, Kamanga's tutor and the director of the initiation.

As a sequence, there is a notable movement in terms of perspective. Whereas he is photographing behind the event to begin with, in a position opposite to that of the local spectators (frames 1–7), he photographs much of the burial activity from a position at the edge of the horn circle, where people such as Sangba, who was not a *binza* but who liked to dance with them, had also gathered (frames 8–10). In the final two frames (frames 11–12) the sense of demarcated ritual space is gone as the *abinza* seem to scatter from the ritual grave, and the perspective is shifted from a centre point looking outwards and backwards towards Evans-Pritchard's hut as the *abinza* dance away. This shift in photographic proximity seems to mirror Evans-Pritchard's movement as a social actor in the ritual events, where this information is known—for instance, in his description of approaching the hole with Kamanga's friends and relations to make gift offerings. Although his photographic engagement is mostly concerned with what is happening to Kamanga while he is in the hole, the significant stage of the offering of gifts is not photographed, since Evans-Pritchard is himself a social actor in these proceedings.

In chapter 7, I examine the connection between the seriality of Evans-Pritchard's photographs and his observation of a Nuer rite in 1936, and here

---

[18] Evans-Pritchard, *Witchcraft, Oracles and Magic*, 241.

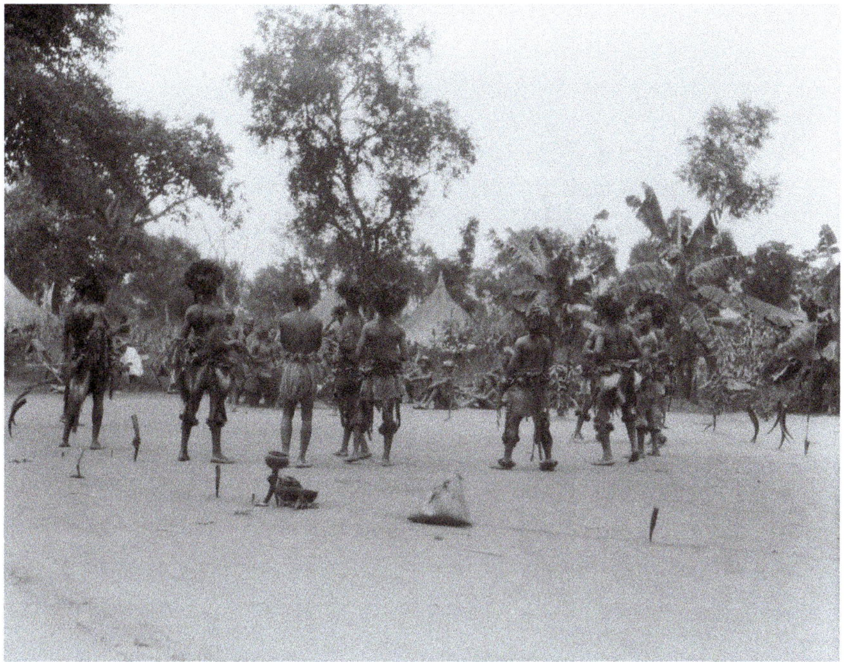

Figure 3.4 Frame 3 from the initiation of Kamanga sequence. Photograph by
E. E. Evans-Pritchard, 1928–9.

also the Kamanga initiation sequence raises important questions about the relationship between photography and participant-observation, particularly in the
context of ritual activity. In the Kamanga sequence there is a dramatic and obvious
movement from observation, in a position opposite the gathered spectators,
directly outside one of Evans-Pritchard's shelters, to participation at the centre
of the ritual stage. The first few photographs in the sequence showing the dance
ground demonstrate a visual concern with keeping the drummers in frame, a
concern that is mostly abandoned in the resulting images, but that was an
important experiential feature of the so-called 'séance'. As the ritual burial gets
underway, however, Evans-Pritchard's distanced, indeed dislocated, proxemics
are transformed—the subsequent images place the photographer at the heart of
the activity, with *abinza* moving around the camera instead of performing in front
of it. This interpreted sequence is certainly in accord with the published description, which first situates Evans-Pritchard as an observer of events, and then as a
participant at the edge of the ritual burial, as sponsor of the initiate. That he makes
this spatial progression within the dance-ground is not without indigenous meaning. To cross over into the dance area demarcated by horns thrust into the earth
was forbidden for an uninitiated person, 'and were he to do so he would risk
having a black beetle or piece of bone shot into his body by an outraged

magician'.[19] Evans-Pritchard's proximity to the *abinza* towards the end of the ritual was a result of his playing the important role of sponsor, a role that allowed him to move into this ritual space. However, the sponsor of an initiate was normally a senior local witch doctor, and so his categorization was ambiguous—as is often the case with European anthropologists—somewhere between high status local patron and sponsor of the initiate. The well-known portrait of a *binza* that appears towards the end of the sequence (frame 11) is certainly a reminder that Evans-Pritchard was not only the sponsor of the initiate Kamanga, but also the employer of the officiating *binza*, Badobo, whose portrait this might well be.

That the sequence is in accord with what we know of Evans-Pritchard's participant-observation of Kamanga's initiation should also be balanced with an understanding of what is not photographed, in particular his offering of gifts as sponsor into the ritual hole, as well as the blowing of medicines up Kamanga's nostrils. Neither of these aspects was recorded visually, although they were important to both the Zande texts recorded after the event as well as Evans-

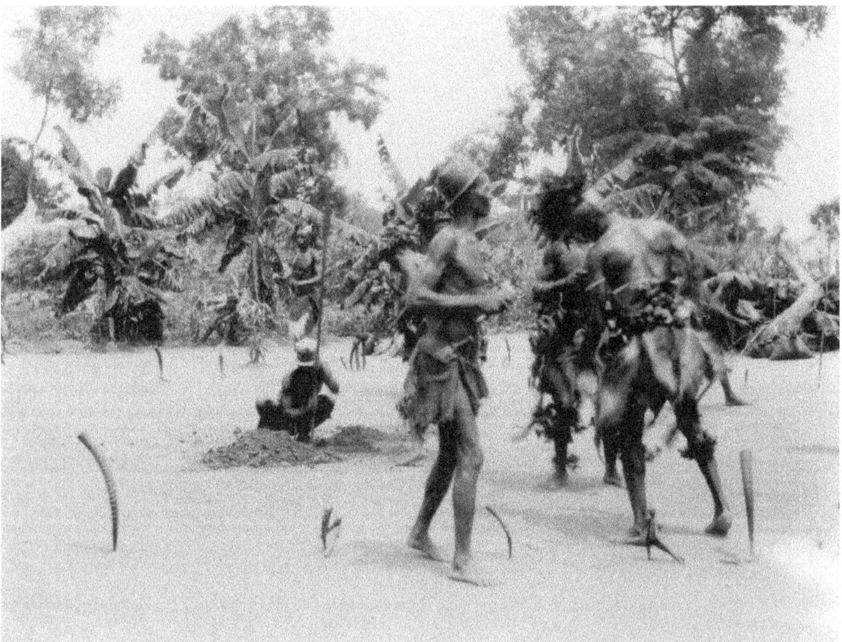

Figure 3.5 Frame 4 from the initiation of Kamanga sequence. Photograph by E. E. Evans-Pritchard, 1928–9.

---

[19] Evans-Pritchard, 'Zande corporation of witchdoctors (part one)', 301.

Pritchard's description. As I argue in chapter 7 in relation to Evans-Pritchard's photography of Nuer ritual, certain modes of participation are self-evidently incompatible with a photographic-engagement with events, irrespective of its visual interest—the offering of gifts by the ethnographer (being a manual task) is one such example. The difficulty of being such a participant-photographer was quickly evident to early fieldworkers such as W. Baldwin Spencer in Australia, who stated that:

> The illustrations will give some idea of the ceremony, but the reader will understand that it is very difficult to watch carefully what is taking place, and at the same time be in a position, at the critical moment, to take a snap-shot of any specifically interesting part of the performance, when one has not the slightest idea, from moment to moment, of what is about to take place.[20]

Of course we know that Evans-Pritchard had in fact witnessed a similar initiation event on a previous occasion and so would have known the general outline of the events to follow. Even so, the photographic record is still essentially inscribed, even circumscribed, with the uncertainty of ritual action as it unfolds, and in Evans-Pritchard's case the additional uncertainty of how his participation as sponsor of the initiate would unfold. Unlike Malinowski, Evans-Pritchard seems not to have ever considered staging events for the purpose of photographing them, although he did frequently do so for the purpose of eliciting information about them. Kamanga's lengthy training as a *binza*, and his ritual initiation into their corporation, was entirely orchestrated by Evans-Pritchard in order to elicit ethnographic information about Zande witchcraft. He writes approvingly, for instance, about the manner in which he used the rivalry and jealousy of two rival witch doctors, Badobo and the itinerant Bögwözo, to reveal more and more secrets of their trade: '[w]hen informants fall out', he wrote, 'anthropologists come into their own... [and] Kamanga and I reaped a full harvest in this quarrel'.[21] In this sense the initiation of Kamanga could be considered within the tradition of ethnographic re-enactment, here not principally for the camera, but nonetheless orchestrated to make certain practices visible to the ethnographer, whose subsequent photographs denote his embodied presence.

Another notable series of images that relate to ritual sequence in *Witchcraft, Oracles and Magic* are the six images published across three plates illustrating the consultation of the *benge* poison oracle. Here images from three seemingly different consultations are presented to illustrate different stages of the activity, involving the preparation of the poison, administering it to a chick, watching its reaction to the poison, and holding it up as it expires. In the last plate, the two

---

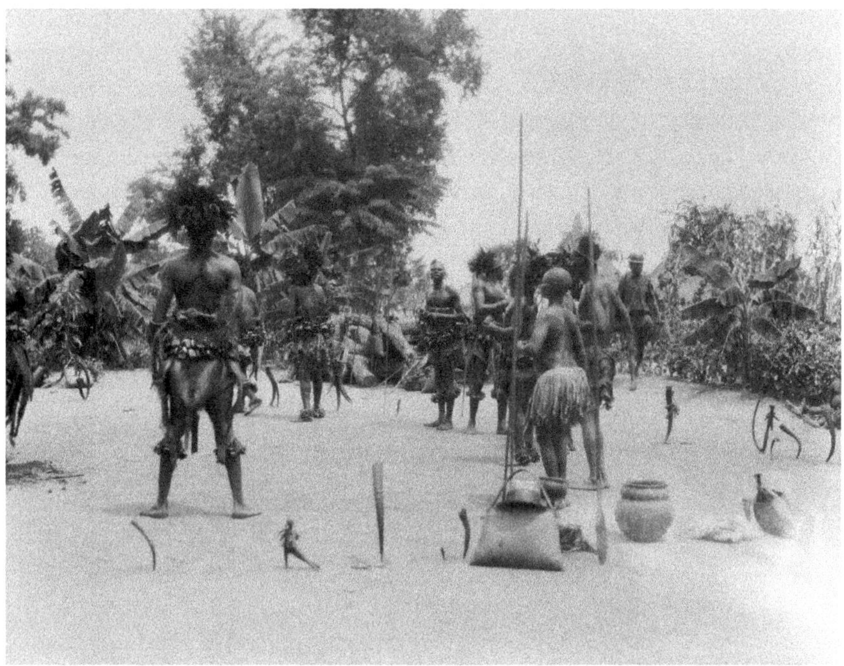

Figure 3.6 Frame 5 from the initiation of Kamanga sequence. Photograph by E. E. Evans-Pritchard, 1928–9.

images are from further away and again show the poison about to be administered to the chick, and then the gesticulation of the man addressing the oracle. The text references to these plates offer no more explication than that they illustrate the way the operator of the oracle is seated and prepares the poison, and how the questioner gesticulates as if speaking at the Zande court. However, it is in the plate captions themselves that the photographic series is revealed as an alternative visual account of the ritual sequence. This is emphasized using the present tense in the caption—for instance, 'The operator is twirling a brush in the poison with his right hand', which then shifts into a future tense to describe what is about to happen, which is that 'he will then place the brush in the leaf-filter held in his left hand'.[22] The reader is held somewhere between the stasis of the image and the temporal dynamic of the caption, which is then augmented by further images that show the next stages, and the whole series serves to sequence the consultation of the *benge* oracle in terms of its significant stages. But there is also a spatial tension, with the first two plates showing the operator in the bush up close but alone, but the third plate showing the *benge* oracle operator with a man

---

[22] Caption for Plate XIXa (Evans-Pritchard, *Witchcraft, Oracles and Magic*, 292).

consulting it from a lot further back and with the camera low to the ground as if photographing through the vegetation. We can only assume that this movement from proximity to distance in the photographs represents a social movement, with Evans-Pritchard himself being the questioner of the *benge* oracle in the first two plates, and when he is observing another questioning the oracle he keeps a socially appropriate distance, presumably since the questions being asked of the oracle were a private matter. We know that Evans-Pritchard frequently consulted the poison oracle, keeping a supply of *benge* for the use of his household, and he stated in *Witchcraft, Oracles and Magic* that 'we regulated our affairs in accordance with the oracle's decision. I may say that I found it as satisfactory a way of running my home and affairs as any other I know.'[23] Given his later reputation for living in a somewhat chaotic manner, this statement has always been understood as a theoretical statement about the practical validity of Zande rationality, as he, in Mary Douglas's phrase, 'learned to expand his West European view of rationality to include worlds built upon other assumptions than we subscribe to'.[24]

Inscription and ethnography

The first-hand witness approach to writing evident in the work of both Evans-Pritchard and Malinowski (what Geertz describes as 'I-witnessing') is also a product of the sort of visualization encapsulated in the presentation of vernacular texts and photographs. As Berger once noted, 'photographs quote from appearance',[25] but likewise vernacular texts, in their dislocation from a purely oral tradition, also quote from the flow of everyday reality. So it seems reasonable enough to approach Evans-Pritchard's Zande photography from the perspective of his core fieldwork methodology, that of creating vernacular texts from an oral tradition, and the interrogation of such texts as primary sources of evidence. I am not arguing that field photographs *are* vernacular texts, but rather that they are *like* vernacular texts—or that both forms of inscription bear interesting comparison. Some of the texts were written by Reuben Rikita, a literate Zande clerk, and some taken down by Evans-Pritchard himself from informants. Some of these stories he also got local people to speak into a wax cylinder recorder, which are today indistinct records, but evoke the time and place of fieldwork in a wonderfully direct and evocative way.[26] Both texts and photographs were the result of a process of translation and

---

[23] Evans-Pritchard, *Witchcraft, Oracles and Magic*, 220.

[24] M. Douglas. 1980. *Evans-Pritchard*. London: Fontana Paperbacks, 45.

[25] J. Berger and J. Mohr. 1989 [1982]. *Another Way of Telling*. London: Granta, 128.

[26] I recently shared these recordings with one of his later Zande informants, Angelo Beda, who wrote down many of the Ture trickster stories for Evans-Pritchard in the 1960s when he was a student in Khartoum. Evans-Pritchard would come along now and then as external examiner and pay him to write down Zande stories between visits.

interpretation on the part of the ethnographer, and both contain traces of local stories, random inclusions, indigenous gestures, and an excess of ethnographic description. The process of writing down oral accounts, which includes the problem of non-verbal communication, fragmented narratives, and obscure references, seems to mirror the way in which the content of photographs inevitably leads beyond the photographer's frame, suggesting wider contexts and alternative readings. As archival objects, some of Evans-Pritchard's photographs are annotated in Zande on the reverse in his own hand, suggesting a certain kind of interaction with his photographs in the field. In like manner, many Zande texts in different handwriting remain in his archive, folkloric snapshots that contain areas of focus, such as the trickster figure, but which also contain a wealth of other information.

Placing copies of Evans-Pritchard's two classic monographs, *Witchcraft, Oracles and Magic Among the Azande* (1937) and *The Nuer* (1940) side by side, perhaps the first thing one notices is that the former is a much thicker book. One of the main reasons for this is that *Witchcraft* contains long quotations from Zande texts collected in the field, whereas these are mostly absent in *The Nuer*, reflecting a key difference in Evans-Pritchard's fieldwork between two very contrasting cultures. Many of these Zande texts were written versions of accounts

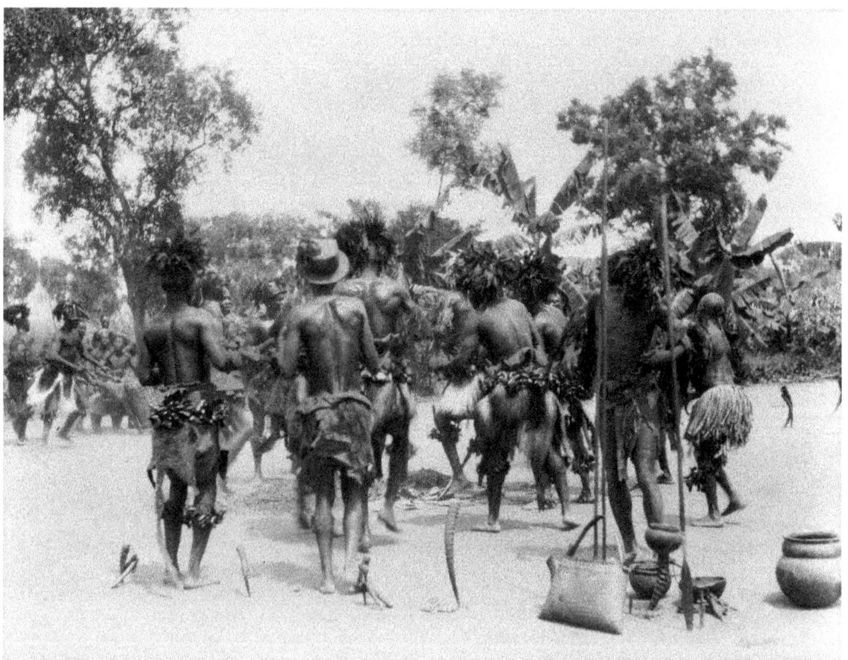

Figure 3.7 Frame 6 from the initiation of Kamanga sequence. Photograph by E. E. Evans-Pritchard, 1928–9.

given by his closest informants and servants over a long period. There were several key individuals that he relied on for this, such as Reuben Rikita, a literate son of Prince Rikita, who occasionally acted as his clerk and who conducted surveys during his breaks in fieldwork. But the most important was his servant Kamanga, whose 'sustained interest and industry' he wrote, 'enabled me to take down the gist of his experiences in a large number of native texts, given week after week for many months, and my constant association with him enabled us to discuss these texts informally and at leisure'.[27]

Reflecting on his fieldwork at the end of his life, Evans-Pritchard noted that the importance of collecting and analysing vernacular texts had been instilled in him by Malinowski, who had in turn been influenced by the Egyptologist Sir Alan Gardiner.[28] Although Malinowski acknowledges his intellectual debt to Gardiner in developing this textual methodology,[29] he is at pains to point out his own separate development in this direction, stating that Gardiner's letter urging him to collect cross-commentaries upon native texts, 'what are in effect glosses (scholia)' had arrived only after he had developed just such a method in the field.[30] Malinowski's work in the area of linguistic classification in Kiriwina led to the basic insight that would underpin his functionalist approach: that grammar can only be studied in conjunction with meaning, and meaning only in the context of situation. The establishment of native texts allowed the ethnographer to understand a linguistic term, not in isolation, but in the context of the sentence from which it took its meaning, and in the situation of usage.

Although deeply influenced by his ethnographic approach, Evans-Pritchard's analytical use of vernacular texts was quite distinct from that of Malinowski's. Whereas Malinowski's texts served their linguistic purpose in an overall functional explanation of culture, Evans-Pritchard's native texts serve to illuminate Zande society, and to lend corroborative force to his arguments about it. This difference of approach came to a head in 1928 after Evans-Pritchard had delivered a paper at Malinowski's seminar between field trips to Zandeland, during which both he and Isaac Schapera believed Malinowski to have accused him of 'cooking' and 'faking' his fieldwork material (discussed in chapter 2). In contrast to Malinowski then, I think we should understand Evans-Pritchard's concern with establishing texts in the context of his training in history, rather

<hr>

[27] Evans-Pritchard, 'Zande corporation of witchdoctors (part one)', 298.

[28] E. E. Evans-Pritchard. 1973. 'Some reminiscences and reflections on fieldwork', *Journal of the Anthropological Society of Oxford*, 4(1), 10.

[29] B. Malinowski. 1922. *Argonauts of the Western Pacific: An Account of Native Enterprise and Adventure in the Archipelagoes of Melanesian New Guinea*. London: Routledge and Kegan Paul, 24.

[30] The letter from Gardiner, found in the Malinowski Papers in the Stirling Library at Yale University (I/3/212A), is quoted in full by M. Goldsmith. 1988. 'Malinowski and Gardiner: the Egyptian connection', *History of Anthropology Newsletter*, 15(1), 8.

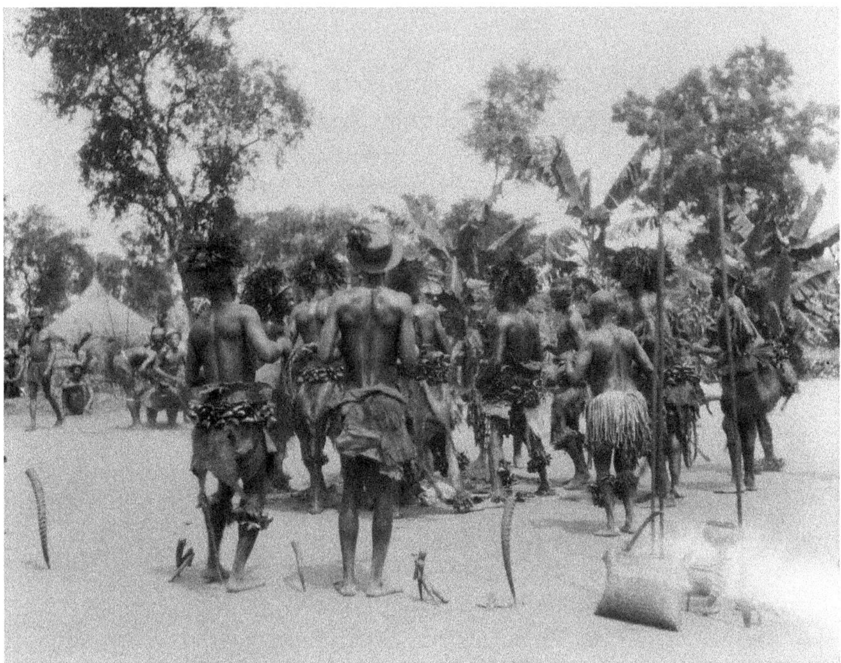

Figure 3.8 Frame 7 from the initiation of Kamanga sequence. Photograph by
E. E. Evans-Pritchard, 1928–9.

than following Malinowski's methodological lead, since his general approach is
to cite textual evidence in much the same way as the historian would do. This
historical approach to the vernacular text becomes more evident still in the
preface to his final edited collection of Zande texts, *Man and Woman Among the
Azande*, where he notes that 'what is most important, I think, about recording
texts in the vernacular and then giving a faithful rendering of them in English, is
that by doing so one allows the native to speak for himself, give his point of view
without the anthropologist interrupting and, I think, being an interpreter'.[31] Of
course, what immediately becomes obvious is the constant need for interpretation of such texts and the explanation of idiom, which often makes the
straightforward presentation of a text virtually worthless. Evans-Pritchard
blamed much of the obscurity of Zande texts on the practice of *sanza* or
'double-talk', in which the meaning of words is intentionally obscured, and
only apparent in highly contextual ways.

Within the anthropological monograph, photography is a historicizing irritant,
particularizing and potentially undermining any generalized narrative that it

[31] E. E. Evans-Pritchard. 1974. *Man and Woman Among the Azande*. London: Faber and Faber, 12.

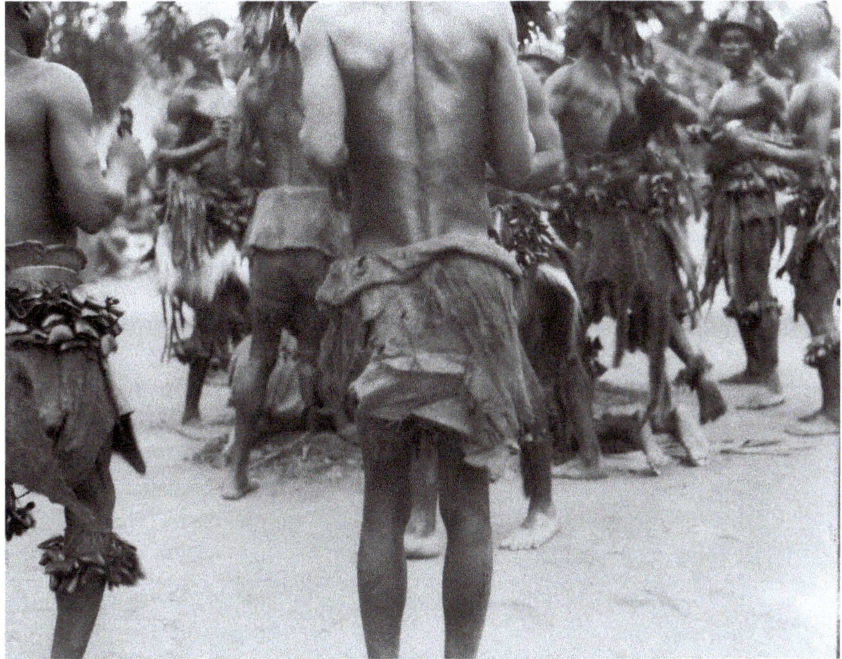

Figure 3.9 Frame 8 from the initiation of Kamanga sequence. Photograph by
E. E. Evans-Pritchard, 1928–9.

is intended to authenticate. Both Evans-Pritchard's Zande photographs and
vernacular texts can be understood as being entangled with similar problems of
translation and ethnographic excess, both being subject to lines of fracture in the
dominant theme, and in constant need of qualification and contextualization. And
nowhere is this relationship more evident than in the dual approach that Evans-
Pritchard brings to the initiation of Kamanga, in which the narrativity of the
vernacular text and the photographic series are brought together, the former
almost providing a 'native commentary' upon the latter. The photographs of
Kamanga's initiation operate as a set of multiple narratives that cannot be
confined or contained by the sets of assumptions we may make about the
ethnographer's intentions. The multiple surfaces, inclusive frames, and unexpected temporal relationships between series of images, reaffirm the notion that
photography is a cultural practice with no fixed outcome. In other words, photographs are frequently double-talk—collections of vernacular 'texts' that say one
thing and possibly mean another. There is a sort of treachery at the heart of
photography: however hard the photographer tries to exclude it, the photographic
frame always includes—produces an excess of—cultural information. This has
always been a point of tension for anthropology: the contingency and immediacy

of the photographic record, and the need to control its inherent noisiness and excessiveness within any sort of useable scientific framework.[32]

In a number of ways, then, it is important to think about Evans-Pritchard's Zande photographs in the context of one of his key fieldwork techniques—that of recording vernacular texts. Both texts and photographs undergo similar processes of intellectual focus, engagement, inscription, and then re-engagement through cross-commentary. Evans-Pritchard's re-engagement with the photographs is evident in the numerous annotations made on the print backs, often in Zande rather than English. These captions mostly record kinship relations between people, such as 'Zambaliru na adia ko ue' (Zambaliru with two of his wives). Such short Zande titles on the photograph itself exert a powerful and complex localizing influence over the photographs, demanding a reinsertion into the relationships surrounding their production, and collapsing the apparent social

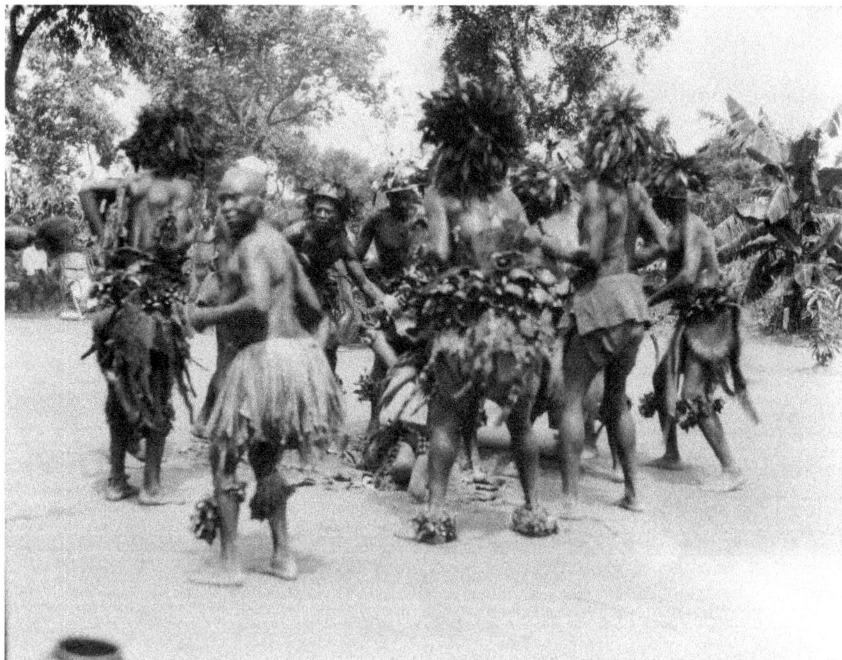

Figure 3.10 Frame 9 from the initiation of Kamanga sequence. Photograph by E. E. Evans-Pritchard, 1928–9.

---

[32] For an excellent overview of anthropology's relationship to photographic excess, see D. Poole. 2005. 'An excess of description: ethnography, race, and visual technologies', *Annual Review of Anthropology*, 34, 159–79.

distance suggested by the composition of the group portrait. As Zande captions, for instance, they resist the essentialism inherent in anthropological categories, and instead reflect the way in which the photographs are immersed in the modes of fieldwork interaction.

This sort of annotation is also found in Evans-Pritchard's own copy of *Witchcraft, Oracles and Magic*, supplied to him by Oxford University Press in 1937 with interleaving blank pages, on which he subsequently made numerous Zande notes, nearly all consisting of the original Zande texts that are given in translation in the printed volume (Figure 3.11). The annotations also include instances of gestured communication that were noted at the time of transcription. On the page opposite Kamanga's description of his own initiation, Evans-Pritchard notes that he demonstrated a witch doctor's posture to him while telling his story, and on the following page that he gestured with his hands, shut his eyes, and then turned his head one way and then another. We also read an additional description of Kamanga seeing stars after the dropping of liquid into his eyes. These gestures are interpreted as additional verbal utterances in the translated text, for the sake of readability. But their parenthetical existence within the Zande texts act as theatrical notes that bring the performative elements of Kamanga's storytelling to the fore, rather than the retrospective content of the story itself. It situates the text

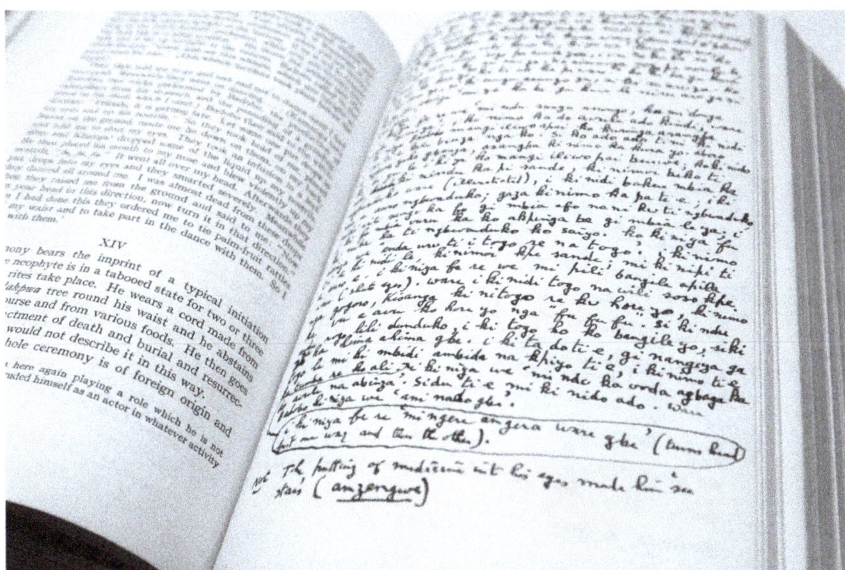

Figure 3.11 Evans-Pritchard's own annotated copy of *Witchcraft, Oracles and Magic Among the Azande*, showing the Zande text relating to Kamanga's initiation opposite the English printed translation. Pitt Rivers Museum Manuscript Collections, Evans-Pritchard Papers, Box 1/1. Photograph by the author.

firmly within the time and place of its communication. It is precisely this sort of peculiar temporality surrounding the communication of meaning that underlay much of anthropology's early suspicion of the photographic image, which, as Deborah Poole has noted, was considered to be 'saturated with the contingency of chance encounters'.[33]

But while the vernacular annotations to his published text are concerned, in both a literary and historical sense, with the notion of authentication and translation, those recorded on the photographs are concerned with social identities or specific activities. One such example is the comment 'Bandutua na soroka benge' (Bandutua consulting the poison oracle) written on the reverse of a working print. This note is suggestive of a specific relationship that Evans-Pritchard had with his photographic archive, and may be suggestive either of printing and cross-commentary during fieldwork or a similar sort of re-engagement with the archival object at one remove, and yet somehow interpreted within the immediacy of the field experience and its modes of communication. Just where and when Evans-Pritchard developed and printed his field photography isn't known, but this might help us understand the role of these vernacular annotations, whether they were written while in a fieldwork frame of mind, at one remove (such as stopovers in Khartoum), or when arranging them at Seligman's home or office at the London School of Economics. For me, the fact that Evans-Pritchard annotated them in Zande suggests that he was in the Sudan when he processed his photographs, understanding their content according to the mode of expression he was using with the Zande informants in his images.

The cross-commentary on vernacular texts, such a feature of Evans-Pritchard's method of gaining what he considered to be reliable data on which to base anthropological analysis, also finds a fascinating parallel in his use of the photograph album during fieldwork. We know that he returned to Zandeland in April 1928 with a set of prints, since they are referred to in a letter sent to his supervisor Charles Seligman en route,[34] and about 220 prints from his first trip bear the physical traces of having been stuck into albums. Only one of these albums remains intact, that of his first fieldwork among the Ingessana of Blue Nile Province in late 1926. Albums, by their nature, are meant to be 'read'—their very form as a book establishes a narrative sequence of disclosed visual clusters, as well as both a sense of concealing that which has previously been revealed, and the expectation of what is ahead. Since many of Evans-Pritchard's Zande album

---

[33]   Poole, 'An excess of description', 172.

[34]   Letter dated 6 April 1928, written on board SS Amarapoora at Marseilles (Pitt Rivers Museum Manuscript Collections, Evans-Pritchard Papers, I/1). In this letter he refers to his attempts to catalogue and arrange all of his 1926–7 fieldwork photographs while at the LSE, but that he had not completed the work. He also notes that, while all his negatives were stored in Seligman's office at the LSE, his Ingessana and Moro prints were kept at Seligman's home at Toot Baldon, whereas his Azande prints were 'with me in the Sudan'.

images are full-face portraits, it seems plausible that the album was used in a variety of ways—not just for remembering individuals, but also to share and talk about with Zande informants and friends.

Although narrative structure is an important feature of the vernacular texts presented in *Witchcraft, Oracles and Magic,* this is only occasionally evident in the presentation of photographs, and indeed the published series of three images of the initiation of Kamanga (Plates XVI, XVIIa and b), illustrating first the preparations for the ritual burial, the digging of the ritual hole, and then the burial itself, is Evans-Pritchard's only published use of the photographic series; the sequence showing the consultation of the poison oracle was taken from different instances and so shows representative stages rather than a sequence. This is not to say that the photographic recording of sequences is not found elsewhere in his archive— for instance, in the recording of beer brewing, or the carving of a stool. In doing so he may have been influenced by the conventional fieldwork advice at the time as found in *Notes and Queries on Anthropology,* which exhorts fieldworkers to record 'successive stages of the making of an object, or of a ceremony',[35] and since he was collecting artefacts during his field trips for sale to museums, he may have wished to document their use or manufacture.

Textual and visual excess

It is in the captions to his published series of images of Kamanga's initiation that Evans-Pritchard specifically addresses the random inclusiveness of the photographic frame. The caption for Plate XVIIb, for instance, explains that, although completely incidental to the ritual event, the man to the extreme left of frame has been mutilated for adultery (Figure 3.12). Such captions demonstrate that the ethnographic excess of the photograph is not necessarily always excluded or ignored by a dominant narrative, but that it is occasionally engaged with to provide multiple entry points from differing ethnographic perspectives (see chapter 5). In various places throughout the book the reader is referred to these illustrations—for instance, in the context of female witch doctors, one of whom is visible in a skirt of split banana leaves,[36] concerning the placing of horns on a dance-ground,[37] and in a discussion about Sangba, a man who danced with other witch doctors, but was not a member of their corporation.[38]

---

[35] A. C. Haddon and J. L. Myres. 1912. 'Photography'. In *Notes and Queries on Anthropology,* edited by B. Freire-Marreco and J. L. Myres. London: British Association for the Advancement of Science (4th edition), 271.
[36] Evans-Pritchard, *Witchcraft, Oracles and Magic,* 156.
[37] Evans-Pritchard, *Witchcraft, Oracles and Magic,* 156.
[38] Evans-Pritchard, *Witchcraft, Oracles and Magic,* 212.

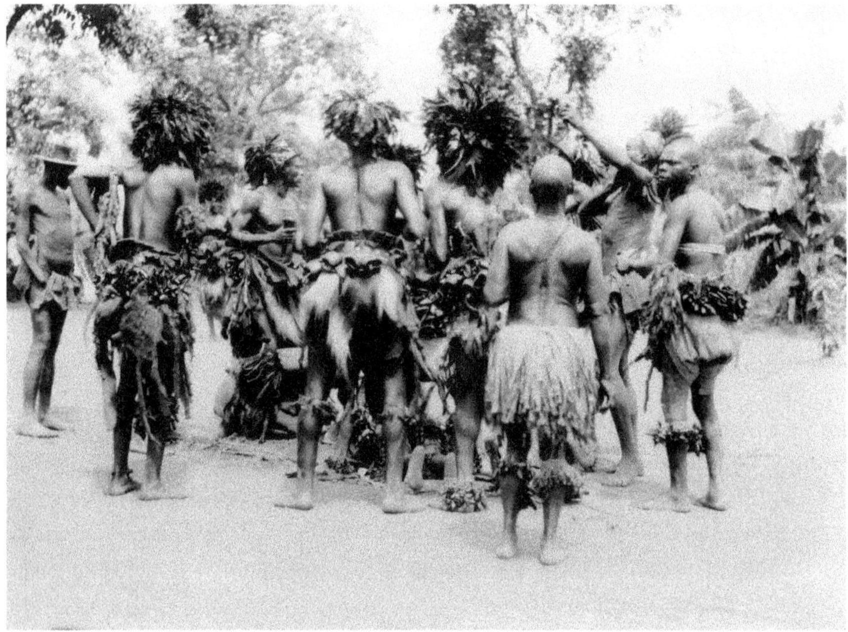

Figure 3.12 Frame 10 from the initiation of Kamanga sequence. Photograph by E. E. Evans-Pritchard, 1928–9.

Starting from their principal role within the book as illustrating a particular ritual event, the range of readings expands outwards within the text to include other referents, biographies, and accidental inclusions. Again, such multiple reference points were partly conventional, as demonstrated in the further exhortation from *Notes and Queries on Anthropology* that 'it is generally possible to secure views that illustrate several points',[39] but in the case of these images their multivalency has less to do with intentionality at the moment of inscription, and more with subsequent analysis. Such random and excessive intrusions from the particularity of time and place into the timeless ethnographic present are certainly not confined to photography. When, for instance, Kamanga begins his description of the ritual experience, he mentions that Kisanga dropped a magic infusion up his nostrils. This unexpected reference prompts a footnote from Evans-Pritchard to explain that 'the ubiquitous Kisanga is again playing a role he is not qualified to play', and that he often obtruded himself as an actor in most activities.[40]

Such uncontrollable intrusions into the visual and textual frame subvert the neatness of the generalized ethnographic categories—not all witch doctors present

<hr>

[39] Haddon and Myres, 'Photography', 271.
[40] Evans-Pritchard, *Witchcraft, Oracles and Magic*, 242.

were male, not all who danced were witch doctors, and so on. The excessive inclusiveness of both vernacular texts and photographic images is presented as part and parcel of the messiness of social reality, through which the reader is guided by anthropological insight. 'I shall ask the reader', Evans-Pritchard writes, 'to accompany me on my visits to séances... here we shall at once find ourselves puzzled by their grotesque movements and obscure revelations. We shall have to organize our rambling reactions to the turbulent scenes at which we shall assist, into a number of coherent problems. These we shall attempt to solve.'[41]

The uneasy relationship between the particularizing and historicizing tendency of photography and the historically ambiguous position of the anthropological analysis is a wider issue that Evans-Pritchard addresses frequently throughout *Witchcraft, Oracles and Magic*. In the case of Kamanga's initiation, the difference between the event as illustrated in the photographs and the 'norm' as described in the text is such that Evans-Pritchard is forced to contextualize and explain. Since Kamanga's initiation took place in Evans-Pritchard's own courtyard, he writes, 'this accounts for the spaciousness of the scene and for the unusual number of magicians present'.[42] Elsewhere we learn that both these particular contexts may be historically linked. In the twenty years between the overthrow of King Gbudwe and the start of Evans-Pritchard's fieldwork, the colonial administration had reorganized settlements along newly built roads, in an attempt to control sleeping sickness and facilitate administration. During this period, the number of practicing *abinza* had increased dramatically, partly as a result of the greater density of settlement, but partly due to social and economic upheaval, and the desire to gain material reward for services as a *binza*. The initiation took place in Evans-Pritchard's own courtyard since he was the sponsor, and the abnormally large number of attending *abinza* was almost certainly due to two related factors, both of which attest to Evans-Pritchard's effect on local social and economic life: that since his own settlement had doubled in size after he first went to live there we can assume that not only was his presence causing local nobles jealousy, but that his employment of two local *abinza* to teach Kamanga had attracted even more local *abinza* to attend the event in the hope of reward.[43]

Armed with caveats about the particular historical contexts of the photographs, we are nevertheless enjoined to consider them as illustrating something essential about this stage of Zande witch doctor initiation—that is, the ritual death, burial, and resurrection of an initiate—a historical model of initiation earlier presented by J. G. Frazer.[44] Frazer's influence is evident, for instance, in Evans-Pritchard's comment that Kamanga's ritual bore 'the imprint of a typical initiation... a ritual

---

[41] Evans-Pritchard, 'Zande corporation of witchdoctors (part one)', 298.
[42] Evans-Pritchard, *Witchcraft, Oracles and Magic*, 239.
[43] Evans-Pritchard, *Witchcraft, Oracles and Magic*, 402.
[44] J. G. Frazer. 1913 [1890]. *The Golden Bough: A Study in Magic and Religion*. Part VII, *Balder the Beautiful*, vol. 2. London: MacMillan (3rd edition), 225–78.

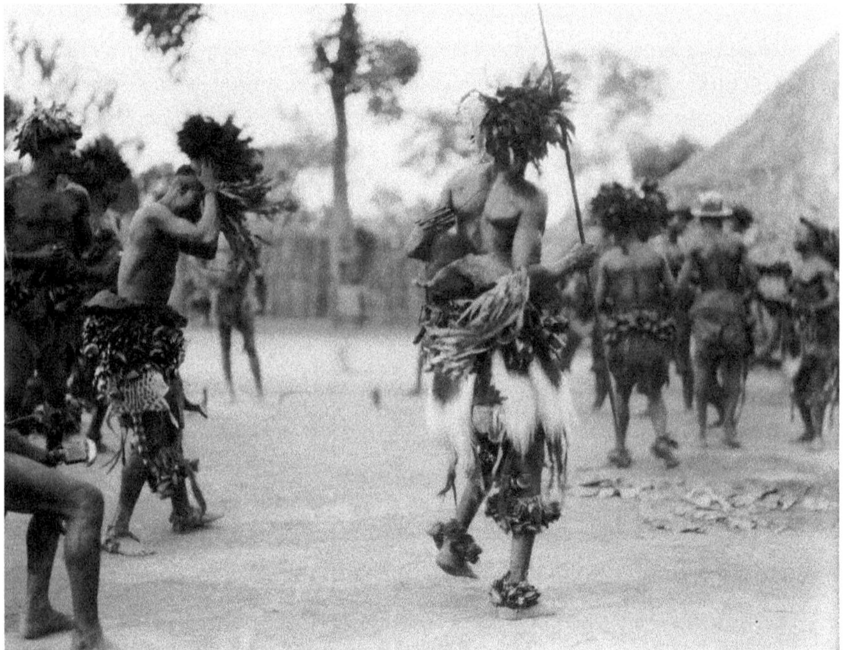

Figure 3.13 Frame 11 from the initiation of Kamanga sequence. Photograph by E. E. Evans-Pritchard, 1928–9.

enactment of death and burial and resurrection'.[45] Although this broad comparative interpretation of the initiation of Kamanga into the corporation of witch doctors in one sense accords with Frazer's model,[46] Evans-Pritchard is nonetheless concerned about the historical credentials of the ritual, and its relevance to his overall analysis of Zande witchcraft. He stresses, for instance, that the burial custom is a relatively recent borrowing, probably not widespread among other Zande groups, is not an essential prerequisite to practising as a *binza*, and that we should consider it as an example of the plasticity of Zande culture.

Given Evans-Pritchard's reservations about the importance of the ritual, the fact that three images of the ritual are reproduced in *Witchcraft, Oracles and Magic* would, on the face of it, appear to give it a disproportional visual prominence compared to the analytic weight given to it in the text. There is an ongoing tension in the relationship between the visual discourse engaged with in the monograph, and the anthropological argument running through the text. Partly this may be due to the fact that the photograph selection was not intended to

---

[45] Evans-Pritchard, 'Zande corporation of witchdoctors (part two)', 89.
[46] This should be balanced with Evans-Pritchard's critique of J. G. Frazer's interpretation of magic (Evans-Pritchard, 'Intellectualist (English) interpretation of magic').

illustrate the ritual alone, but *abinza* in general, evidenced by cross-referencing throughout the book. The reproduction of the initiation series was also serendipitous for at least one other reason—although Evans-Pritchard had frequent interaction with *abinza*, he otherwise took very few photographs of them (perhaps due to their objections or suspicions). Added to this is the fact that nearly all the plates used in *Witchcraft, Oracles and Magic* were produced from blocks already produced for earlier journal articles (presumably for economic reasons), and so image selections made to illustrate previous articles, which may have had slightly different emphases, end up illustrating a different text in a new context and with a wider set of cross-references, a process that I discuss in detail in chapter 5.

The approach I have taken with the series of images of Kamanga's initiation is to consider them from the perspective of his core fieldwork methodology, that of writing vernacular texts. It should be clear from the sorts of comparisons made that I haven't proposed a model for thinking about photographs *as* texts, with all the hermeneutic analysis that would entail, but rather that they are *like* vernacular texts—or rather that both forms of inscription bear interesting comparison. Both texts and photographs are necessarily implicated in processes of intention, performance, translation, and interpretation; both contain traces of local stories,

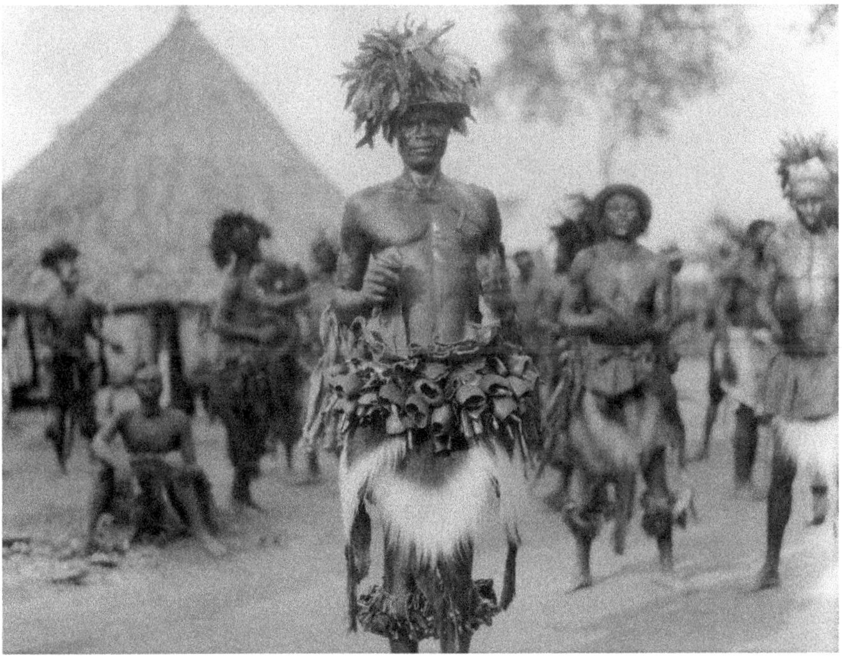

Figure 3.14 Frame 12 from the initiation of Kamanga sequence. Photograph by E. E. Evans-Pritchard, 1928–9.

random inclusions, indigenous gestures, and ethnographic excess. The process of writing down vernacular texts, which includes the problem of non-verbal communication, fragmented narratives, and obscure references, seems to mirror the way in which photographs are framed by the ethnographer, and yet always lead beyond to local understandings of visual imagery and self-representation. As objects, Evans-Pritchard's Zande prints bear traces of annotation in the vernacular, suggestive of a fieldwork mode of interaction with his archive, and the material traces of a lost album bring to the imagination previous performances as part of a fieldwork collection, to be leafed through and shared with Zande neighbours. There are the wider social contexts that shape the texts and which the photographs bring to the fore—local experiences of colonialism, indigenous forms of authority, and social upheaval. And then there are the performances, selections, and visual discourses within the anthropological monograph itself, the material relationships between text and image at a particular point in publishing history, an interweaving between textual and visual approaches to ethnographic material, and which can be seen to offer differing emphases and alternative readings. This reunited or reassociated series of photographs offers a new narrative, albeit fragmentary, about a classic event in the ethnographic literature, a narrative as I have shown that diverges and converges with the published account.

In the case of the initiation of Kamanga, the problems of immediate and visible ethnographic context that the photographs raise in relation to the anthropological description are so numerous that Evans-Pritchard is forced to engage with them directly—problems of unusual spaciousness, numbers of participants, gender, unexpected actors intruding into the scene, and Evans-Pritchard's own social role as host and sponsor of the initiate. Both photographs and vernacular texts provoke footnotes, parenthetical explanations, and contextual preambles. They are both the source of anthropological insight, and yet their excessive description is the source of a tension that pulls us away towards the randomness of actual events.

4

Double alienation

Fieldwork and photography between two worlds

Reflecting late in life on how he went about fieldwork, Evans-Pritchard wrote that 'I had no interest in witchcraft when I went to Zandeland, but the Azande had; so I had to let myself be guided by them. I had no particular interest in cows when I went to Nuerland, but the Nuer had, so willy-nilly I had to become cattle-minded too.'[1] The notion of Evans-Pritchard as the 'cattle-minded' ethnographer, entering fully into an alternative way of perceiving the world, struck me as potentially important in understanding the results of such perception: his field photography. How might we approach the archive differently, I began to think, if we see in it both the imprint of local agency acting upon the ethnographer, as well as differently patterned local responses to the act of photography itself, played out in front of the camera. I was also drawn into this approach in the search for an explanation, as I began cataloguing his archive, as to why Evans-Pritchard's Zande photographs were so different in nature to those he took of the Nuer. I could rule out a transformation in his photographic approach or having undertaken some professional training; Evans-Pritchard remained mediocre as a photographer in both a technical and compositional sense throughout his career. Why should they be so different, given that they were taken by the same fieldworker, and at a similar time? Most writing on the history of photography and anthropology gives prominence to shifting academic frameworks that shape modes of visual representation, but relatively little has suggested how the archival record might be shaped by differently patterned indigenous responses to the fieldworker and their camera. Herle has suggested that John Layard's photographs taken on Malakula in 1914–15 may indicate a more participatory form of fieldwork, but also that they reveal 'the complex intersubjective relations involved in their production',[2] which suggests that archival patterning can be as much about indigenous relationships to the fieldworker and their camera as the intentions of the fieldworker.

In this chapter I compare these sets of photographs and explore the way that different historical and cultural relations to exogenous influences within Zande

---

[1] E. E. Evans-Pritchard. 1973. 'Some reminiscences and reflections on fieldwork', *Journal of the Anthropological Society of Oxford*, Vol 4(1), 2.

[2] A. Herle. 2009. 'John Layard Long Malakula 1914–1915: the potency of field photography'. In *Photography, Anthropology and History: Expanding the Frame*, edited by C. Morton and E. Edwards. Farnham: Ashgate Publishing, 261.

and Nuer society in the early 1930s can be seen to be inscribed within the archival record and played out in modes of self-presentation to Evans-Pritchard's camera. Questions of self-presentation inevitably also open up questions about the way in which people posed for his camera. How do we 'read' pose cross-culturally? Although we might make suggestions about this, we should also acknowledge that field photographs can be highly ambiguous documents. Nonetheless, ambiguity can also be seen as a productive quality, in which meaning can be re-established at different times and in different places, not just at the moment the shutter falls.

One concept that I will explore is the notion of visual distance as an index of social distance. As a colonial technology, photography resonated very differently with Zande and Nuer communities in the 1920s and 1930s. Arguably, these differing relationships to both the anthropologist and his camera do pattern the archive, and suggest analytical routes beyond those reductive discussions of asymmetrical power relations so redolent of Foucault-derived approaches to anthropological photography and the 'colonial archive'. Such analyses have always tended to suppress precisely those voices and histories that they were intended to valorize, and a greater analytical awareness of the role of indigenous agency in the shaping of anthropology and its visual results is needed if new forms of indigenous history are to emerge.[3]

Historians of South Sudan would be the first to say that it isn't that surprising that Evans-Pritchard's Zande and Nuer photographs are so different, when one considers the marked difference between the two societies on a whole range of social, cultural, and historical levels. While this seems straightforward, it actually opens up a complex area of investigation into the social and cultural processes involved in the production of field photography, as well as the role of photographic intentionality in the shaping of the visual record. Why are there no posed group portraits of Nuer families? Or posed groups of age mates? Why are there relatively few informal images of Azande involved in everyday tasks and activities? Such questions certainly open up interesting areas of investigation into how indigenous agency might have shaped Evans-Pritchard's archive. We get glimpses of the very real differences in fieldwork that Evans-Pritchard experienced among these two peoples in statements such as: 'Azande would not allow me to live as one of themselves; Nuer would not allow me to live otherwise. Among Azande I was compelled to live outside the community; among Nuer I was compelled to be a member of it. Azande treated me as a superior; Nuer as an equal.'[4]

---

[3] See E. Edwards and C. Morton. 2009. 'Introduction'. In *Photography, Anthropology and History: Expanding the Frame*, edited by C. Morton and E. Edwards. Farnham: Ashgate Publishing, 3.

[4] E. E. Evans-Pritchard. 1940. *The Nuer: A Description of the Modes of Livelihood and Political Institutions of a Nilotic People*. Oxford: Clarendon Press, 15.

In order to fully accommodate such a role for indigenous agency, we must critique the prime role that photographic intentionality is given as the supreme arbiter of what is visually recorded—of what is seen and what is left unseen—and the resulting pattern of the archive. While Evans-Pritchard's attitude to his field photography suggests that he used it as a visual notebook, my argument in this chapter will be that, just as with a textual field notebook, the visual one is patterned according to a whole range of historical and sociocultural factors affecting the situational nature of the ethnographic encounter, and indigenous attitudes towards both the fieldworker and the camera.

Situating the field

As I described in chapter 2, in early November 1926 Evans-Pritchard arrived in what is now the Blue Nile Province of Sudan to carry out research among the Ingessana (Gamk) people of the Tabi Hills. This short period of initial fieldwork, consisting of two months spent in the vicinity of Soda, the site of an old Sudanese government station, was carried out to help provide information for his supervisor Charles Seligman's ethnographic survey of the country, published some years later. Evans-Pritchard's photographs from this first period of fieldwork were in some respects quite different from those of his subsequent Zande fieldwork. Among the Ingessana, Evans-Pritchard undertook a limited photographic sequence of physical type photographs, usually both profile and full-face, with his coat for a backdrop. Such scientific-reference imagery is entirely absent in his Zande photographs, although many of them were presumably taken on the same first visit to the Sudan. Although Evans-Pritchard took a large number of Zande portraits, they are characterized by a much less shallow and scrutinizing focal plane, have no backdrop, and although sometimes repetitive (such as the series of portraits of the sons of Prince Rikita) each image is inflected by the personality of the individual, with no attempt made to strip the subject of 'modern' or incongruous possessions or clothing.

On the surface, then, a cross-section through Evans-Pritchard's field archive could superficially suggest a shift in fieldwork methodology—a development represented by a retreating focal depth of the images—from scientific scrutiny to relaxed portraiture; from an approach where context is intentionally excluded to one where context crowds in. Another interpretation would be that the Ingessana photographs demonstrate the particular concerns of a more limited survey, whereas the Zande portraits emerge from deeper social relationships established over time—the product of a more immersive fieldwork methodology. Working from the surface of the image, it could be argued that Evans-Pritchard's archive visually demonstrates the disciplinary shift within British anthropology in the 1920s, with radically different notions of what constituted a 'scientific' approach laid bare in the photographic record. The evidence for this line of interpretation, however, is undermined by the written record, which in fact indicates not a linear progression in Evans-Pritchard's methodology but the coexistence of parallel ethnographic investigations with differing methodological concerns. Evans-Pritchard did in fact carry out physical measurements during his Zande fieldwork,[5] and although not taken according to accepted methods, six of his Zande portraits were cropped and enlarged to provide a comparison of 'Zande types' in the Seligmans' book.[6] So those Ingessana physical anthropology photographs can in a sense be understood as those of a research assistant, operating according to the needs of his supervisor's project. When it came to his Zande fieldwork, close relationships established over months of living in that community enabled an intimacy and level of access within a non-Western society that Evans-Pritchard had never experienced before, and his camera traces its progression.

Zande self-presentation

Evans-Pritchard's Zande photographs are quite diverse in subject matter, including individual and group portraits, social activities such as dances, techniques, material culture (such as spirit shrines, pottery making), and ritual. Most of his Zande negatives are quarter-plate size film negatives, possibly taken with a camera adapted for film packs. In fact this is the main format for his photography between 1926 and 1930, and is therefore present throughout much of the Zande, Moro, Ingessana, and Bongo material. It is also a significant format in his first Nuer fieldwork between 1930 and 1931.[7] The technology here is significant since his lack of confidence with early cameras meant that he 'tried to take two or three photos of whatever it was I was taking a picture of, varying the time exposure or stop, so one of them was certain to be reproducible'.[8] This comment also suggests the extent to which he understood the illustrative and corroborative importance of his field photographs for subsequent publications.

The Zande photographs are also characterized by a strong sense of self-presentation to Evans-Pritchard's camera, which might suggest an awareness of

---

[5] C. Seligman and B. Z. Seligman. 1932. *Pagan Tribes of the Nilotic Sudan*. London: Routledge, 496.

[6] See Seligman and Seligman, *Pagan Tribes*, Plate LVI (opposite page 496). Evans-Pritchard made all of his Zande photographs available to the Seligmans, who cropped around the faces of Zande portraits. In only one or two instances did Evans-Pritchard ever photograph a Zande subject in profile.

[7] This film size (designated 118) was used by a number of cameras. Kodak, for example, produced the No.3 Autograph camera from 1914 to 1926. This used 3 1/4 by 4 1/4 inch negatives, usually six exposures to a spool, yet the 1928 Kodak dealer catalogue notes that 118 film would also be supplied in 12 exposure spools, on request. The mechanically printed number on the bottom of many of the negatives is evidence that they actually come from a film pack. These were packs of sheet film that could be used with an adaptor in place of dark slides holding glass plates.

[8] E. E. Evans-Pritchard. 1973. 'Some recollections on fieldwork in the twenties', *Anthropological Quarterly*, 46(4), 241.

photography among many Azande, even though very few would have owned photographs of themselves. In a series of some twenty portraits of the sons of Prince Rikita, for instance, each sitter poses in the same camp chair with a grass fence behind. Despite the uniformity and repetitive nature of the series, Evans-Pritchard's framing lacks any sense of scientific intention such as recording physical types, and instead is more suggestive of having been commissioned by Rikita to create portraits of his sons, possibly as a marker of status. Most of the prints from this series in Evans-Pritchard's archive contain traces of having once been placed in an album, possibly used by him during fieldwork. We know that Evans-Pritchard returned with prints on his second Zande expedition, and can only surmise that he also showed them and discussed them with Zande informants.

Many of the Zande portraits are characterized by a style of pose that has the subject looking straight at the camera, feet together and arms straight to the side of the body. The rigidity of this pose feels awkward; the subject has obviously been asked to pose for the camera, and the response is formal and acquiescent. There are also some formal Zande group portraits, such as one of Chief Ongosi with his wives and children (Figure 4.1). He also photographed Prince Gangura, seated, with wives and daughters standing behind him and sons on the ground in front (Figure 4.2), as well as Gami, a commoner provincial governor, with a line of sons to his left, daughters to his right, and wives and younger children seated on the ground (Figure 4.3). These family portraits strongly suggest the important role photography played in the social and political network that Evans-Pritchard relied upon during his fieldwork, and that there was a strong local demand for portraiture, to affirm kin ties and political prestige. These group portraits first prompted my thoughts about the differences between Evans-Pritchard's Zande and Nuer images. Why are these sorts of group portrait not only absent from Evans-Pritchard's Nuer photographs, but also inconceivable? The answer cannot reasonably lie in any shift in his photographic style or interest, or shift in ethnographic focus, but reflects social and cultural differences between Zande and Nuer, as well as different experiences of colonialism and its tools of control and observation such as the camera.

With King Gbudwe having been overthrown in 1905, Azande had been under colonial control for a number of years before Evans-Pritchard arrived in 1926. The opinion of early colonial observers among the Azande, such as P. M. Larken, was that the Zande cultural area had grown significantly in the nineteenth century as a result of warfare, and particularly through the assimilation of neighbouring (often acephalous) groups.[9] Cultural assimilation was therefore a long-established part of what political assimilation into the greater Zande system meant for most people.

---

[9] P. M. Larken. 1926. 'An account of the Zande', *Sudan Notes and Records*, 9(1), 21.

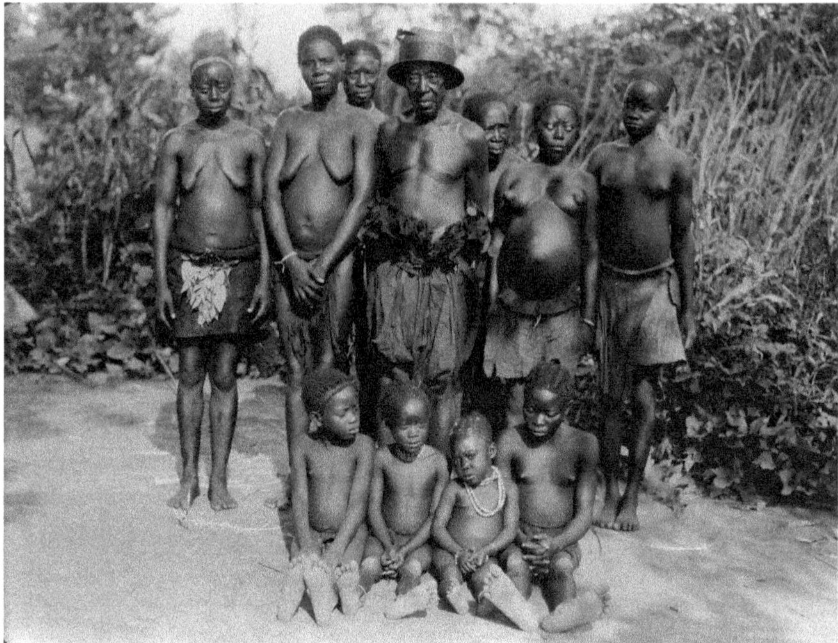

Figure 4.1 Ongosi, a Zande courtier of Prince Basongoda's court, with some of his wives and children, Yambio, Western Equatoria, South Sudan. Photograph by E. E. Evans-Pritchard, 1927–30.

In Evans-Pritchard's opening account of Zande culture in *Witchcraft, Oracles and Magic among the Azande,* he psychologizes this historical process, stating that:

> in the experience of the author . . . the Azande are so used to authority that they are docile; that it is unusually easy for Europeans to establish contact with them . . . that they adapt themselves without undue difficulty to new conditions of life and are always ready to copy the behaviour of those they regard as their superiors in culture[10]

Relationships between closely associated photographs from Evans-Pritchard's Zande fieldwork are often suggestive of the social interplay surrounding his photography. Let us examine, for instance, two photographs of one of Evans-Pritchard's closest informants, Ngbitimo (also known as Zambaliru).

The first image is a portrait of Ngbitimo standing next to medicines growing in the centre of his homestead, two of his wives sitting on a termite mound in the

---

[10] E. E. Evans-Pritchard. 1937. *Witchcraft, Oracles and Magic Among the Azande.* Oxford: Clarendon Press, 13.

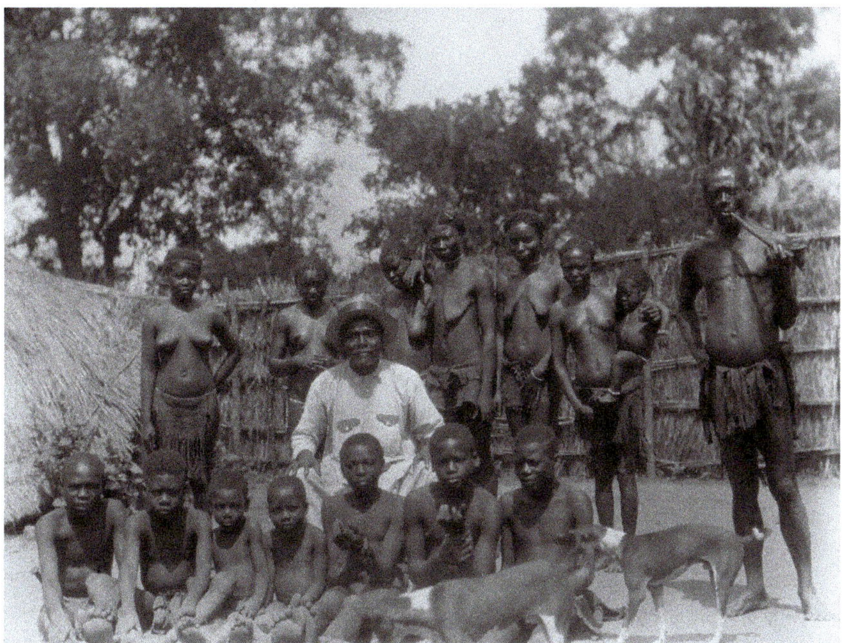

Figure 4.2 Prince Gangura and his family, Yambio, Western Equatoria, South Sudan. Photograph by E. E. Evans-Pritchard, 1927–30.

distance (Figure 4.4). In the second portrait, Evans-Pritchard has shifted his position to the left in order to include offerings placed on a *tuka* to the right of frame (Figure 4.5). This time two of Ngbitimo's wives stand either side of him, one of whom is gesturing either towards her husband, or else the *tuka*. I think it is unlikely that Evans-Pritchard has prompted this gesture, which seems to be a spontaneous act. But what is this gesture? Is it a Zande gesture of a wife presenting her husband to the camera, a way of visually indicating status to the viewer? If so, what sort of local understandings about photographic representation does it presuppose? Or if the gesture is towards the *tuka*, what is her communication intended to indicate? That the *tuka* is the subject of the photograph, not her? Or is it just a gesture that has nothing to do with the act of photography, and was just caught accidentally? Either way, the presence of this gesture transforms the image into something more than Evans-Pritchard's intention, and appropriates it.

There are two important strands to this idea, the first being that such acts of self-representation suggest a cultural awareness of photography, or at least of its expected outcome (a picture). The second is that cultural responses to the act of photography, such as the gesture, may often be articulated through already existing modes of public gesture and comportment, such as in formalized

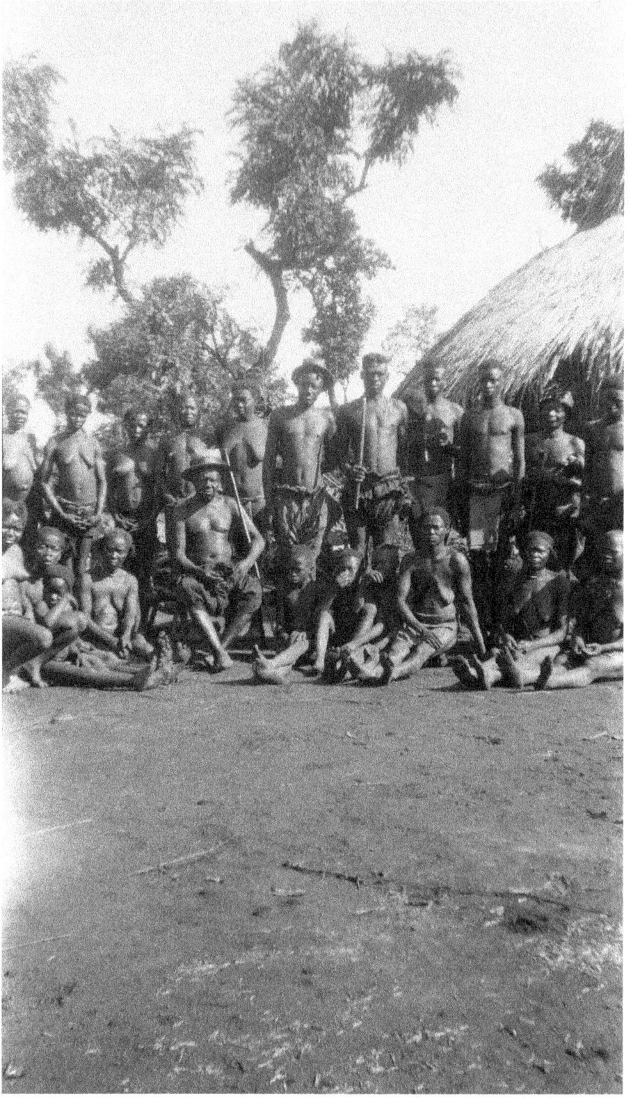

Figure 4.3 Gami, a commoner governor, with his family, Yambio, Western Equatoria, South Sudan. Photograph by E. E. Evans-Pritchard, 1927–30.

greetings and spatial arrangements at social gatherings. Elizabeth Edwards has discussed the way in which these sorts of indigenous socio-spatial configurations can sometimes be seen as emergent through the dominant narrative in which photographs have been embedded over time, in her example of two photographs of rival Samoan claimants and their supporters seated on the deck of HMS

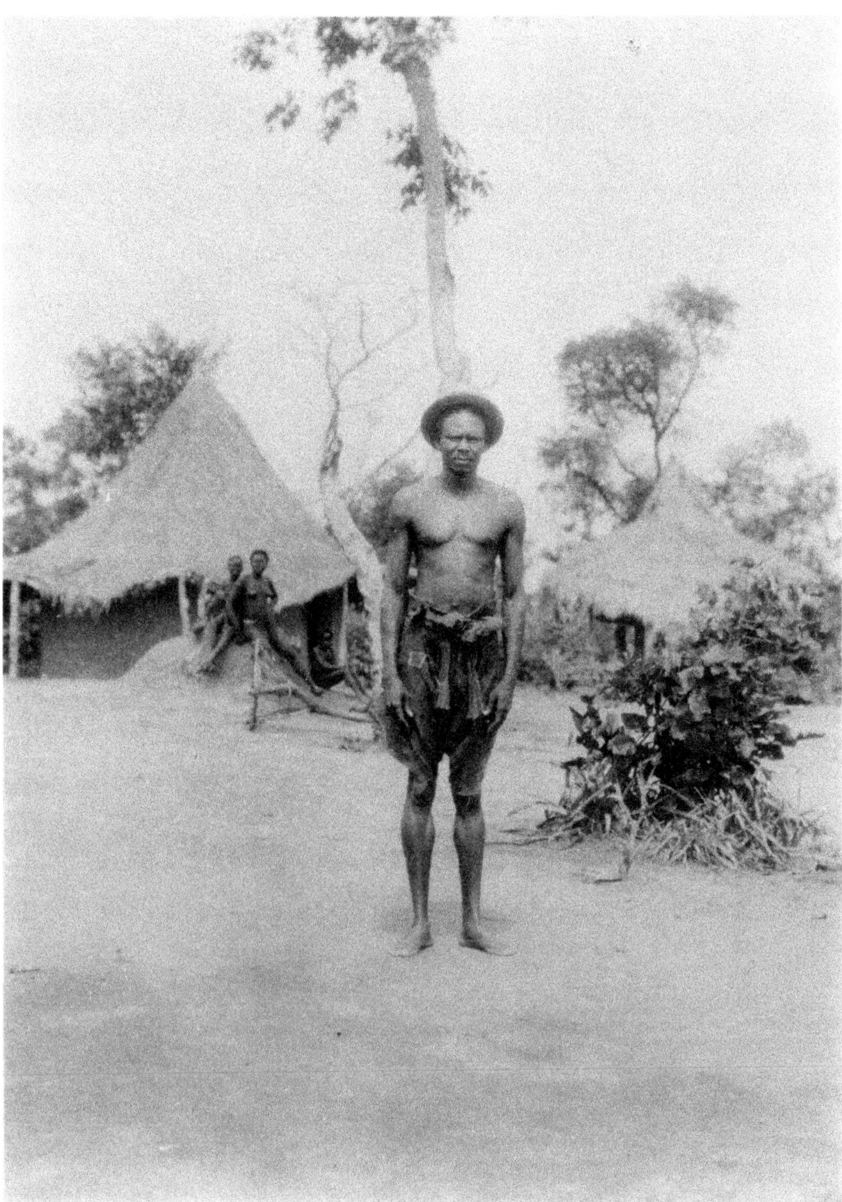

Figure 4.4 Ngbitimo with medicine plants growing in his homestead, Yambio, Western Equatoria, South Sudan. Photograph by E. E. Evans-Pritchard, 1927–30.

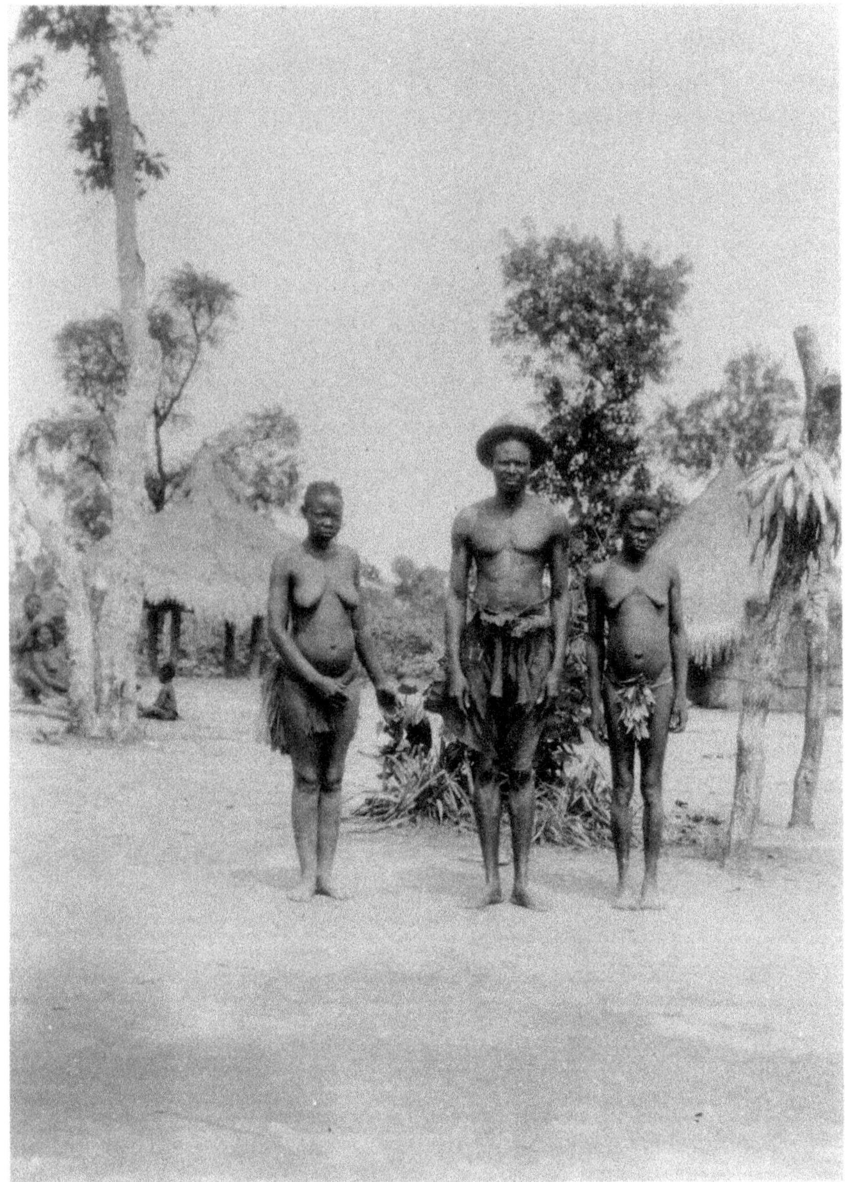

Figure 4.5 Ngbitimo with two of his wives, Yambio, Western Equatoria, South Sudan. Photograph by E. E. Evans-Pritchard, 1927–30.

Miranda. Such photographs, Bronwen Douglas has argued, 'inadvertently register shadowy traces of local agency, relationships and settings'.[11] If we take another look at the group portrait of Prince Gangura and some of his family (Figure 4.2), it is clear that notions of local agency, relationships, and settings are not inadvertent, but subtly undermine the notion of the 'colonial gaze'. In other words, this doesn't feel like a photograph 'about' or 'of' a Zande prince and his family, but 'for' a Zande prince and his family. Again, it is the presence of gesture within the pose, this time by two boys sitting at the front, that arrests our attention as some sort of communication is directed towards us.

In the group portrait of the governor Gami and his family (Figure 4.3), in whose homestead Evans-Pritchard stayed, the use of a chair by the head of the family is also used to indicate status, with older males again standing to the left side. What seems apparent in both group portraits is a process whereby local expectations of photographic representation, possibly derived partly from a limited local circulation of photographs or print media, are mediated by pre-existing cultural practices, especially those derived from spatial organization at Zande group meetings. Since we are told by Evans-Pritchard that Zande men and women never sit together in public, these group portraits, with boys sitting with women and men standing behind, take on additional local inflections and relationships beyond the camera. In one sense, the very existence of such formal group arrangements obviously indicates some sort of local understanding of photography, its technologies, intentions, uses, and manners of representation. But we have as yet little knowledge of what such local understandings were among the Azande in this period.

We might compare such group portraits with others taken just across the border in the Belgian Congo by Herbert Lang in 1913 of the Zande chief Akenge with a number of his wives.[12] Again, there is a temptation to try and understand such photographs in terms of what sort of relationship there is between the photographic pose and pre-existing spatial dynamics at Zande social gatherings, such as attendance at the court of a royal. But it is also tempting to try and understand what sort of indigenous self-representation they may represent, rather than focusing on whether Lang is working with representational norms. More research may reveal the extent to which such portraits actually reveal complex understandings and manipulations of photographic representation on the part of chiefs in particular. We might then compare, for instance, Schweinfurth's portrait

---

[11] B. Douglas. 1998. 'Inventing natives/negotiating local identities: postcolonial readings of colonial texts on island Melanesia'. In *Pacific Answers to Western Hegemony: Cultural Practices of Identity Construction*, edited by J. Wassmann. Oxford: Berg, 70.

[12] For instance photograph #111631 by Herbert Lang from the 1909–15 Congo expedition of the American Museum of Natural History, taken in Akenge in September 1913. The description runs: 'The biggest hut in Azande style in his village. In front, the chief is surrounded by some of his most favored women.'

of the Mangbetu King Munza of 1874[13] with both Lang's portrait of the Akenge chief in 1913, and Evans-Pritchard's portrait of a Zande prince's deputy used as the frontispiece to *Witchcraft, Oracles and Magic* (Figure 4.6). Rather than seeing such similarities as the consolidation of a Western visual trope of central African chieftaincy, it is important to acknowledge the potential historical role of local leaders in their own representation. To not accommodate such a possibility (or even likelihood) would run counter to the evidence presented in the literature, which suggests that Zande chiefs had elaborate conventions about the way authority was visually and spatially presented to onlookers.

The symbolism of the pose of authority is also used in a more subtle way by Evans-Pritchard in his frontispiece to *Witchcraft, Oracles and Magic Among the*

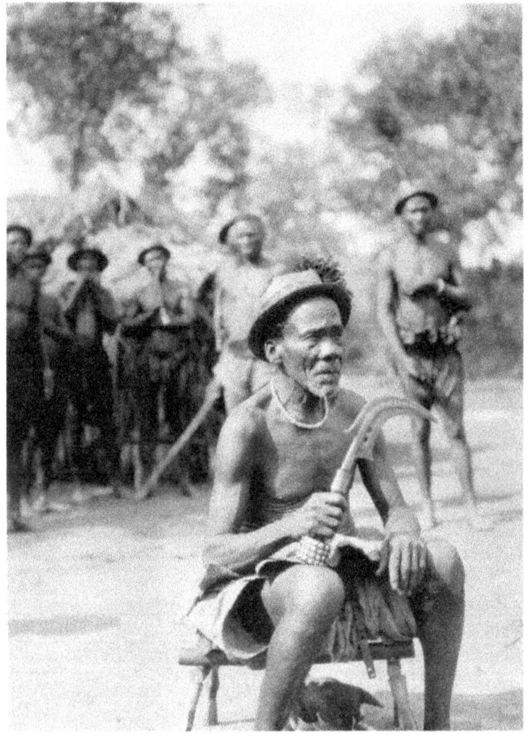

Figure 4.6 Portrait of a Zande chief's deputy, published as the frontispiece to *Witchcraft, Oracles and Magic Among the Azande*, Yambio, Western Equatoria, South Sudan. Photograph by E. E. Evans-Pritchard, 1927.

---

[13] Published as the Frontispiece to Georg Schweinfurth's 1874 book *The Heart of Africa: three years' travels and adventures in the unexplored regions of Central Africa from 1868 to 1871* (Vol. II). London: Sampson Low, Marston, Searle & Rivington, with the caption 'King Munza in full dress'.

Azande. Why, for instance, is this photograph used, when it is made clear throughout the book that witchcraft is neither practised, nor believed in, by the ruling class in Zandeland? The metonymic burden of the frontispiece image in this instance is perhaps related to the language of its caption. Here we have a society, the caption tells us, with a prince, a prince's court, a deputy, and a knife of office; in other words, the values of aristocracy, order, hierarchy, and stability. Given Evans-Pritchard's attempt in the following analysis to demonstrate the validity of Zande rationality as expressed through witchcraft and oracular practices, the frontispiece image resonates with the wider conclusions of his thesis concerning the workings of the social system, in which he explicitly acknowledges the influence of Radcliffe-Brown. While it is possible that Evans-Pritchard's choice of frontispiece illustration intentionally echoes that of Schweinfurth's frontispiece image of King Munza, thereby consolidating a long-established representational trope of Zande political authority, we should not discount the possibility, given that a number of similar images were taken by Evans-Pritchard of other deputies posed in this way, that Zande courtiers themselves were complicit in the composition of images that enhanced and demonstrated their political status.

'Nuerosis'

When Evans-Pritchard first arrived in Nuerland in January 1930, the society that he encountered was markedly different to that of the Azande: not politically centralized, without elaborate social and political hierarchy, either no deference to European authority or openly hostile towards it, and little enthusiasm for outside ideas or material culture. As the historian of South Sudan Douglas Johnson has discussed, the 1920s was a tumultuous period in Nuer history, during which time the Sudanese government was embroiled in various attempts to control and administer the cattle-keeping Nuer groups of Upper Nile Province.[14] These actions had reached a critical phase by the end of 1927, when government attempts to intimidate the Nuer prophet Guek Ngundeng using aeroplanes failed. Government actions the following year brought another Nuer prophet Dual Diu into open rebellion, and troops were sent throughout Nuer country east of the Nile in an attempt to capture the leaders of these uprisings.[15] Desperate for more information about Nuer society and political organization in order to exercise control, the Sudanese government informed Evans-Pritchard that the Nuer would now be an urgent priority for any subsidy for research. Reluctant to abandon his

---

[14] D. H. Johnson. 1982. 'Evans-Pritchard, the Nuer, and the Sudan Political Service', *African Affairs*, 81(323), 231–46, and D. H. Johnson. 1993. *Governing the Nuer: Documents by Percy Coriat on Nuer History and Ethnography 1922–1931*. JASO Occasional Papers No. 9. Oxford: JASO.

[15] Johnson, 'Evans-Pritchard', 231.

Zande studies at a critical stage, Evans-Pritchard nonetheless agreed to begin work among the Nuer, and even expressed enthusiasm about doing so, 'partly because I feel sorry for the Nuer and would be glad to help them settle down peacefully by making myself intimate with their life'.[16]

After a troubled beginning to his arrival in Nuerland, Evans-Pritchard eventually met up with his Zande companions Mekana and Kamanga, and drove to Muot Dit in Lou Nuer country with a Nuer youth named Nhial.[17] In a letter to the Civil Secretary Harold MacMichael in March 1930, however, Evans-Pritchard described the problems of conducting research among the traumatized and suspicious Nuer:

> From our point of view the natives of this area are too unsettled & too resentful and frightened to make good informants & the breakdown of their customs & traditions too sudden & severe to enable an anthropologist to obtain quick results.[18]

The picture of obstinacy and evasiveness towards the anthropologist painted by Evans-Pritchard in his introduction to *The Nuer* needs to be understood in the context of Nuer attitudes towards someone who they rightly saw as an agent of an alien government—which, as Johnson points out, 'had bombed them, burned their villages, seized their cattle, took prisoners, herded them into dry "concentration areas", killed their prophet Guek and had blown up and desecrated the Mound of his father Ngung-deng, their greatest prophet'.[19] Evans-Pritchard wrote, for instance, that 'When I entered a cattle camp it was not only as a stranger but as an enemy, and they seldom tried to conceal their disgust at my presence, refusing to answer my greetings and even turning away when I addressed them.'[20] Frustrated at getting nowhere with his research, Evans-Pritchard felt like he was being driven crazy by his Nuer interlocutors giving him the run-around—a craziness that he termed 'Nuerosis'.[21]

His second period of fieldwork the following year (this time in eastern Nuerland), from February to June, began to yield some results. In a letter to Malinowski in May 1931, however, he expressed continued frustration:

---

[16] Typewritten report from E. E. Evans-Pritchard to Harold MacMichael, 8 February 1929, quoted in Johnson, 'Evans-Pritchard', 232.

[17] Johnson quotes a letter from Evans-Pritchard to Matthew dated 4.12.30, in which he states that the 'only informant whom I managed to procure on my last trip was a half-witted youth from Yoinyang' (Johnson, 'Evans-Pritchard', 237). Nhial also assisted Evans-Pritchard during his fieldwork in 1931 and in 1936 Evans-Pritchard stayed with Nhial at Nyueny as 'a friend of the family' (E. E. Evans-Pritchard. 1956. *Nuer Religion*. Oxford: Clarendon Press, 35), proving that Nhial was a central figure in facilitating Evans-Pritchard's Nuer fieldwork.

[18] Letter from E. E. Evans-Pritchard to Harold MacMichael, 27 March 1930, quoted in Johnson, 'Evans-Pritchard', 236.

[19] Johnson, 'Evans-Pritchard', 236.   [20] Evans-Pritchard, *The Nuer*, 11

[21] Evans-Pritchard, *The Nuer*, 13

I am still sweating away at the Nuer. They are really quite impossible—possibly like Bateson's 'Bainings'.[22] I have spent weeks learning the language and it is only now when I am preparing to leave more or less that info comes in—not pours in but trickles… it is a most depressing piece of work altogether. Still on the other hand it is rather fun after the easy Zande work tackling a really difficult culture.[23]

It was clear that the Nuer frequently considered photography in general as a tool of a hostile and alien government. In western Nuerland in 1930 his attempts to photograph cattle led to an undescribed, yet serious, incident, and 'for the remainder of that expedition I abstained from photographing a single cow'.[24] For the Nuer, government interest in their cattle had hitherto taken the form of fines, confiscation, or bombing. 'On no account', advised Evans-Pritchard in the government journal *Sudan Notes and Records*, 'should the cattle be photographed till friendly relations are established… It was only when I acquired a few cattle of my own [in 1931] and had a stake in the kraal that I was able to establish real contact with the people.'[25] Here we begin to understand something essential about Evans-Pritchard's acceptance within Nuer society, that without cattle he had no social existence to speak of, and no means of establishing social relationships with those he sought to live with and gain intimate information from about their kinship connections. For the Nuer, such knowledge was something that came with real social connections, which centred on cattle, whereas among the Zande, knowledge flowed through hierarchical power structures into which Evans-Pritchard fitted quite easily.

From a total of over one thousand photographs taken during his Nuer field-work, only about a quarter relate to his much longer eight and a half months of fieldwork during 1930–1, with three-quarters having been taken during the shorter three months of fieldwork between 1935 and 1936. Many of the photographs taken in 1930–1 are inflected by the sort of social distance experienced by Evans-Pritchard described above, with images of homesteads and cattle camps taken unobserved from the periphery, or when deserted. In Figure 4.7, for instance, Evans-Pritchard has wandered away from Yakwach camp, where he has pitched his tent, to take a photograph of the scene. Incidentally, it was under the awning of this tent that he took the photograph that he reproduces as Plate XIV in *The Nuer*, captioned 'August shower', and which I discuss in detail in the next chapter (reproduced as Figure 5.1). When people are included, it is almost

---

[22] A reference to Gregory Bateson's fieldwork among the Baining people of New Britain (Papua New Guinea) in 1927–8, which was notoriously difficult.

[23] London School of Economics archive, Malinowski Papers, Mal 7/11, letter from Evans-Pritchard to Malinowski, May 20 1931.

[24] E. E. Evans-Pritchard. 1937. 'The economic life of the Nuer: cattle (part 1)', *Sudan Notes and Records*, 20(3), 242.

[25] Evans-Pritchard, 'The economic life of the Nuer: cattle (part 1)', 242–3.

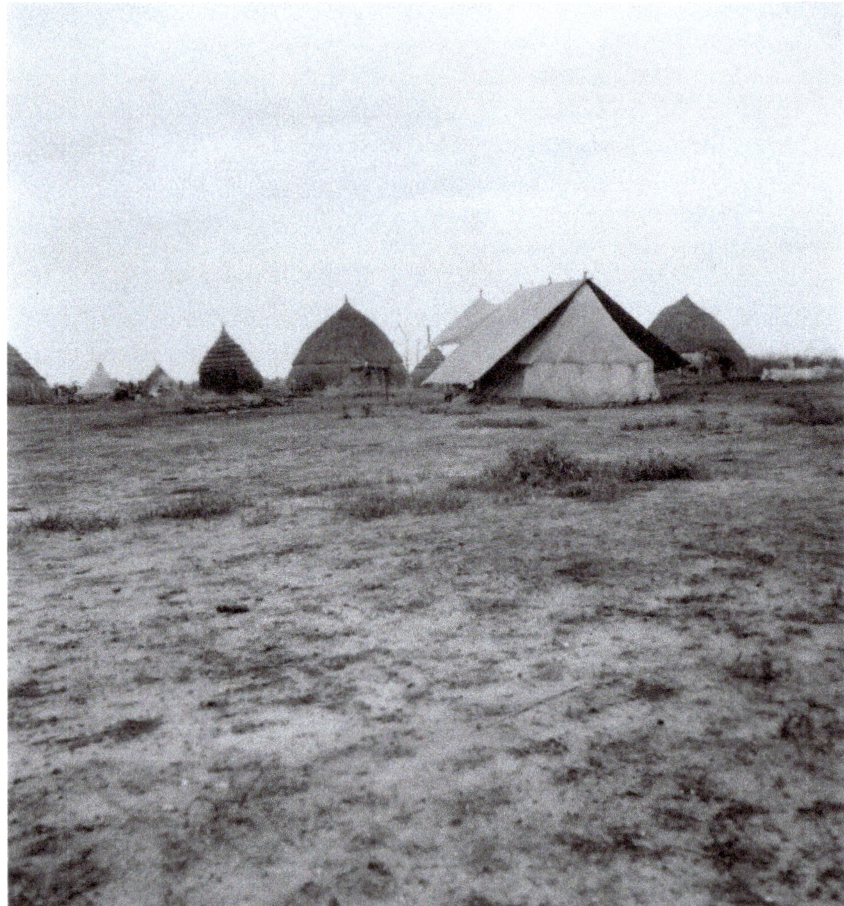

Figure 4.7 Evans-Pritchard's tent pitched at Yakwach cattle camp, Sobat River, Upper Nile, South Sudan. Photograph by E. E. Evans-Pritchard, 1935.

always the youths and young children that he spent most time with, and with whom he was on friendly terms. Occasionally striking portraits of these youths appear, especially from Yakwach cattle camp on the Sobat River in 1931 (Figure 4.8), but there are no portraits of adult men or women, possibly since few were at the dry-season camps. Although a feature of the photography of his second period of fieldwork, there are also very few images of Nuer dance events in his earlier fieldwork.

As has been mentioned, the nature of the images shifts considerably in 1935–6, with numerous photographs of differently marked cattle, milking activity (unthinkable in 1930), domestic activities, and dances, often taking place right outside his tent. Now mostly using a Rolleiflex camera, photography became a much more central tool of his fieldwork, no doubt highly aware of the limited time available to record

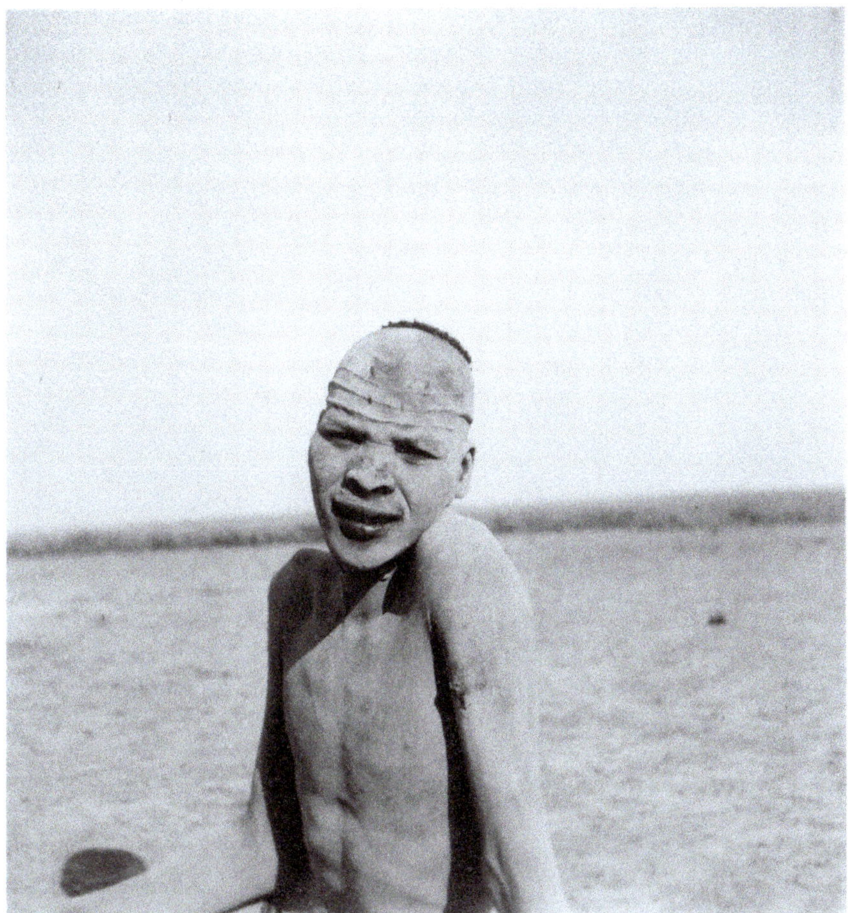

Figure 4.8 Nuer youth in western Nuerland, possibly Nyueny village, Unity State, South Sudan. Photograph by E. E. Evans-Pritchard, 1936.

details for subsequent analysis, as well as the need for decent illustration in any publication (almost all images published in *The Nuer* were taken in 1935–6).[26] In 1936, for example, he was able to photographically record Nuer ritual activity for the first time. In chapter 7 I discuss in detail his photographic record of the rite of *gorot*, a fertility rite involving the sacrifice of an ox by suffocation, which took place in 1936 at Nyueny village. Another ritual event that Evans-Pritchard witnessed in 1936 proved

[26] He had returned to the Nuer in 1935 only by chance since his Leverhulme Research Fellowship to study the Galla (Oromo) in Ethiopia was curtailed by the Italian invasion. The Leverhulme Trust also supported his fieldwork in Kenya in 1936, after which he paid a final visit to the Nuer in October/ November.

much more difficult to photograph successfully, since most of it took place at dusk, although one photograph taken early the following morning proved successful enough to be used in his later publication *Nuer Religion* as Plate IX, captioned 'Invocation'. This was the *colwic* ceremony for the spirit of a girl (called Nyakewa) killed by lightning. Another photograph from the sequence (Figure 4.9) situates Evans-Pritchard at the periphery of the ritual events, witnessing the sacrifice standing alongside the women and youths.

Evans-Pritchard keeps his distance at the *colwic* sacrifice in a way that is quite different to his movement through the ritual space during the *gorot* rite, where he takes photographs from very close to the sacrifice itself. In the *colwic* photograph, a senior maternal uncle with raised spear invokes *kwoth* (God) as he sacrifices an ox, next to a shrine made for Nyakewa. The shrine is visible in

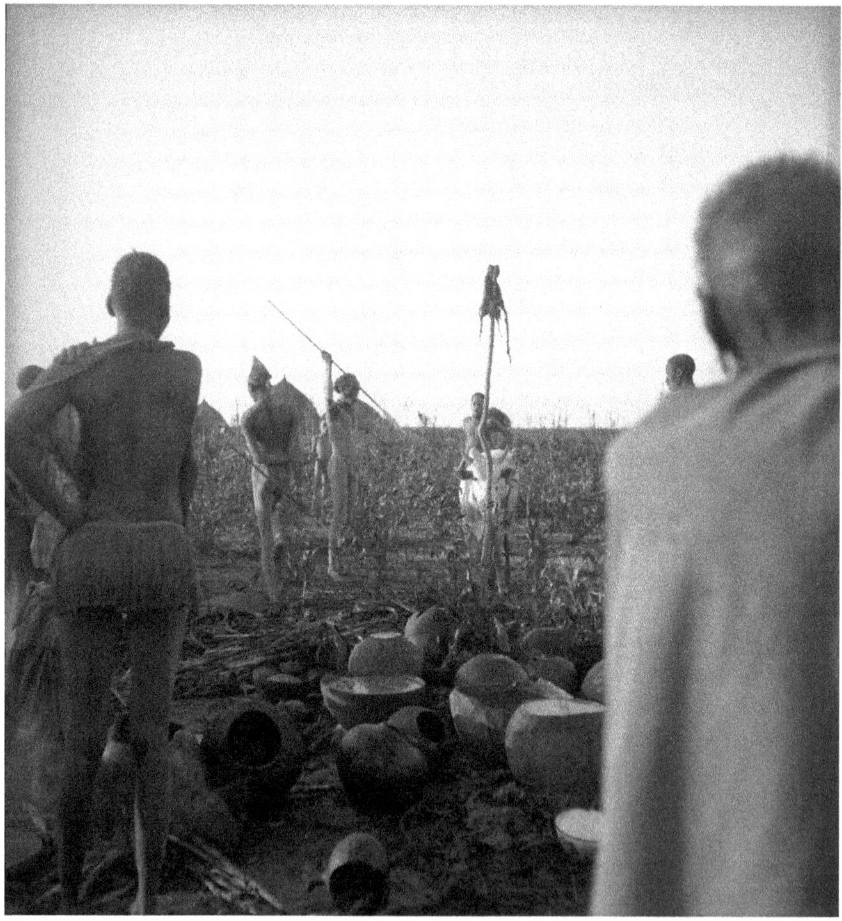

Figure 4.9 'Invocation' in the *colwic* sacrifice, Nyueny village, Unity State, South Sudan. Photograph by E. E. Evans-Pritchard, 1936.

the foreground just beyond the beer vessels, consisting of a low earthen mound with a shrine-stake (*riek*) at the centre and part of another sacrifice placed on top. Nyakewa was considered to have become a *colwic*, a spirit taken directly by God. The specific intervention by the divine via lightning was considered so dangerous to all associated with the deceased that sacrifice was made by all relatives (in all, more than twenty animals were sacrificed over several days). Not intruding into the sacrificial space, Evans-Pritchard's photographic record of the *colwic* sacrifice retains that strong sense of collective witness that I discuss in relation to his record of the *gorot* rite in chapter 7; he and his camera take their place alongside other witnesses, all of whose social presence is essential to the efficacy of the ritual. Evans-Pritchard does not intrude with his camera as though he were a central actor in the ritual; his view, and thereby our view, is alongside the other onlookers.

Context as author

With his anthropological investigations being framed so differently between the two groups, with enquiries among the Azande focused on witchcraft and magic, and among the Nuer more generally on social and political organization, one might expect these intellectual areas of focus to influence the photographic record. However, this is hardly so. For instance, there are examples of oracle consultations, *tuka* (spirit shrines), and magic-related material culture in his Zande photography, but they do not dominate; much more extensive photographic sequences, such as beer brewing, food preparation, and house construction, barely get a mention in his written ethnography.

In the introduction to this chapter I argued that the role I was proposing for indigenous agency, or more broadly local context, in the shaping of the field archive would involve rethinking the primacy given to photographic intentionality. The notion that photography is a way of seeing the world mediated by a photographer, and that photographs are the result of repeated choices between possible images made by that photographer, underlies much critical writing on the medium. John Berger writes for instance that:

> Every image embodies a way of seeing... Every time we look at a photograph, we are aware, however slightly, of the photographer selecting that sight from an infinity of other possible sights... The photographer's way of seeing is reflected in his choice of subject.[27]

---

[27] J. Berger. 1972. *Ways of Seeing*. London: BBC/Penguin Books, 10.

The photographer as author or collector of images is a concept that underlies, for instance, much modernist thinking on photography as both art and reportage. Vilém Flusser, for instance, defined a photographer as 'a person who attempts to place, within the image, information that is not predicted within the program of the camera';[28] and for Sontag 'photographs really are experience captured, and the camera is the ideal arm of consciousness in its acquisitive mood. To photograph is to appropriate the thing being photographed.'[29] For other photographic theorists, such as John Tagg, photographic intentionality is subordinate to the institutional and social practices and power structures which give photography its instrumental force. This approach is also found in the work of Allan Sekula, who has examined how photographs function in systems of commodity exchange within capitalism, and in particular photography's dual historical role in the creation of likenesses, both of the bourgeois self, and of the criminal.[30] For both Tagg and Sekula, the photographer is a technician within the institutional processes in which photographs are generated and consumed, such as colonial governance (including its social science department, or anthropology).

Although Evans-Pritchard's sponsorship by the colonial Sudanese government during his fieldwork would seem to provide a rich context in which to examine his photographs from this perspective, there is little evidence that his fieldwork photography was at all useful within colonial power structures. Only weakly can Evans-Pritchard's Zande or Nuer photography be considered as 'instrumental' photography, in which 'colonised peoples... were constituted as the passive... objects of knowledge' within social science discourse.[31] Although Evans-Pritchard's Zande and Nuer photographs were taken within a colonial context, Tagg's notion of instrumental photography is much more relevant to nineteenth-century forms of disciplinary image production and consumption, and somewhat less relevant to images that emerged from the intensive, long-term, individual fieldwork of the twentieth century. To constrain them within such an asymmetrical power reading would deny them a local identity, which they undoubtedly have and will have to a greater extent in the future. Indigenous agency in the form of resistance to the camera is also something that is occasionally apparent, for instance, throughout Malinowski's photography in the Trobriand Islands from 1915 to 1918, despite its aestheticized nature. Towards the end of his stay on Mailu Island, for instance, he recorded in his diary:

Went to the village hoping to photograph a few stages of the bara [dance]. I handed out half-sticks of tobacco, then watched a few dances; then took

---

[28] V. Flusser. 2000 [1983]. *Towards a Philosophy of Photography*. London: Reaktion, 84.

[29] S. Sontag. 1979 [1977]. *On Photography*. London: Penguin Books, 3–4.

[30] A. Sekula. 1986. 'The body and the archive', *October*, 39, 3–64.

[31] J. Tagg. 1988. *The Burden of Representation: Essays on Photographies and Histories*. Basingstoke and New York: Palgrave Macmillan, 11.

pictures—but results very poor. Not enough light for snapshots; and they would not pose long enough for time exposures. At moments I was furious with them, particularly because after I gave them their portions of tobacco they all went away.[32]

Young's conclusion about Malinowski's preference for framing people and objects in their social context in the middle distance, rather than up close as portraits, is that his style was 'methodologically driven' by an incipient 'functionalist' approach. However, it is less clear whether Trobriand Islander attitudes about posing for Malinowski to take close portraits was of more relevance to their absence from his archive.

The problem here is that photography is only a weak carrier of operator intentionality. Partly this is due to photography's inherent analogical nature—'a message without a code' as Barthes memorably described it[33]—which means that photographic intentionality is only one factor in the process of inscription. This leaves the question of photography's communication of meaning far from resolved. 'Insofar as photography is (or should be) about the world', wrote Sontag, 'the photographer counts for little, but insofar as it is the instrument of intrepid, questing subjectivity, the photographer is all.'[34] There is an inherent problem with Sontag's notion of a questing photographer, which is that it excludes the way in which context, and in particular the agency of those involved in social situations, shape the photographic record. The instability of photography's meaning undermines any dominant analytical position we might give to photographic intentionality. The random inclusiveness (and hence visual excess) of photographic inscription, its fixity of appearance and yet potentially infinite recodability, as well as its temporal and spatial slippages across both literal and metaphorical border zones, mean that interpretations that privilege the subjective vision of the photographer tend to dissolve when scrutinized from a historical perspective. Reading subjective intention as the dominant force behind the creation of a photograph is more likely to mirror the analyst's own critical position than illuminate the social contexts in which photographs are created. As Elizabeth Edwards has written, 'photographic inscription is not unmediated; the photograph is culturally circumscribed by ideas of what is significant or relevant at any given time, in any given context...the inscription itself becomes the first act of interpretation'.[35] Photographs are subject to subsequent layers of intentionality, of course, as found in Evans-Pritchard's subsequent treatment of his photographs in various publications, orderings, cross-commentaries, and annotations, and this

---

[32] Quoted in M. Young. 1998. *Malinowski's Kiriwina: Fieldwork Photography 1915–18*. Chicago and London: Chicago University Press, 6.

[33] R. Barthes. 1985. *The Responsibility of Forms*. New York: Hill and Wang, 5.

[34] Sontag, *On Photography*, 122.

[35] E. Edwards. 2001. *Raw Histories: Photographs, Anthropology and Museums*. Oxford: Berg, 9.

layering of intention makes the notion of a single moment of authorial intent a highly dubious one.

This more situational understanding of the nature of photographic inscription enables us to reinsert indigenous agency in the creation of field imagery in a more analytical way. If field photographs are culturally circumscribed by context-driven ideas of significance or relevance, then this is never wholly determined by the field photographer, but is partly determined by local contexts. If inscription is the first act of interpretation, then the visual interpretation of both Zande and Nuer culture needs to be understood in the context of cultural co-production— situationally determined, and historically circumscribed. Just as our expectations of photography as a medium are grounded in its ability to perform a version of reality—photography's indexical relationship to the world—so must any argument about the role of indigenous agency be grounded in the materiality of photography; it has to be demonstrated.

The relational image

Throughout this book I focus on the archival photograph as a highly revealing relational and biographical object through which new histories can be written, tracing the complex archival relations between some of Evans-Pritchard's well-known published photographs. My use of the term 'relational' here refers to the way in which photographic meaning emerges from an individual image's relationship to others in a series. Fieldwork photographs are relational in a number of different ways and on a number of different levels, both spatially and temporally. For instance, they may form part of a sequence of images relating to an event or ritual, or a technological theme such as pot making, which is more fragmented over the course of fieldwork. Images also usually contain relations to other images in time and space through the process of inscription. The relational dimension of a photograph is here a recognition of the way in which any photograph is suggestive of relationships beyond itself to other photographs, rather than merely within its own frame. Materially, photographs are related as numbered frames on a film, or dated slides, or as digital images with embedded metadata about their production, and hence have relationships to other images. It is only by examining the archival image in this relational context that we can investigate the question of indigenous agency on a sound methodological footing, because the relationships between moments of inscription are particularly revealing about the social and cultural contexts that surround particular photographs. The relational understanding of photographs is also connected to ongoing debates about the 'agency' of the image within social relations, or their role as social objects that are entangled with material and sensory processes in the communication of meaning. Ethnographic studies have shown, for instance, how photographs sometimes stand for deceased kin within existing social networks, as well as the social incorporation of archival photographs of deceased relatives by families as part of processes of so-called visual repatriation.[36] Other studies have focused on the use of photographs of deceased family members and elites as part of processes of commemoration, in which the mobilization of the photograph effectively extends the social agency of the deceased person beyond death. Outlining the relevance of Gell's concept of agency to photographic studies, Richard Vokes has argued that the agency of the photographer's subject is also readily emergent from the process of photographic inscription: 'practically all photographic theory begins from a reading of the photographer's intentions, and all photographs may also be interrogated in terms of their subjects' intentionality'.[37]

In the last chapter I looked in detail at the archival relations between twelve photographs that Evans-Pritchard took of the initiation of Kamanga into the Zande corporation of witch doctors, and the textual account of events that they relate to. This case study enables us to gain a widened understanding of how photographic intentionality interweaves with indigenous agency in such contexts. These images cannot simply be read in terms of Evans-Pritchard's intention to visually represent stages of a Zande ritual, but must be seen within the social and cultural dynamic of his social involvement in Kamanga's initiation, as a social actor in the event itself, and the actions of the Zande participants. Why was the important stage of the offering of gifts into the ritual hole not photographed? Or the dropping of a liquid into the initiate's eyes and nose? The relations between the images from this sequence suggest that events such as these generate their own opportunities that shape the visual record in situational ways, and that indigenous agency plays an influential role in shaping it.

The question of intentionality and indigenous agency also hangs over the series of photographs that I discuss in detail in chapter 7, the sequence that Evans-Pritchard took in 1936 of the Nuer rite of *gorot*. I re-associated three films of still photographs relating to this event but which had become subsequently dispersed throughout his collection. In these photographs what emerges is a strong sense of the collective social nature of the *gorot* ceremony, with family members gathered closely around, some assisting at points, others watching. The importance of collective witness and group involvement is a common feature of Nuer religious practice, and especially sacrifice, which involves numerous relatives who travel considerable distances to attend, and which ends with the distribution of meat among relatives. The group witnesses that a sacrifice has been carried out as part

---

[36] See for instance B. Smith and R. Vokes (eds). 2008. 'Haunting images: the affective power of photography', special edition of *Visual Anthropology*, 21(4); C. Morton and G. Oteyo. 2009. 'Paro manene: exhibiting photographic histories in western Kenya', *Journal of Museum Ethnography*, 21, 155–64.

[37] R. Vokes. 2010. 'Reflections on a complex (and cosmopolitan) archive: postcards and photography in early colonial Uganda, c.1904–1928', *History and Anthropology*, 21(4), 377.

of the family's obligation to spirits, they witness which direction the beast falls after sacrifice, and they gather to hear the lengthy invocations that precede it. Evans-Pritchard as participant-photographer is also part of this dynamic collective witness, moving with onlookers as they witness different aspects of the ceremony. The nature of his photographic engagement seems to sway with the collective witness of the group, shown by the presence of other onlookers on either side of the frame. The images of the circling of the hut by the youth with the boiled ox hump in particular demonstrate that the socio-spatial dynamic of the earlier suffocation element of the rite, where onlookers sat patiently nearby to watch, had transformed into a more participatory and informal rite, in which Evans-Pritchard had to jostle for position to gain a view of the scene. Yet again, the question of why certain elements were not photographed emerges, if part of Evans-Pritchard's intention was to create a visual record of stages of the rite. As I later discuss, there is the strong possibility that there are no images of certain parts of the rite because his presence or participation was not appropriate, or that photographing particular situations was not socially appropriate, such as the couple eating meat together, something considered humiliating, since married couples did not eat in each other's presence. Instead, Evans-Pritchard's participation and observation remains firmly at the social level of the uninitiated, such as children, witnessing alongside them and being guided by their movement and focus (Figure 4.10).[38]

A double alienation

Recent anthropological writing on the history of photography has sought to stress the multiple forms of history that can be written taking the visual as the starting point, rather than as secondary illustration of written history, and the way the medium always seems to leak beyond its frames to suggest alternative stories that cannot ultimately be contained within a single narrative.[39] Rather than seeing photography as a fundamentally Western technology appropriated by others, anthropologists, artists and critics have sought to highlight the way in which photography has been remade and rethought in contemporary culture; how archival images and their troubling colonial contexts are engaged with in

---

[38] In the published account the indigenous voice comes through only fleetingly, although in the case of eating in front of his wife we are informed that 'the husband told me afterwards that this was the most humiliating part of the rite' (Evans-Pritchard, *Nuer Religion*, 218).

[39] Excellent examples being Elizabeth Edwards's *The Camera as Historian: Amateur Photographers and Historical Imagination, 1885–1918*. Durham, NC: Duke University Press, 2012, and C. Pinney and N. Peterson (eds). 2003. *Photography's Other Histories*. Durham, NC, and London: Duke University Press.

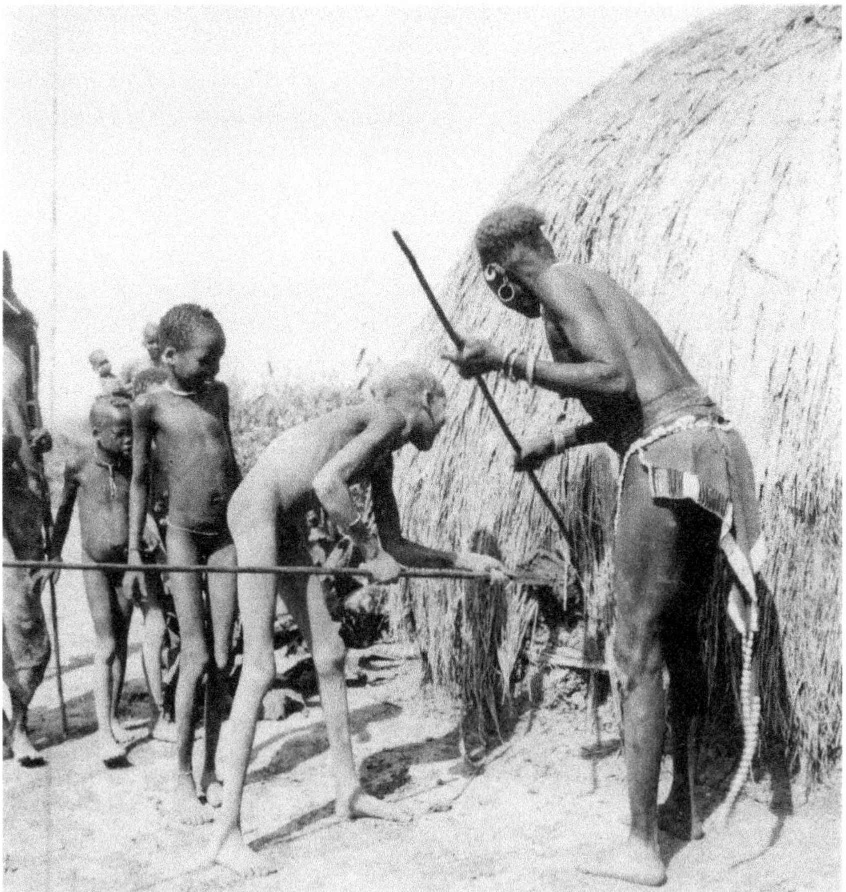

Figure 4.10 Offering the boiled hump of the sacrificed ox to a couple inside a hut, part of the Nuer rite of *gorot*, Nyueny village, Unity State, South Sudan. Photograph by E. E. Evans-Pritchard, 1936.

order to reappropriate the likenesses of ancestors and achieve 'visual sovereignty'.[40]

My intention in this chapter has been to extend the anthropological recognition of multiple and overlapping histories in Evans-Pritchard's Zande and Nuer photographs, and argue for a greater acknowledgement of the field photograph as a cultural co-production, doubly alienated from the cultural contexts of both fieldworker and local community. If 'photographs are necessarily contrived

[40] H. J. Tsinhnahjinnie. 2009. 'Dragonfly's home'. In *Visual Currencies: Reflections on Native Photography*, edited by H. Lidchi and H. J. Tsinhnahjinnie. Edinburgh: National Museums of Scotland, 10–13.

and reflect the culture that produces them',[41] the field photograph is a particularly odd cultural hybrid in this regard. Arguably, the inherent cultural ambiguity of the field photograph, being a product of the cultures of both the fieldworker and the culture being studied, lies at the heart of anthropological fieldwork. As Evans-Pritchard noted, 'one enters into another culture and withdraws from it at the same time . . . one becomes, at least temporarily, a sort of double marginal man, alienated from both worlds'.[42] Those working in the areas of museology and intellectual property rights, for instance, increasingly recognize the culturally ambiguous nature of the field photograph. Collaboration and consultation with indigenous communities regarding the right to use and exploit historic photographs is a process that implicitly acknowledges the co-productive nature of the archive.

This dynamic has historically opened up performative spaces where ideas of culture and identity have been enacted. A striking example of such a performative space is found in the images Evans-Pritchard took at the American Mission at Nasir of a collection he had made of Nuer children's toy oxen made of mud (Figure 4.11). Although he collected other figures made by children, including a man, a hedgehog, and a giraffe, he only photographs the oxen in the field in this way, all placed on a stool, either inside the mission building, or just outside against the woven grass fence, or else by the river bank (Figure 4.12). We can only surmise why this series of images was made. Perhaps Evans-Pritchard was fearful that the items were so fragile that they would not survive the journey home intact, and so made a record of how they were meant to look. Many of the examples he sold to museums have since had extensive repairs, especially to the horns, so he was right to be concerned about them. He only rarely photographed other items of material culture that he collected in the field, despite making quite extensive collections on each trip, so we cannot place the toy oxen photographs within a systematic practice that Evans-Pritchard had of documenting field collections. Although he hinted at a theoretical place for material culture in his monograph, suggesting that 'material objects are chains along which social relations run',[43] he was evidently reluctant to develop this thinking any further. The images, and the oxen themselves, seem to sit in a place between two worlds, indexed by the mission infrastructure of the stool, window, roofline, and sheets of paper on the table, and the Nuer world of song oxen and their huge presence in the imagination of Nuer children. The photographs open up a performative space in which these two worlds intermingle at a point in time and space; they perform a little drama about the interconnections between the Nuer and outsiders. But, as I have

---

[41] C. Pinney, 2003. 'Introduction: "how the other half . . ."'. In *Photography's Other Histories*, edited by C. Pinney and N. Peterson. Durham, NC, and London: Duke University Press, 7.

[42] Evans-Pritchard, 'Some reminiscences and reflections on fieldwork', 4.

[43] Evans-Pritchard, *The Nuer*, 89.

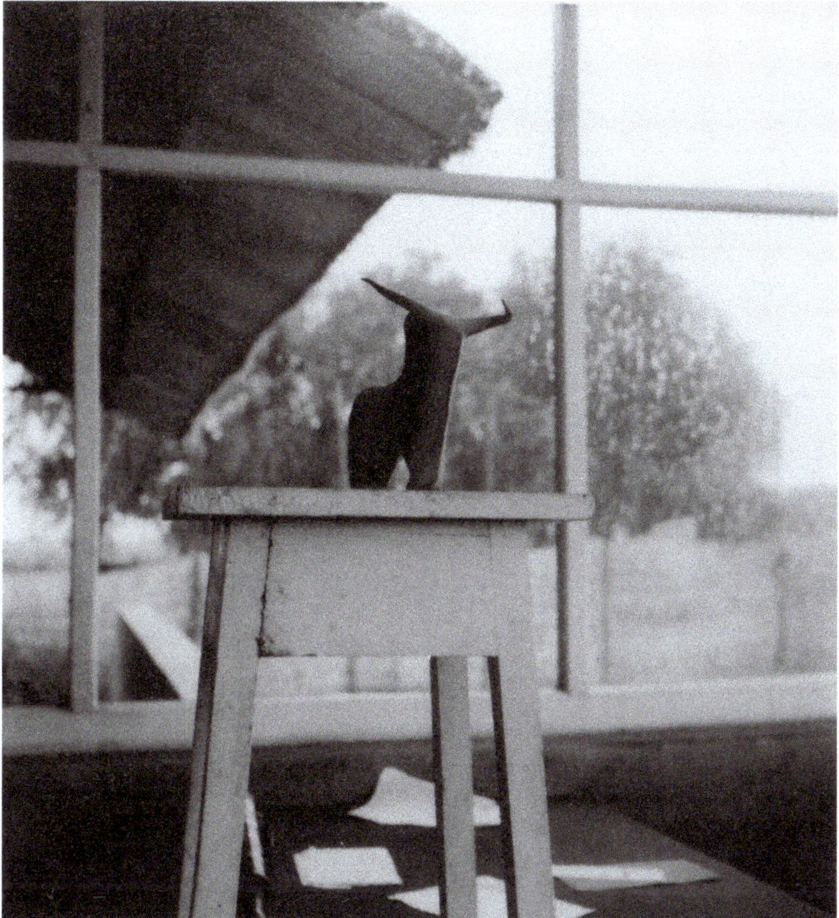

Figure 4.11 A Nuer child's toy mud ox, on a stool at the American Mission at Nasir, Upper Nile, South Sudan. Photograph by E. E. Evans-Pritchard, 1935.

argued throughout this chapter, this is not a matter of photographic intentionality; Evans-Pritchard did not intend to create such culturally hybrid objects as these photographs. These photographs emerged from—indeed were in a sense authored by—the social contexts of their own production, and Evans-Pritchard was just one of the contributing factors in their creation. In this sense the photographs are no different from the clay oxen themselves, which have been on display in Oxford ever since; we say that Evans-Pritchard collected the clay oxen but we do not infer any greater role or agency for the ethnographer in their creation. Perhaps collecting and photographing are not such different acts after all, and may be subject to similar claims from those with cultural connections to them.

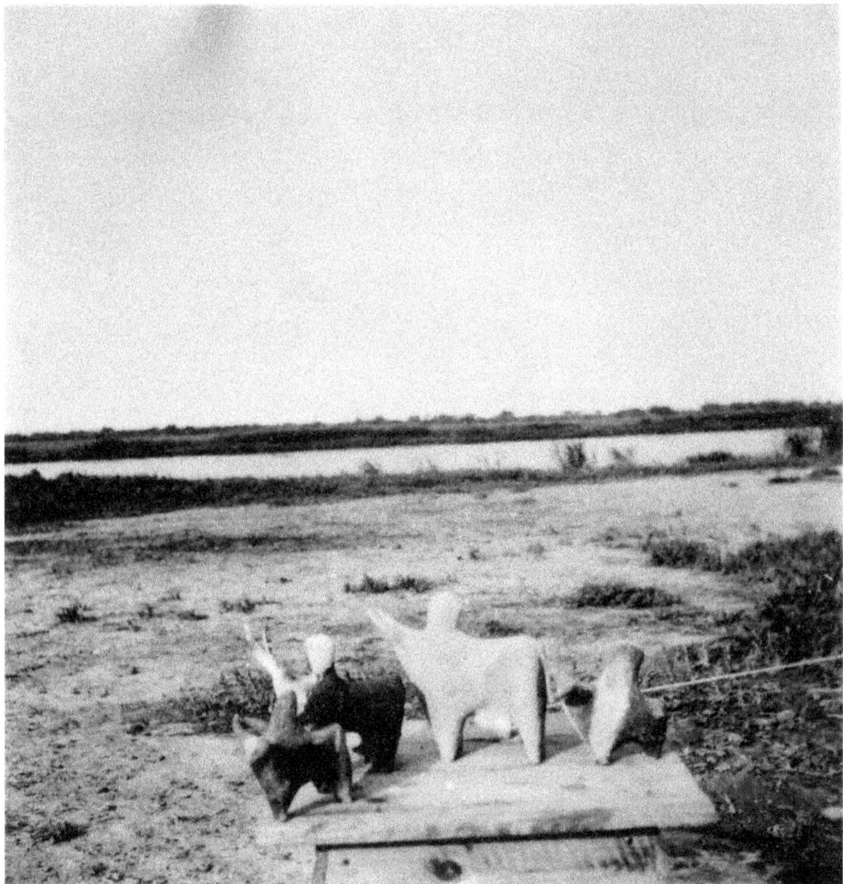

Figure 4.12 Group of four Nuer children's toy mud oxen, on a stool near the river at the American Mission at Nasir, Upper Nile, South Sudan. Photograph by E. E. Evans-Pritchard, 1935.

I have argued in this chapter that the double alienation that lies at the heart of field photography is not a static process, but one that is dynamically formed in the fieldwork situation, and influenced by political and cultural factors. I have argued that the historical, political, and cultural factors affecting Zande and Nuer attitudes towards Evans-Pritchard and his camera could not have been more contrasting. This, I have argued, is inscribed within the archive on a number of different levels, such as forms of self-presentation, distance and proximity, and across periods of fieldwork, as with the increasing diversity and familiarity evident in Evans-Pritchard's second phase of Nuer photography. I have also argued that the examination of indigenous agency in the shaping of the field archive should also be methodologically grounded in the archive itself, rather than at the level of analysis. Archival images need to be understood as relational objects in terms of their spatial and temporal connections to other images; this approach allows a greater understanding of the shaping of the visual record in the field, and the influence of local agency in its creation, extent, and character. Evans-Pritchard's photographic engagement with certain events needs to be reconnected to processes of collective witness in which the fieldworker is included, rather than as a participant-observer, which situates the photograph outside of local contexts of production. This is a theme that I return to in chapter 7. As Evans-Pritchard notes, his own fieldwork, and hence his photographic record, was to a great extent guided and mediated by certain key local collaborators, 'through whose eyes I saw the social world around us'.[44]

[44] E. E. Evans-Pritchard. 1951. *Kinship and Marriage Among the Nuer*. Oxford: Clarendon Press, 106.

5

Image, archive, and monograph

Dangerous liaisons

Modern anthropology's *Las Meninas*

My first encounter with Evans-Pritchard's anthropology was also my first encounter with his photography, having been asked, like most students, to go away and read a much-worn, heavily underlined, library copy of *The Nuer*. Although I must have looked at his photographs in the book, I remember little about this visual experience. That is hardly surprising; I had been asked by my supervisor to compare Evans-Pritchard's discussion of Nuer time reckoning with other ethnographies, and so the photographs barely registered in my hasty student search for pertinent quotes for my essay. And yet, if someone asks me about the Nuer I immediately conjure up images in my mind that come straight from Evans-Pritchard's publications, and these images are surely integral to my understanding of what he said about Nuer social and cultural life. Surely then the crucial point is that for the same reasons that illustrations were seen to be an important element of the anthropological monograph, they are important to how we culturally translate, process, and retain anthropological knowledge. In other words, it isn't enough to say that photographs were (or are) just used to 'illustrate'—whatever that means—what would otherwise be a rather dry text, they were (and are) published for a reason, and that is because we are visual animals whose visual sense dominates our sensory processing of the world around us.

One photograph that I do remember from first reading that chapter on time and space in *The Nuer* is also one that has captivated other commentators— Plate XIV, the one succinctly captioned 'August shower (Lou)' (Figure 5.1). In the text, Evans-Pritchard refers to this plate as being a good illustration of the ferocity of the rainy season. In fact, multiple cross-referencing of illustrations is something Evans-Pritchard did frequently. 'August shower' stood out to me as a student because of the tent pole, ropes, and flap that are visible in the image, placing you as a viewer there in the scene in a very immediate way, sheltered from the downpour, unlike the cattle, who have turned their backs to the rain. I remember thinking to myself, 'Oh, you lived in a tent!' I think somewhere in the back of my mind I had assumed Evans-Pritchard would have been given a house to stay in, or maybe I assumed anthropologists had to live in a hut, not a tent. In any case, what I retained from this visual encounter was the curious feeling that the tent flap had

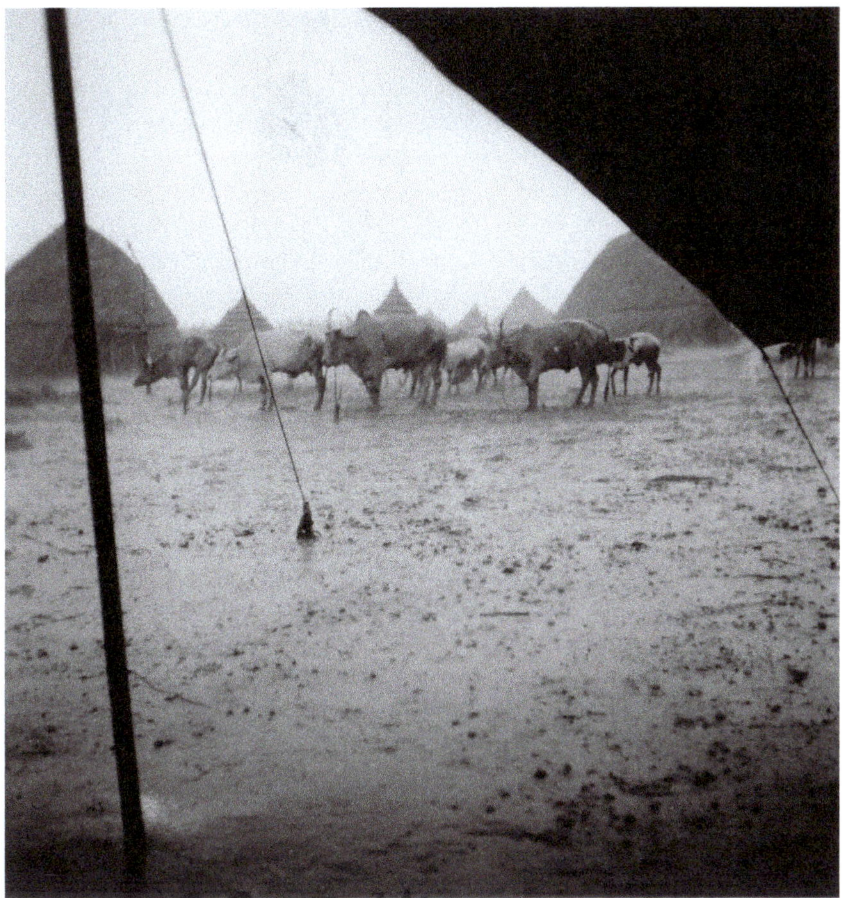

Figure 5.1 'Cattle in rain—Lou', published as Plate XIV with the caption 'August shower (Lou)' in *The Nuer* (1940). Photograph by E. E. Evans-Pritchard, 1935.

disrupted something, shown something of the mechanism of doing anthropology that perhaps we weren't meant to see. Maybe I even thought that it had subtly undermined the effortless authority with which he otherwise wrote about Nuer society; it reminded me that he was an outsider looking in, that we were outsiders on the edge of Nuer society looking in, whereas the text tried to understand Nuer concepts from the inside and translate them outwards to us.

In this chapter I want to look closely at the work that photographs do in Evans-Pritchard's anthropology by comparing his published ethnography *The Nuer* in detail with his overall archive, and ask what the limits of interpretation are when it comes to the visual construction of his argument. 'August shower' is in fact an excellent case study to start with, since I am not the only anthropologist to have been struck by its interpretative implications for the reader.

'August shower' was taken at the Nuer cattle camp of Yacwach in August 1935. A few years later, in a journal article, Evans-Pritchard described that, 'In July of the same year I was practically imprisoned at Yakwac for water lay everywhere several inches deep at the back of the hamlet and progress through the rank grasses was laborious and even dangerous because it was impossible to detect the deep water-filled holes in which a leg might easily be broken.'[1] We get a good view of this wider scene from the back of the cattle camp in another image from his fieldwork that I discuss in chapter 4, in which Evans-Pritchard looks back with his camera at his tent, pitched right alongside the huts looking into the central space where the cattle were kept (Figure 4.7). Back in England, sorting his fieldwork images, he listed this photograph on a typewritten sheet with the caption, 'Cattle in rain – Lou', Lou being the Nuer subgroup among whom he was staying. When it came to writing the monograph he selected the image for use in his chapter on Nuer 'oecology', but instead of using his existing caption 'Cattle in rain – Lou' he changed it to 'August shower (Lou), and refers to it in the text: 'How terrific are these rains may be judged from Plate XIV, taken from under the awning of my tent during a moderate shower in August'.[2] The shift of emphasis in the caption from 'Cattle in rain' to 'August shower' shows just how mutable the meaning of the photographic image can be depending on how it is deployed. In the monograph, the image is mobilized to augment Evans-Pritchard's argument about the way in which ecology and social institutions are interrelated.

'August shower' may have continued a long journey into anthropological obscurity if it wasn't for anthropology's 'crisis of representation' in the 1980s, a phase of disciplinary soul-searching ushered in by George Marcus and Michael Fischer in their 1986 book *Anthropology as Cultural Critique* in the wake of deep uncertainty within the human sciences about how the social realities of other people were represented academically. Since no interpretive account, they argued, can ever directly or completely capture lived experience, what we are left with is a series of texts that mediate social realities; inscriptions that cannot hope to translate culture perfectly, and which are at best forms of literature and history. Such a view presented a serious challenge to anthropology's claims to knowledge creation. Anthropological texts, it was claimed, merely referred to other texts, such as fieldwork accounts, representations, and interpretations, and the language of representation was only rhetoric. Related to this of course was a crisis of authority—who is the anthropologist to speak about another culture? The other key crisis of representation text was also published in 1986, was also edited by George Marcus (this time with James Clifford), and was called *Writing Culture:*

---

[1] E. E. Evans-Pritchard. 1938. 'The economic life of the Nuer: cattle (part 2)', *Sudan Notes and Records*, 21(1), 37.

[2] E. E. Evans-Pritchard. 1940. *The Nuer: A Description of the Modes of Livelihood and Political Institutions of a Nilotic People*. Oxford: Oxford University Press (1968 printing; lithographic reproduction from original sheets), 64.

the Poetics and Politics of Ethnography, which drew attention to the way in which anthropology can be critiqued as literature.

But of course these texts did not in themselves provoke a crisis within anthropology; that was already well underway, mostly as a result of the ongoing politics of decolonization, but also due to a whole range of other developments inside and outside the discipline. These texts were widely read and cited within anthropology, and did provoke what has often been seen as anthropology's postmodern turning point—the rise of a more reflexive approach in which the anthropologist has both visibility and agency in the creation of knowledge about other cultures.

And so, in the light of these debates, we return to 'August shower'. In his influential essay, 'The parallel histories of anthropology and photography' in the groundbreaking 1992 volume *Anthropology and Photography*, Christopher Pinney reproduces the photograph as part of a discussion on the way in which photography frequently betrays its own historicity and productive contexts. He cites first a photograph from Iowa in which the presence of a white man in the photograph is 'a sort of scratch on the negative, a blemish which betrays the presence of the photographer and his culture'. Turning to Evans-Pritchard's photograph, he continues the argument, suggesting that it:

> depicts in the main an August shower in full pelt, but betrays through the peripheral presence of tent flaps the presence of the photographer behind the camera. Precipitation has here precipitated the exposure of the camera's presence and perhaps it is not too far-fetched to see this mirroring of the viewers' own culture in the tent pole and flap as modern anthropology's Las Meninas.[3]

In a recent book Pinney reprises this point, but the gap of nearly twenty years has introduced a slightly new theoretical twist:

> A tent flap and pole frame our view of a line of distant cattle and huts and unwittingly incarnate the photographer in a rain-sodden phenomenology. Suddenly we are profoundly aware of the camera as a physical object, held by an ethnographer sheltering from the rain. There is an immediacy, a sense of presence, but also a qualification: a sense of literal and metaphorical framing: the ethnographer is a foreigner in his tent, not a Nuer sheltering in one of the distant huts.[4]

As 'modern anthropology's Las Meninas', this photograph was of course symbolic for Pinney of anthropology's crisis of representation; it was seen to reveal, albeit

---

[3] C. Pinney. 1992. 'The parallel histories of anthropology and photography'. In *Anthropology & Photography 1860–1920*, edited by E. Edwards. New Haven, CT: Yale University Press with the Royal Anthropological Institute, 76.

[4] C. Pinney. 2011. *Photography and Anthropology*. London: Reaktion, 97.

unwittingly, the cultural mediation involved in the anthropological endeavour as published in one of the foundational texts of British social anthropology. Without the period of self-reflection and soul-searching that anthropology underwent in the 1980s, it hardly seems possible that Pinney would have made the conceptual leap that draws a parallel between this image and Velazquez's famous painting. In particular, it was possibly the work of French theorist Michel Foucault that Pinney had in the back of his mind when he made his formulation. In *The Order of Things: An Archaeology of the Human Sciences* (1970), Foucault reproduces *Las Meninas* as a frontispiece and then devotes his opening chapter to an extensive analysis of the representational issues arising from the painting. For Foucault, 'the entire picture is looking out at a scene for which it is itself a scene.'[5] He goes on to point out that 'around the scene are arranged all the signs and successive forms of representation; but the double relation of the representation...to its author as well as to the person to whom it is being offered, this relation is necessarily interrupted'.[6] It is this *double relation* of course that connects *Las Meninas* to 'August shower', since, as Pinney points out, the extraneous presence of the tent which frames the image disrupts the representational illusion that this is an unmediated and timeless window onto a Sudanese cattle camp, and reveals it rather as mediated by an anthropologist, whose presence is shown in the tent flap and pole. As Foucault adds further in relation to *Las Meninas*, 'representation undertakes to represent itself here in all its elements, with its images, the eyes to which it is offered, the faces it makes visible, the gestures that it calls into being...And representation, freed finally from the relation that was impeding it, can offer itself as representation in its pure form'.[7] 'August shower' is undeniably a far less representationally complex image than *Las Meninas*. It does not con-sciously play with mirroring the representer or the represented directly. But Pinney's underlying point is that it draws part of its mirroring effect from the sets of assumptions that the viewer brings to any photographic image—that it is somehow an unmediated view of what it purports to show. Despite the fact that we understand that photographs are taken by somebody in a particular time and place, the photographic image beguiles us, seduces us look through the frame, and to forget the presence of the framing camera, held by a photographer. 'August shower', unusually for a photograph by a field anthropologist, situates the image in a particular social-spatial relationship, referred to in the visible comparison between the anthropologist's tent, and the Nuer huts further away. Not only is the camera on the boundary of the camp looking in, the anthro-pologist is living there, and we are invited to stand under the tent awning to shelter from the rain with him.

---

[5] M. Foucault. 1994 [1970]. *The Order of Things: An Archaeology of the Human Sciences*. London: Routledge, 14.

[6] Foucault, *The Order of Things*, 16.   [7] Foucault, *The Order of Things*, 16.

But my conclusion is not that we should consider this image, or rather Pinney's formulation of it as 'anthropology's Las Meninas', as symbolic of the analytical cul-de-sac that the discipline's 'crisis of representation' involved, but rather symbolic of anthropology's route out of crisis. For it was precisely this sort of attention to points of reflexivity and historical fracture in dominant readings of visual imagery, and especially historical and colonial imagery, that opened up the discipline to completely new areas of analytical investigation. Whereas many scholars in the 1980s and early 1990s still felt the full weight of Foucault-inspired analysis of colonial imagery in terms of its inherently asymmetrical power relations, as well as the instrumentality of the state, 'anthropology's Las Meninas' is a subversive interpretation, one that resists such attempts to reduce the photographic image to a universal political reading. In so doing, the anthropology of photography was opened up to new and minority histories, alternative readings, and creative reworkings. As a result, the photographic archive is no longer in representational crisis, but in resurgence.

Reading *The Nuer* visually

The major theoretical statements that followed in the wake of *Writing Culture* also sought to unravel the role of the anthropologist as an author who asserted 'ethnographic authority' in a variety of literary ways.[8] Clifford Geertz characterized Evans-Pritchard as a particularly important case study in this respect, putting forward the argument that his writing style was an important device in his analytical approach, which was to make other cultures intelligible, reasonable, and rational to his intended audience. In order to do this, Geertz argued, he intentionally deployed a writing style characterized by 'anthropological transparencies', visualizable descriptions of culture that carry the theoretical argument along with it. In 1990, the anthropologist John Hutnyk wrote a dubious critique of *The Nuer* as part of the 'crisis of representation' debate, which nonetheless illustrated the hand-wringing state of the discipline at the time. 'A crisis of reputation seems to haunt much of the past of anthropology', he wrote, 'and Evans-Pritchard has been given no exemption from this necessary clearing work.'[9] Hutnyk's analysis of the way Evans-Pritchard's photographs perform a sort of 'instamatic anthropology', reducing the Nuer themselves to stereotypes and signs to be simplistically compared, now feels painfully reductive. Later commentators, such as Barbara Wolbert, made the observation that photography as a key aspect

---

[8] See for instance J. Clifford. 1988. *The Predicament of Culture: Twentieth Century Ethnography, Literature and Art.* Cambridge, MA, and London: Harvard University Press, 32–4, and C. Geertz. 1988. *Works and Lives: The Anthropologist as Author.* Oxford: Polity Press.

[9] J. Hutnyk. 1990. 'Comparative anthropology and Evans-Pritchard's Nuer photography', *Critique of Anthropology*, 10(1), 97.

of the anthropological monograph had been completely overlooked within the debate on ethnographic authority. Wolbert suggested, for instance, that photography could be seen to act as a potentially subversive element within the overall presentation of such authority, since reading the images in a certain way could be seen to undermine it. While this argument is valid in one sense, it only holds if one reads the images metaphorically and accept the proposition that Evans-Pritchard (her case study was *The Nuer*) made a conscious attempt to use photography in the monograph as part of a 'dramaturgical strategy'.[10] But if analysis is focused solely upon image content, it does not grapple with the important ways in which the photographs in *The Nuer* are utilized within the text itself. Not only this, there are the historical specificities of ethnographic publishing that always shape picture selection, and this of course has to be understood first before anything concrete can be said about the visual construction of authority. It is also only by positioning the published photographs in their archival context that one can talk about ethnographic authority in any meaningful way, since one can then begin to understand the types of selections made, and the relationships between individual images. Underpinning this approach is the notion that the image has a biography—that its original inscription in the negative is only a starting point for a complex series of related objects through time and space.[11] An awareness of the 'genealogical' relations between photographic objects is particularly important when dealing with the way in which different 'performances' of the same image in different contexts are related. Geertz's suggestion of a link between the visualizable as a dimension of ethnographic writing and the visual presentation of photographs within *The Nuer* is an important interplay worthy of fuller treatment. In the next chapter, I discuss in some detail Geertz's elaboration of this idea in the context of Evans-Pritchard's Anuak ethnography. But here my main focus is on the relationship between text and image in modern anthropology, and in particular *The Nuer*. Although the field photography of anthropologists post circa 1930 has been a relatively neglected area when compared to nineteenth-century studies, some of this generation have had critical attention, such as Bronislaw Malinowski, Isaac Schapera, Margaret Mead, and Gregory Bateson.[12]

[10] B. Wolbert. 2000. 'The anthropologist as photographer: the visual construction of ethnographic authority', *Visual Anthropology*, 13, 324.

[11] Recent work that highlights the biographical dimensions of photographs as cultural objects can be found in E. Edwards. 2001. 'Material beings: objecthood and ethnographic photographs', *Visual Studies*, 12(1), 67–75, and E. Edwards and J. Hart (eds). 2004. *Photographs Objects Histories: On the Materiality of Images*. London and New York: Routledge.

[12] See for instance E. Samain. 1995. 'Bronislaw Malinowski et la photographie anthropologique', *L'Ethnographie*, 91(2), 107–30; M. Young. 1998. *Malinowski's Kiriwina: Fieldwork Photography 1915–1918*. Chicago and London: University of Chicago Press; Ira Jacknis. 1984. 'M. Mead and G. Bateson in Bali: their use of photography and film', *Cultural Anthropology*, 3(2), 160–77; J. Comaroff, J. Comaroff, and D. James (eds). 2007. *Picturing a Colonial Past: The African Photographs of Isaac Schapera*. Chicago: Chicago University Press.

Here, however, I explore Barbara Wolbert's analysis of the photographs reproduced in *The Nuer*, which, she argues, operate as a 'visual construction' of ethnographic authority, working to 'draw the viewer in and position the author as interpreter', through a 'dramaturgical strategy' of image ordering and disclosure.[13] In her analysis, which is similar to (but much more nuanced than) Hutnyk's, she reproduces a number of page spreads from the monograph to make explicit the way in which visual material is used by Evans-Pritchard to establish both the bovine idiom that lies at the heart of Nuer social experience, as well as the authoritative presence of the anthropologist in Nuerland. The argument is presented that 'the disruptive nature of photography in the ethnographic context is based upon the independence of photography from picture arrangement'—that is, that the image is infinitely recodable.[14] The problem here is that analysis can so easily stray from the consideration of how illustrations are put to work in a published monograph into conjecture about Evans-Pritchard's photographic output and fieldwork encounters. It is one thing, even an interesting thing, to argue for the subversive potential of published images, embedded as they are within a textual account. It is another thing to make suppositions about 'the legibility of a photograph', when analysis of the original photographs (as opposed to the reproduced *images*) does not support such readings. It is here that we need to separate analytically visual readings of the monograph and readings of the archive, and look in material detail at the correspondences and divergences that such readings may take.

Reading the monograph

Importantly, the ethnographic monograph is often not one book, but many, since reprints, revisions, and changes in format over time (such as paperback) are all essentially new productions involving new sets of editorial procedures and financial considerations (such as sales, costs etc.). So, for instance, while Wolbert reproduces plates from the first edition of *The Nuer* published in 1940, her bibliographic reference is to the 1969 first American paperback printing. While in the 1969 paperback edition the text pagination of the first edition is retained, since it is produced from the original sheets, the photographs are printed double-sided on plain paper and not spaced throughout the book in the same way. In fact, difficulties in obtaining the original photographic blocks meant that Oxford University Press' New York division decided to rephotograph the images from the first edition itself.[15] Without the first edition (with its different picture

<hr>

[13] Wolbert, 'The anthropologist as photographer', 324.
[14] Wolbert, 'The anthropologist as photographer', 333.
[15] Letter dated 15.5.1969 from Oxford University Press, New York Office to Head Office, Oxford, on the subject of the first paperback edition of *The Nuer* (Oxford University Press Archive ref: PB/ED/ 001071 OP214).

arrangement) to hand, how can the aim to 'leaf through the book as someone would who picks it up for the first time' be possible? Subsequent changes to picture arrangement are important aspects of the 'dramaturgical strategy' that Wolbert attempts to demonstrate, since it affects when the reader encounters certain images while reading the text.

In the case of one image that I discuss in detail later, that of 'Milking a restless cow', in the 1969 printing it no longer faces Evans-Pritchard's description of milking that it was intended to illustrate in the first edition (Figure 5.2), but is instead encountered by the reader several pages earlier. The same thing happened in the 1977 reprinting of Evans-Pritchard's other influential work, *Witchcraft Oracles and Magic Among the Azande* (1937)—all the (now poorer quality) plates are printed double-sided and repositioned at the back of the book, instead of throughout the text as in the first edition and reprintings prior to that date. Does this change represent a shift in 'dramaturgical strategy' by forcing us to do some work by flipping to the back of the book as we come across image

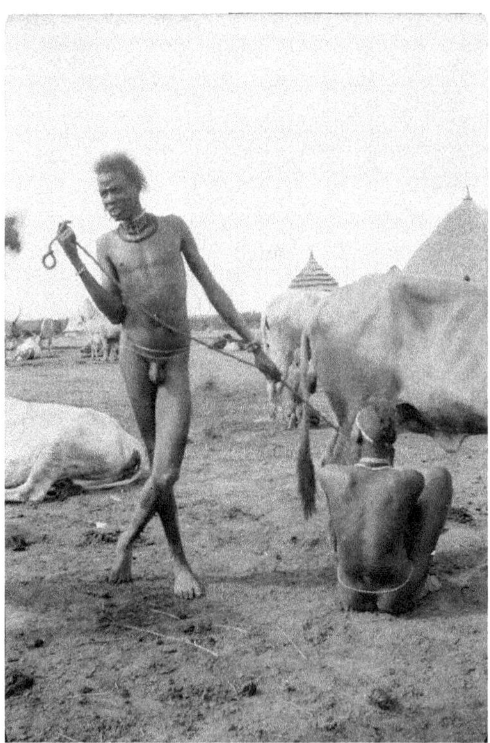

Figure 5.2 Nuer man holding a rope tied to a cow's rear legs to keep it still while being milked, Yakwach cattle camp, Sobat River, Upper Nile, South Sudan. Published as Plate III with the caption 'Milking a restless cow (Lou)' in *The Nuer* (1940). Photograph by E. E. Evans-Pritchard, 1935.

references within the text? Certainly not on the part of Evans-Pritchard himself, who died four years before the edition was published. The change seems to have been brought about by a move to a different printer in Northamptonshire, no doubt due to cost considerations. To see Evans-Pritchard as the 'author of a picture story' then doesn't hold up to much scrutiny when one considers the historical contexts and constraints within which pictures were selected and arranged for publication over time—contexts that problematize the notion that the published images represent a straightforward visual statement of ethnographic authority.

Wolbert does makes the important point that not all of the photographs published in *The Nuer* were taken by Evans-Pritchard. In fact, six other sources of photographs are acknowledged, one of which (Plate IX) is almost certainly not even Nuer but Shilluk.[16] Wolbert's argument is that Evans-Pritchard 'published a certain kind of photo from other sources than his own large photo collection', and that those selected were mainly close-up portraits, as opposed to his own images that were more distant.[17] Strangely, one of the three examples that Wolbert presents of other photographers' work (that of Plate XXIX, 'Man (Nasser Post)') was in fact taken by Evans-Pritchard himself. Perhaps a more important point about the use of plates in *The Nuer* is the fact that eight of them were made from printing blocks made up for previous articles in the journal *Sudan Notes and Records* and elsewhere (such as in the Seligmans' book *Pagan Tribes*), a fact made clear in the List of Plates.

One of the images that Wolbert analyses in more detail (Plate VIII, 'Sandy ridge with cattle byres on the horizon') is an interesting case in point. This same image was originally published in the first of a two-part article in *Sudan Notes and Records* in 1937, with the caption 'Sandy ridge with homesteads in the background (Duk Country)'. The publisher's block was then reused by Oxford University Press for *The Nuer* some three years later. Analysis of the original negative (Figure 5.3) shows that the published image has been cropped markedly on the right by the original publisher (who has also marked the original negative), a

---

[16] Plate IX 'Harpoon-fishing from canoe (Sobat River)' (also used on the front cover of the paperback edition) is credited as having been taken by Frank D. Corfield, the colonial administrator whose four-year tour of duty in Nasir District of Upper Nile Province 1931–5 coincided with E-P's fieldwork. However, this image depicts Shilluk and not Nuer men, and seems to have been originally taken by G. W. Titherington who was Assistant and District Commissioner in Upper Nile Province 1931–4 (Douglas Johnson, personal communication, 2004). Other photographic sources in *The Nuer* are: Royal Air Force (Plate XVI); American Presbyterian Mission at Nasir (possibly via Blanche Cora Soule, who also gave him other photographs); Yuzbashi (i.e. Captain) Talib Ismail, a Sudanese officer who served in Upper Nile Province as a *sub-mamur* at Akobo from 5 June 1920 to 1 November 1927, almost certainly via Charles and Brenda Seligman who may have procured them in Sudan in 1921–2; E. S. Crispin (medical officer in Sudan from 1904); Frederick L. Hamer (Assistant and District Commissioner for Eastern Nuer from 1932 to 1936 when he died of blackwater fever).

[17] Wolbert, 'The anthropologist as photographer', 333.

manipulation which has then been reproduced through the use of the same block in *The Nuer*.

The biographical movement from negative to published plate reveals the important fractures between the photographer's frame and subsequently imposed frames, which reproduce an altered reading of the original photograph. In the case of the sandy ridge photograph, the standing figure was framed centrally by Evans-Pritchard, showing that the youth was probably an opportunistic portrait, or 'type' photograph. Further evidence that the seated youth was not an intended subject is provided by further close-up portraits of the central youth. By cropping the space to the right, the publisher of *Sudan Notes and Records* was attempting to rebalance

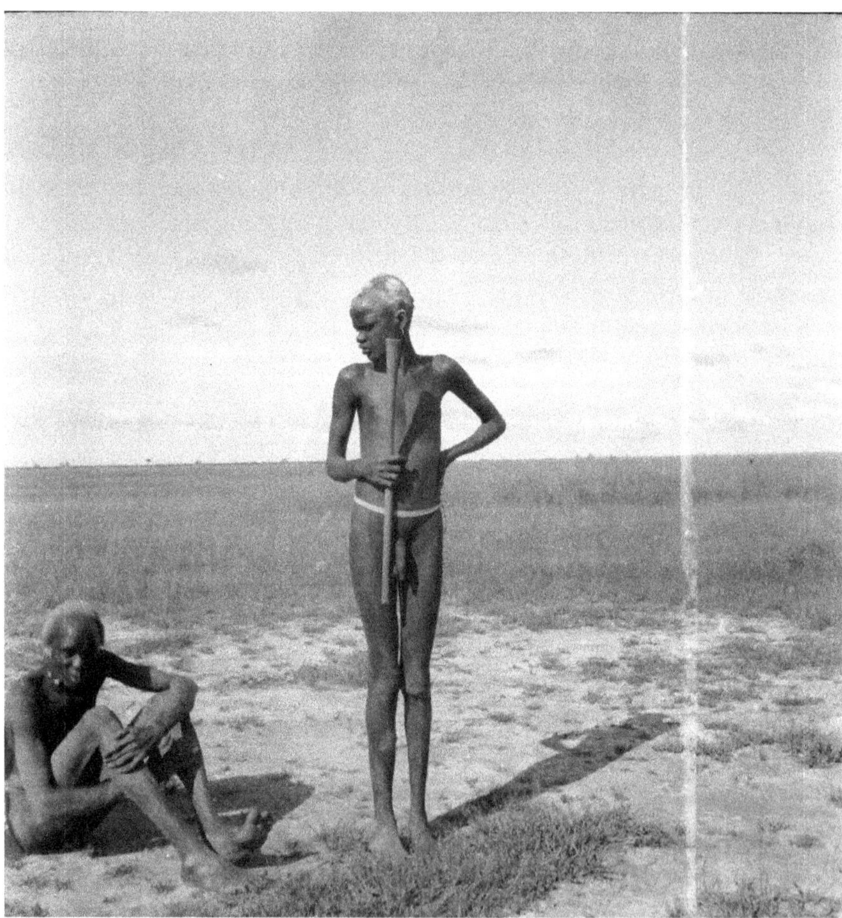

Figure 5.3 Nuer man holding a club (negative). Published as Plate VIII in *The Nuer* with the caption 'Sandy ridge with cattle byres on the horizon (Dok)'. Photograph by E. E. Evans-Pritchard, probably 1936 at Ler, Unity State, South Sudan.

the image and change the marginal status of the seated youth by re-emphasizing the relationship between the two figures. Since the original photograph was in a square format, it is also likely that the publisher was correcting the proportions of the image for publishing in portrait orientation. The interplay of contexts, intentions, and meanings between the original photograph and the way it is manipulated for publication in differing situations is surely the thing of central importance here, since the assumption that the published image 'is' the photograph overlooks in an essential way the critical interventions of the publishing process. More than this, the fact that blocks made for previous publications were reused in *The Nuer* further problematizes the notion of a straightforward presentation of ethnographic authority since it suggests a level of serendipity, or at least expediency, in picture selection. There is even the possibility that Evans-Pritchard's decision to reuse previously published images within *The Nuer* was due to the increased cost of producing new blocks from original negatives at the onset of war.[18] As the detailed publication history of Evans-Pritchard's images shows, some of the previously made blocks were kept together as plates in *The Nuer*, and some mixed to form new plates, which suggests both a continuity of visual narrative from previous articles, as well as an attempt to reorder and rethink the visual presentation within the monograph.[19] This approach to illustration mirrors Evans-Pritchard's own view of his books as the bringing together of previously published articles in a new form.

Criticizing Geertz's claim that the illustrations in *The Nuer* are 'unreferred to',[20] Wolbert makes the important point that, in fact, Evans-Pritchard refers to them frequently throughout the book. This is an important aspect of the relationship between textual and visual authority, of course, since textual references to illustrations can be considered extended captions that operate to both narrow down and open out the potential range of meanings within the image. This is a key point, since some commentators such as Hutnyk have held up the

---

[18] In a letter (unsigned) from Oxford University Press to Evans-Pritchard, dated 11 June 1945, the writer argues that book production charges had risen 50 per cent on pre-war levels, and that illustrations for his proposed book on the Sanusi would have to be modest (Oxford University Press Archive ref: PB/ED/001071 OP214).

[19] Plate VIIa (facing page 62) in *The Nuer* was first published as Plate VIb (facing page 224) in *Sudan Notes and Records* (*SNR*) 20(3), 1937. Plate VIIb (facing page 62) was first published as Plate VIIa (facing page 232) in *SNR* 20(3), 1937. Plate VIII (facing page 68) was first published as Plate V (facing page 216) in *SNR* 20(3), 1937. Plate XVa and b (facing page 134) was first published as Plate IIIa and b (facing page 74) in *SNR* 17(1), 1935. Plate XXIa (facing page 200) was first published as Plate VIa (facing page 224) in *SNR* 18(3), 1937. Plate XXIb (facing page 200) was first published as Plate VIIb (facing page 232) in *SNR* 18(3), 1937. Plate XXVIa and b (facing page 236) was published with the youth with ash-covered hair to the right, as Plate II (facing page 42) in *SNR* 18(1), 1935. These two images are credited to the District Commissioner F. D. Corfield in *The Nuer*, but not in *SNR*. Plates XXV and XXVIII in *The Nuer* (five images) are taken from blocks made for C. G. Seligman and B. Z. Seligman (1932). As with the blocks from *SNR*, some of these blocks were subsequently kept together to form plates in *The Nuer*, although the picture editor at Oxford University Press swapped several of them around to form new plates and thereby a new visual narrative.

[20] Geertz, *Works and Lives*, 66.

brevity of the captions, such as 'Youth' or 'Girl milking', as exemplifying some form of distanced essentialism.[21] A good example of the type of image reference that Evans-Pritchard makes is: 'I ask the reader to look at some of the illustrations, for example the frontispiece and plates III, V, and XVII, which will convey to him better than I can do in words the crudity of kraal life'.[22] This sort of comment, found throughout the book, is highly revealing in a number of ways. Firstly, it establishes a break in the flow of ethnographic prose that surrounds it, an intervention that asks the reader to become active in seeking out the plates referred to and drawing parallels between the separate images. In particular, Evans-Pritchard is asking both the reader and the images to corroborate his preceding statement that 'the stark nakedness of Nuer amid their cattle and the intimacy of their contact with them present a classic picture of savagery'.[23] There is no doubt that these often detailed textual references to the plates act as extended captions, and seek to place the readings of the images within the overall argument that Evans-Pritchard is attempting to build. Such extended captioning of the images throughout the text in part explains the brevity of the plate captions, which merely serve to summarize, in conventional publishing format, the image content. When we take this fully into account we can see that far too much analytical weight has been placed on the relationship between image and caption in *The Nuer*, without fully taking into account Evans-Pritchard's complex strategic usage of them from the text outwards.

Evans-Pritchard's numerous references to the plates also suggest a dynamic interplay between picture selection and the writing process. Often the references have been seemingly inserted into the flow of a previously written block of text, such as 'how terrific are these rains may be judged from Plate XIV',[24] and frequently the same image will be referred to at different places if it serves to illustrate some different subject matter or item of material culture. This strongly suggests that Evans-Pritchard had the final picture selection organized at an early stage of writing the book. Such frequent cross-referencing of plates also suggests that the photographs that he had selected were laid out for reference during the writing process. A good example of this is his description of the scars left by Nuer initiation (*gar*), stating that 'they are particularly clear in Plates XXVI(b), XXVII, and XXVIII'.[25] While his cross-referencing of images within *The Nuer* is thereby very much about illustration, the complex framework of textual references makes

---

[21] Hutnyk, 'Comparative anthropology', 90.   [22] Evans-Pritchard, *The Nuer*, 40.

[23] Evans-Pritchard, *The Nuer*, 40. It is important to not read this statement as Evans-Pritchard saying that the Nuer are 'savages'. He is again using an anthropological transparency, to use Geertz's phrase, to translate his visual experience of Nuer life in the context of his reader's categories of non-Western culture: savagery, barbarism, and civilization, the stages of cultural development set out by Lewis Henry Morgan in his 1877 book *Ancient Society* that still had a wide currency in early twentieth-century anthropology.

[24] Evans-Pritchard, *The Nuer*, 64.   [25] Evans-Pritchard, *The Nuer*, 249.

it clear that he saw the photographs as providing multiple points of entry from differing ethnographic contexts.

Reading the archive

I have so far argued for the analytical separation of the published image from the photograph as an archival object, and also raised various issues about the historical contexts in which Evans-Pritchard's photographs were eventually reproduced in *The Nuer*. I now want to move on to show how an archival understanding of the published images is an essential part of any notion of the visual construction of ethnographic authority. I do so in order to show how problematic it is to read the photographs in *The Nuer* symbolically, or as a hypothetical general reader might interpret them. Let us look in more detail then at the archival situation of one of the plates that Wolbert analyses in detail, Plate III ('Milking a restless cow (Lou)'), about which she says:

> This laconic comment ['Milking a restless cow'] gives us a little story which we attempt to verify through the picture. Not only is a man with his back to the camera milking in the foreground, but more milking is going on in the background. The young man is standing there casually, holding the line with which the cow's rear legs are tethered. Either the cow cannot be that restless, or the man must be able to register the cow's slightest movement…he seems completely absorbed by what the person to his right is saying or doing…it might well be another man milking.[26]

In her analysis, Wolbert reproduces the plate back to front, but this seemingly trivial error is actually vital when one looks again at its relationship to the frontispiece of *The Nuer*, titled 'Section of homestead and kraal (Eastern Gaajok)' (Figure 5.4).

Although the frontispiece and Plate III were captioned by Evans-Pritchard as having been taken among neighbouring, but quite distinct, Nuer tribes—the Lou and the Gaajok—their original film numbers, clearly written on the reverse of both the negative and the original contact print, indicate that not only do they belong to the same film, but that they are probably sequential exposures. According to these film numbers he first took the frontispiece image (64 A183) and then the image of the 'casual' man (64 A184). The evidence of the documentation is confirmed when the two images are placed side by side, with the frontispiece enlarged slightly to form a composite (Figure 5.5), showing that not

---

[26] Wolbert, 'The anthropologist as photographer', 325.

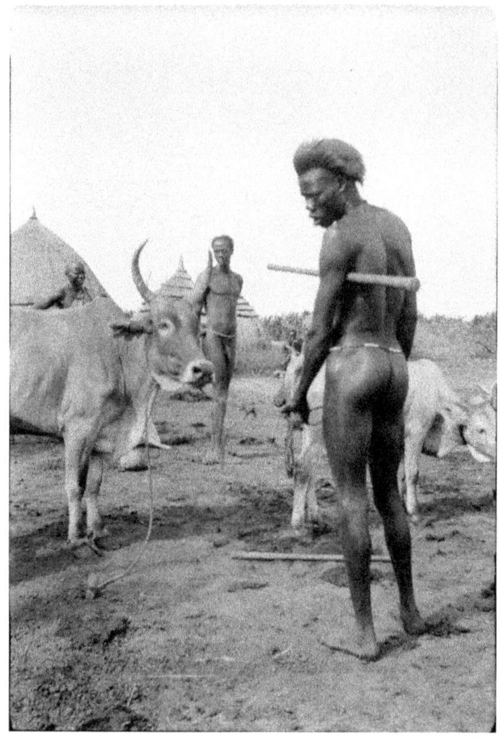

Figure 5.4 Nuer man with club, Yakwach cattle camp, Sobat River, Upper Nile, South Sudan. Published as the Frontispiece to *The Nuer* with the erroneous caption 'Section of homestead and kraal (Eastern Gaajok)'. Photograph by E. E. Evans-Pritchard, 1935.

only were they taken in the same location rather than separate ones, but that they were taken immediately after one another, with the camera turned a few degrees.

With this new composite image there are now two men restraining the cow, which is also tethered to the ground, its calf being held back from suckling by an unseen figure to the right of the frame. These two men are joined by a third man, all three of them watching something happening beyond the frame to the left, probably a youth performing a praise song about a favourite ox, rather than 'another man milking'. Concrete evidence for this is found in another photograph from the archive (original negative number 64 A182) in which we see the milking activity from further back, with two youths to the left of the frame, one of whom is wearing metal arm-rings (known as *thiau*).

As Evans-Pritchard moved forward to take the next photograph in the sequence (Figure 5.6, the frontispiece to *The Nuer*), a shadow, probably from the youth wearing the *thiau* arm-rings, can be seen cast across the ground in front of

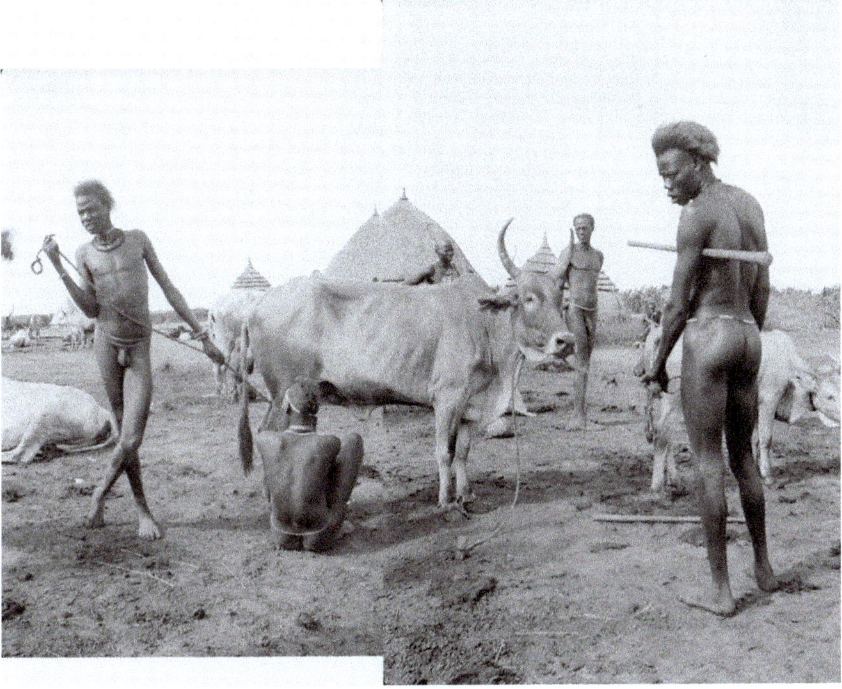

Figure 5.5 A composite image of the 'milking a restless cow' scene at Yakwach cattle camp, made from the original negatives of Plate III and the Frontispiece to *The Nuer*.

the man, near the cow's tethering peg; a shadow with arms raised in imitation of the trained horns of a favourite ox.[27] This is the characteristic gesture made by Nuer youths during the recitation of a praise song about a favourite ox, or merely the calling out of their ox-name which they gain after initiation. Although in the next photograph in the sequence (Figure 5.2), this shadow is no longer evident, the blurred hand of the gesturing youth can just be made out intruding into the frame on the left.

It is here that image analysis and textual illustration compete—Wolbert sees a 'man with his back to the camera milking a cow', yet Evans-Pritchard's statement on the facing page is that 'men are forbidden to milk cows'.[28] The fact that it is almost certainly a woman milking the restless cow is, as indicated in Evans-Pritchard's own textual reference to the image, that 'the milker squats by the cow and milks a single teat at a time into the narrow mouth of a bottle-necked

---

[27] A photograph of this type of gesture can be seen in another of Evans-Pritchard's books, *Kinship and Marriage Among the Nuer*. Oxford: Clarendon Press (1990 [1951], Plate VII), titled 'A youth singing in praise of his ox. His arms are raised in imitation of its horns'.

[28] Evans-Pritchard, *The Nuer*, 22.

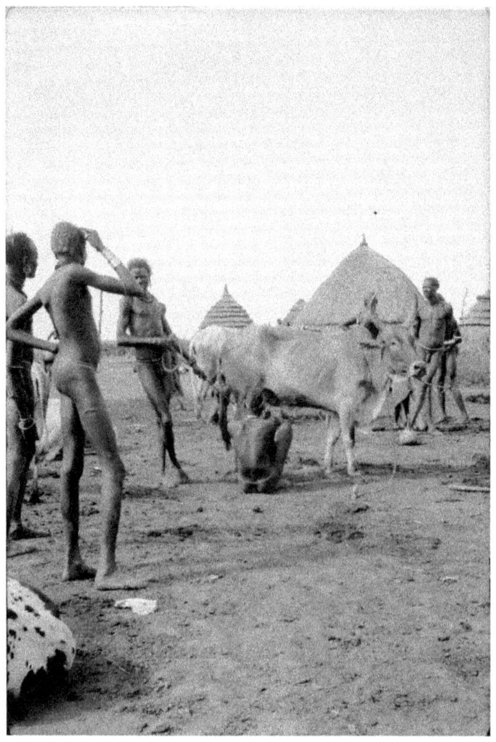

Figure 5.6 The 'milking a restless cow' scene from another position. Yakwach cattle camp, Sobat River, Upper Nile, South Sudan. Photograph by E. E. Evans-Pritchard, 1935.

gourd balanced on *her* thighs (see Plates III and V)...if a cow is restless a *man* may hold it still'.[29] Understood in relation to the ethnographic description, a more likely interpretation of the 'casual' manner of the man (incidentally similarly described by Geertz as 'a tall, naked cowherd leaning, negligently, legs crossed, against the tension of a tether')[30] is possibly his unease at being indirectly involved with the ritually dangerous activity of milking. Evans-Pritchard elsewhere wrote that Tot, one of his servants, had died in 1936, and that 'the reason given for his death was that after initiation he had milked a cow secretly at night in a byre and drunk its milk'.[31] This prohibition was also noted by the colonial administrator Percy Coriat in 1923, who wrote that 'an adult Gaweir may not milk cattle or grind corn. It is said that a man who milks his own cow will die.'[32] While Geertz and

<hr>

[29] Evans-Pritchard, *The Nuer*, 22, emphases added.   [30] Geertz, *Works and Lives*, 66.
[31] Evans-Pritchard, 'Economic life of the Nuer: cattle (part 2)', 217.
[32] Cited in D. Johnson. 1993. *Governing the Nuer: Documents by Percy Coriat on Nuer History and Ethnography, 1922–1931*. JASO Occasional Papers No. 9. Oxford: JASO, 33.

Wolbert are tempted into an interpretation of the man's posture in 'milking a restless cow' as either casualness or negligence, I suggest a further possibility, based on Evans-Pritchard ethnography, of the man's dissociation from a polluting activity: the evidence of the sequence of photographs is really little more than that the man leans away from the cow to keep the tether taught, while he chats with the other men to his side; this is a daily activity that he has no doubt carried out hundreds of times. What young person anywhere carries out such a habitual domestic task in anything other than a casual way?

A consideration of the archive as a visual totality can allow us to move beyond the framed boundaries of individual photographs, towards a more relational understanding of the seriality of photographs—their relationship to other photographs. In the case of Evans-Pritchard's collection, the photographs are relational in several senses: on one level, they are part of a series of negatives—a film or set of related films—that links them together temporally and through subject matter; and on another level, they are related through their subsequent archival situations, selections, and groupings. Both sets of relational possibilities are important aspects of the biography of the photographic object, encompassing both inception and subsequent usage. Such an archival interrogation of the collection can also undermine the authority of the photographer; aside from Evans-Pritchard's frontispiece there are other instances where Evans-Pritchard was confused about the precise location of his photographs, his shorter fieldwork trips of 1935 and 1936 being especially ripe for confusion. This approach of course is quite distinct from the semiotic approach that Wolbert takes to the plates in *The Nuer*, but to my mind shows how little we actually learn from such approaches, either about the photographer-author or the reader.

In my view, the limitations of a semiotic reading of Evans-Pritchard's illustrations as some form of authoritative visual construction is exemplified in one of Wolbert's most interesting explications, being Plate XXIX from *The Nuer*, 'Man (Nasser Post)':

we see a man with two spears and an item that may be a quiver. He goes along a path cut by automobile tires. The man is walking beside the path, presumably to get out of the way of a vehicle. Someone is coming, or – more likely, if one considers the direction of the blur of the man's feet and the angle of the two spears and the quiver he is carrying – someone is driving away. This reading of the photograph can be presumed not only on the basis of photo-technical observation of the blur and knowledge of movement, but also due to the composition, dominated by a movement corresponding to the Western world's main direction of reading from upper left to lower right. This increases the impression that the photographer has turned around again to look at the place he is leaving. The man in the picture is watching the other being driven away. The composition of the picture, determined by the verticality of man and path, the row of trees on the horizon, and the spears and pipe in the foreground, conveys the image of a barrier closing behind the brave researcher who had raised it for a while. The viewer leaves the by now more familiar, foreign region at the author's side.[33]

In the context of this argument, we could reasonably expect analysis to confine itself to the visual construction of authority from a viewer's perspective, or indeed, as Wolbert also argues, how it works to subvert such authority. Yet it soon strays into conjecture about the circumstances of the photographic encounter, and none of these readings withstand any archival scrutiny. Is this really a track cut by tyres? If so, where are the tyre tread marks in the sand; surely it's just a footpath? Is the photographer really in the back of a vehicle being driven away? If so, how does he manage not to blur the image, and where is the dust thrown up by the wheels? Are the man's spears really like 'a barrier closing behind the brave researcher who had raised it for a while'?

To answer these questions we can go back to the archive, which shows that Evans-Pritchard took three photographs of this man on the path in quick succession.[34] In the first image taken (Figure 5.7), we see that the man (who is, incidentally, carrying a *ghur* or ambatch (*Aeschynomene elaphroxylon*) parrying shield, and not a quiver or pipe),[35] is walking, not on an automobile track, but on a single path edged with stones near the Sobat River at Nasir. Evans-Pritchard is not in the back of a vehicle being driven away, but is following the man on foot, with another man smoking a pipe looking back at him.

In the second image (Figure 5.8), Evans-Pritchard has moved off the path to the left, probably to stand beside the man smoking the pipe, and takes another shot of the spear carrier who has turned to them. In the third (published) image (Figure 5.9), we can see that Evans-Pritchard has moved forwards and to his right, approaching the spear carrier. Perhaps some words were exchanged (he spoke Nuer well by 1935 when this image was probably taken), and he then raised the camera to take another shot. The man has also moved off the path to the right, probably during their short verbal exchange between shots, and now turns to leave (or lead the way?) down the path as the photograph is being taken. With this new archival interpretation, the visual metaphors of leaving and of barriers closing, behind both author and viewer,

---

[33] Wolbert, 'The anthropologist as photographer', 330.

[34] Figure 5.7 has the original film number [28/4 A232], Figure 5.8 [28/4 A234], and Figure 5.9 [28/4 A235], all annotated by Evans-Pritchard on the negative and contact print reverse.

[35] The ambatch wood (*Aeschynomene elaphroxylon*) parrying shield that the man is carrying is referred to explicitly on page 86 of *The Nuer*. An illustration of this type of object is reproduced in E. E. Evans-Pritchard. 1974 [1956]. *Nuer Religion*. New York and Oxford: Oxford University Press, 251, captioned 'Fig.5 Hollowed-out ambatch log, used as stool, &c.' It was drawn from the shield that Evans-Pritchard collected in 1936 among the western Nuer and donated to the Pitt Rivers Museum in 1937 [1937.34.44]. The Museum's accession volume includes the description: 'Ghur, short parrying-shield of ambatch, with pockets for tobacco & trifles'.

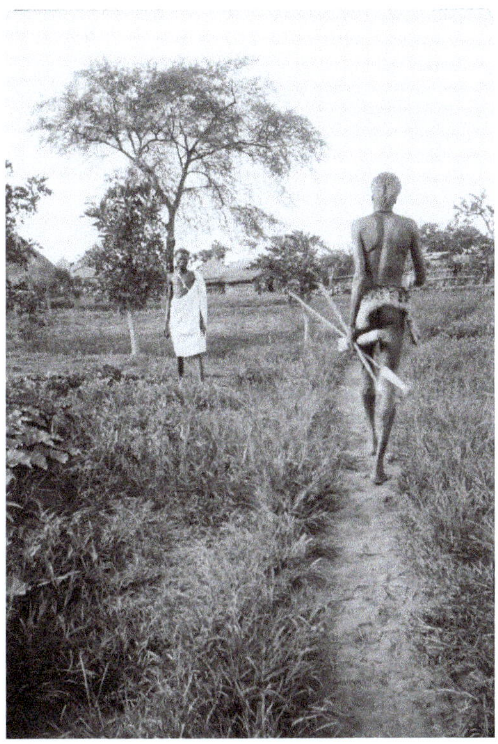

Figure 5.7 Photograph of a Nuer man on a path at the American Mission at Nasir, Upper Nile, South Sudan. Photograph by E. E. Evans-Pritchard, 1935.

are seen to be erroneous—if anything, the sequence suggests metaphors of approaching and entering the Nuer world. This would not be necessarily problematic if the argument was made that, whatever the archival sequence of images actually shows, the published plate in the book suggests a metaphor of 'leaving' to the reader. But to move beyond metaphor and to presume leaving as the actual context of the image's creation on the basis of 'photo-technical observation . . . corresponding to the Western world's main direction of reading' is seen as erroneous when the sequence of exposures shows that Evans-Pritchard is actually approaching, and the Nuer man, while certainly looking back, is leading the way.[36]

The subtitle of this chapter is 'dangerous liaisons', and I have tried to show how problematic semiotic and metaphorical propositions about the link between Evans-Pritchard's photography and the published monograph can be, when archival evidence suggests otherwise. Wolbert's use of published plates as evidence about Evans-Pritchard's photographic practice is a particularly good case in point.

---

[36] Wolbert, 'The anthropologist as photographer', 330.

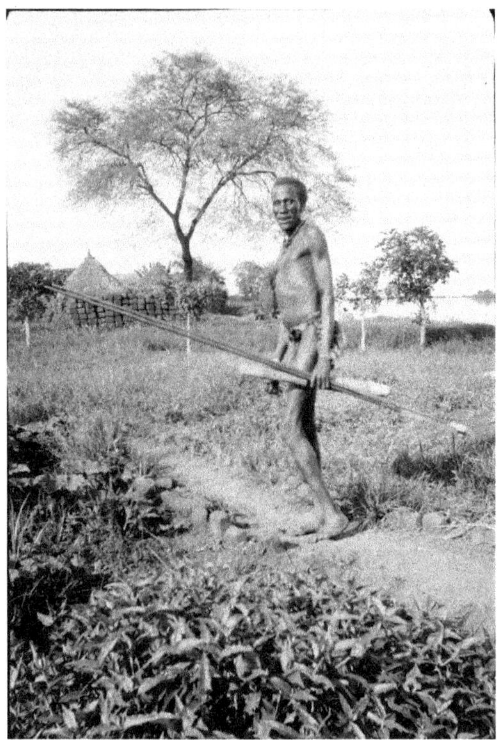

Figure 5.8 Photograph of a Nuer man on a path at the American Mission at Nasir, Upper Nile, South Sudan. Photograph by E. E. Evans-Pritchard, 1935.

The main conclusion made is that a comparison of the horizons in the frontispiece, Plates III and VIII, indicates that they were all 'taken in secret by the camera which happened to be hanging around Evans-Pritchard's neck'—that is, by a Rolleiflex or Rolleicord camera which has a viewing pane on top which the photographer looks down into to frame the image before taking the photograph.[37] However, only Plate VIII—the 'sandy ridge' photograph (Figure 5.3)—was in fact taken by a Rolleiflex or Rolleicord, the other two being 3 1/4 x 2 1/4 inch format (probably a Kodak). So the assumption that 'the negatives from Evans-Pritchard's Nuer research are all 6x6cm',[38] and thereby taken by a Rolleiflex or Rolleicord, isn't correct, there being five main negative formats in his collection, three used during 1930–1, and two (the 6 x 6 cm format for a Rolleiflex/Rolleicord and a 3 1/4 x 2 1/4 inch format for a Kodak) used during his 1935–6 fieldwork. Wolbert is right to point out that, in many of the images taken with his Rolleiflex

[37] Wolbert, 'The anthropologist as photographer', 334.
[38] Wolbert, 'The anthropologist as photographer', 333.

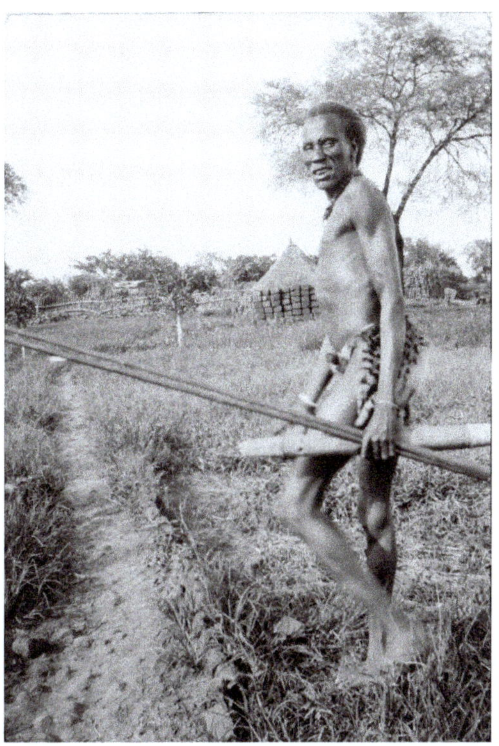

Figure 5.9 Photograph of a Nuer man on a path at the American Mission at Nasir, Upper Nile, South Sudan, published as Plate XXIX in *The Nuer* with the caption 'Man (Nasser Post)'. Photograph by E. E. Evans-Pritchard, 1935.

or Rolleicord camera, the gaze of the subject is often not into the lens, but either just above it at the level of the photographer's head, or often elsewhere.

But, from a historical perspective, the important point is not that the Rolleiflex/ Rolleicord images 'trick' us into reading a 'lack of proximity into ethnographic authority',[39] but that Evans-Pritchard's two distinct phases of Nuer fieldwork (1930–1 and 1935–6) were carried out in different political and social contexts in the region, and that this is inscribed within the images. Whereas the political situation in 1930 meant that he 'abstained from photographing a single cow',[40] his return to eastern Nuerland in 1935 led to a frenzy of photographically recording cattle and milking techniques in the cattle camps. This photographic practice was brought about by a transformed set of relations to the Nuer in his later fieldwork. In 1935, he spent a month at the home of his cook, Tiop, who had earlier worked

[39] Wolbert, 'The anthropologist as photographer', 337.
[40] E. E. Evans-Pritchard. 1937. 'The economic life of the Nuer: cattle (part 1)', *Sudan Notes and Records*, 20(3), 242.

for him in 1931, and whose community at Mancom made him 'welcome on his account'.[41] In 1936 he spent five out of seven weeks of fieldwork in the home village of Nhial, a youth who had worked for him in both 1930 and 1931, and whose community considered him a 'friend of the family'.[42] Far from lacking proximity, these later images are often striking in their relaxed immediacy, with extended sequences of dance and religious rites a particular feature. Knowledge of these sequences and relationships have only been reconnected within the archive through detailed research of individual images across the collection, as I show in chapter 7 in relation to his photography of a particular Nuer rite, and demonstrates just what can be done when analysis moves beyond the confines of the published image to a more nuanced history of the inscription and subsequent biography of the photograph.

[41] Evans-Pritchard, *Kinship and Marriage*, 106.   [42] Evans-Pritchard, *Nuer Religion*, 35.

6
Akobo Realism

Conversations with the Anuak

Writing about Evans-Pritchard's writing style, the anthropologist Clifford Geertz chose to give, by way of an example, a rare autobiographical piece published in *The Army Quarterly* at the end of his life: 'Operations on the Akobo and Gila Rivers, 1940–41'. Discussing how influential Evans-Pritchard had become in the discipline, he argued that '[e]ven most Americans sound, by now, a bit like "Operations on the Akobo"'.[1] The Akobo and Gila Rivers are in south-eastern South Sudan, and the Akobo marks the border with Ethiopia. The Anuak (also known as Anyuak or Anywaa) call this region home. Evans-Pritchard undertook two and a half months' fieldwork among the Anuak in 1935 after an initial attempt to work with the Oromo (Galla) in Ethiopia was thwarted, and when he believed no further opportunity to return to the Nuer might be possible. In Anuakland he walked 400–500 miles along the Akobo River, taking over 200 photographs and assembling a substantial artefact collection. He wrote up his investigations on the political system of the Anuak in 1940, with a further note in 1947. When World War II broke out, and his attempts to join the Welsh Guards ended in disappointment; Evans-Pritchard went to the Sudan, formally to conduct further fieldwork, but instead immediately joined the Sudan Auxiliary Defence Force. There he patrolled the eastern border with Italian-controlled Abyssinia with a unit of Anuak fighters, but also managed to continue with ethnographic enquiries, spending two months improving his knowledge of the language, during a 'strenuous, if very minor, campaign'.[2] This chapter engages with Geertz's well-known analysis of Evans-Pritchard's writing style in his account of that wartime experience, titled 'Operations on the Akobo', by extending his theme of Evans-Pritchard's literary 'optical idiom' into the visual record he created, comparing his photographic archive with his anthropological writings on the Anuak and situating it in its immediate historical contexts. The analysis reveals a new understanding of an ethnography written during a phase of colonial manipulation of the Anuak as rival chiefs were played off against each other by colonial officers. Not for the first time, the raw photographic record offers an 'inscriptive

---

[1] C. Geertz. 1988. *Works and Lives: The Anthropologist as Author*. Oxford: Polity Press, 59.

[2] E. E. Evans-Pritchard. 1947. 'Further observations on the political system of the Anuak', *Sudan Notes and Records*, 28, 62.

abundance'[3] which allows us to access Evans-Pritchard's fieldwork and its cultural encounters in a new way.

Geertz obviously had a complex relationship with Evans-Pritchard's work, and possibly with the man himself. His account is essentially an explication of why he finds the 'maddening brilliance' of Evans-Pritchard's writing style so beguiling in the way it binds author and reader into a 'very carefully observed narrative contract' that is 'anxious to picture Africa as a logical and prudential place – orderly, straightforward and level headed, firmly modelled and open to view'.[4] For Geertz, Evans-Pritchard's biographical sketch of his army service in Anuakland sums up this narrative contract perfectly since 'the presumptions that connect the author, and his audience ... are so strong and pervasive, so deeply institutionalized, that very small signals carry very big messages'.[5] As a result of this contract, the text-building strategy is to make the strange both interesting and sometimes amusing, challenging the reader's categories, but not tearing them up; nothing that Evans-Pritchard experiences (and therefore, by extension, the reader) is beyond reasoned description. This text-building strategy he terms 'Akobo Realism'—the sense that everything encountered can be reasoned with and made comprehensible. The Anuak themselves come across as 'not other but otherwise (sensible enough when you get to know them, but with their own way of doing things)'.[6] It is a style and tone which is both deeply English and class laden, and also deeply sympathetic to its subjects—as Geertz argues, he does one by doing the other. However, there is also a sense of nostalgia in Geertz's account. He ends his analysis with the thought that although we might see Evans-Pritchard's self-assured style as the 'bringing of Africans into a world conceived in deeply English terms, and confirming thereby the dominion of those terms', it is 'not smug nor ungenerous nor uncompassionate. Nor for that matter, is it untrue'.[7] It is fascinating to compare this sympathetic appreciation by Geertz for Evans-Pritchard's endeavour of cultural translation with that expressed by Godfrey Lienhardt, one of Evans-Pritchard's students, and someone who also carried out some fieldwork among the Anuak:

> The Anuak, he [Evans-Pritchard] told me, were the people he felt most at one with ... their nobility is a real nobility but, dependent for political powers on popular acclaim, has not the oppressive force of Zande nobility. Aristocracy and hierarchy, absent among the Nuer, are accompanied by effective rebellions against any mere imposition of the ruler's will ... He observed too in watching the ceremonial deference still offered to village rulers who were losing their support that a following could only be held together if a leader's authority

---

[3] E. Edwards. 2014. 'Between the local, national, and transnational: photographic recording and memorializing desire'. In *Transnational Memory, Circulation, Scales*, edited by C. De Cesari and A. Rigney. Berlin and Boston: De Gruyter, 174.

[4] Geertz, *Works and Lives*, 49, 58, 70.   [5] Geertz, *Works and Lives*, 58.

[6] Geertz, *Works and Lives*, 70.   [7] Geertz, *Works and Lives*, 71.

was readily conceded at heart by his followers. Evans-Pritchard never tried to govern – he never needed to.[8]

Lienhardt's ruminations here on Evans-Pritchard's character and ability to exert influence without the use of authoritative control certainly chime with Geertz's identification of Evans-Pritchard's 'Oxbridge Senior Common Room' approach, which meant that 'on the Akobo as on the Isis [River Thames in Oxford], men and women are brave and cowardly, kind and cruel, reasonable and foolish, loyal and perfidious, intelligent and stupid, vivid and boring, believing and indifferent, and better the one than the other'.[9]

But it is Geertz's identification of the specifically visual quality of Akobo Realism that I am mainly interested in here. Geertz argues that 'the main source of his persuasive power is his enormous capacity to construct visualizable representations of cultural phenomena', which he terms 'anthropological transparencies' and 'magic lantern ethnography'. This isn't simply to say that Evans-Pritchard uses vivid descriptive language to make unfamiliar places and people intelligible to his reader, although he frequently does so. Geertz's argument is more subtle than that. He suggests that Evans-Pritchard's use of the visualizable is part of a concerted attempt to 'demonstrate that the established frames of social perception, those upon which we ourselves instinctively rely, are fully adequate to whatever oddities the transparencies may turn out to picture'.[10] What is seen by the ethnographer is then perceived and made intelligible to the reader; images 'flip by, driving the argument home'. For Geertz, Evans-Pritchard's 'natural idiom is, so to speak, optical, his "being there" signature passionately visual'. As a result, Evans-Pritchard's writings on the Nuer people 'makes theirs perhaps the most seeable society in the whole of ethnography'.[11]

The interconnection between the visualizable nature of Evans-Pritchard's writing and his published photographs, which Geertz also discusses, is something that I dealt with in the previous chapter. What I want to engage with here is the way in which Akobo Realism might act as a useful concept to guide us to a better contextual understanding of Evans-Pritchard's account of the Anuak and their social and political setting. The reason I think it might be is that, above all, Evans-Pritchard's account of the Anuak is at one level supremely intelligible, allowing the reader readily comprehensible and sympathetic access to a social and political world with only cursory historicization. We tramp the grassy plains and swamps with the ethnographer and perceive a world that we can accommodate as part of the narrative contract that Geertz describes. Yet if you scratch the surface of

<hr>

8 G. Lienhardt. 1974. 'E-P: a personal view: Sir Edward Evans-Pritchard, 1902–1973', *Man*, 9(2), 303–4.

9 Geertz, *Works and Lives*, 71.   10 Geertz, *Works and Lives*, 64.

11 Geertz, *Works and Lives*, 65.

Akobo Realism, points of historical tension readily emerge—tensions between colonial policy and colonial administrators, tension between anthropological endeavour and colonial ambivalence, political tensions between colonial powers, tensions over borders and boundaries, and tensions over authority, status, and the symbols of colonial chieftainship. These tensions are papered over partly by his Anuak photographs that beguile us into perceiving Anuak social and environmental reality as carrying on outside such tensions, when in fact they frame them in important ways. Before I return to this theme, however, it is worth exploring how and why, after years spent carrying out long-term detailed fieldwork among the Azande and Nuer, Evans-Pritchard came to do fieldwork on the Ethiopian border, and even take up arms there as a soldier during World War II.

Heading for the Galla

In his 1974 obituary for Evans-Pritchard, his student and friend Godfrey Lienhardt suggested that, although only there for relatively brief periods in 1935 and 1940–1, Evans-Pritchard had left a lasting impression:

> Ten years or so later, and on the Ethiopian border from which E-P's activities were mounted, I heard from Anuak who remembered Odier waraCang (his Anuak ox-name which associates a brilliant black and white beast with the bright sun) how he had concealed himself in trees, along with his rifle, and bewildered the Italians by picking them off one by one in their own camps. He himself recalled this campaign rarely and briefly, and looked back with pity sometimes on the game, even, which he had killed for food. During that brief campaign, he collected information … for his writings on the Anuak and compiled the only Anuak grammar and dictionary. Who else could have done it?[12]

In fact, the Anuak dictionary Lienhardt refers to was compiled by Major E. C. Tunnicliffe, the Assistant District Commissioner of Anuak-Beir District, in 1932. A handwritten note at the top reads, 'Corrected by EEE-P'.[13] I will return to Evans-Pritchard's wartime experiences with the Anuak shortly, but to understand how the 'Guerilla Don'[14] eventually ended up there fighting on one of the front

---

[12] Lienhardt, 'E-P: a personal view', 300. Lienhardt himself carried out fieldwork among the Anuak during 1952–4 as a Research Fellow of the International African Institute, with funding initially provided by UNESCO, for a study of African cosmological ideas and social values. He later wrote a two-part article entitled 'Anuak Village Headmen', *Africa: Journal of the International African Institute*, 1957, 27(4), 341–55 and 1958, 28(1).

[13] This dictionary is held in the Evans-Pritchard Papers, Box 8, item 46, Pitt Rivers Museum, University of Oxford.

[14] 'Oxford Don as Guerilla' was the title of a short article in the *Daily Telegraph*, 14 August 1941, based on a conversation between the journalist and Evans-Pritchard. It includes the humorous note

lines of the war against the Italians, we must first go back six years or so to understand the train of events that were eventually to take him there. Some of the earliest, and previously unpublished, evidence of his interest in certain peoples of Ethiopia at this time comes from letters that he wrote in 1934 to the explorer Wilfred Thesiger.[15] Thesiger's account of his 1933–4 Awash expedition in the remote Danakil region of the country was published by *The Times* in a series of four articles titled 'An Abyssinian Quest', in 1934. In November of that year, he gave a lecture to the Royal Geographical Society titled, 'The Awash River and the Aussa Sultanate', which subsequently appeared in *The Geographical Journal* in 1935. Evans-Pritchard had obviously been developing an ethnological interest in the country, and Thesiger's articles in *The Times* prompted the following letter:

Aug 13, 1934

Paris

Dear Mr Thesiger,

My friend Mr Louis Clarke of Cambridge suggested that I ought to write to you about Abyssinia as he was sure that you would give me advice. I am acquainted with the Anglo-Egyptian Sudan, having made four ethnological expeditions there but the ways and means of Abyssinian travel is unknown to me.

I have received a Leverhulme Fellowship to study the Pagan Galla of Abyssinia on two expeditions & intend to begin with the people of Walaga in the West.

I shall be very grateful if I can have a talk with you and would suggest that if you will be in London on Aug 16th and will lunch at the Royal Societies Club, St James Street, S.W.1. I shall be greatly honoured. About 1 o'clock.

I have read your articles in The Times with great interest and they have helped to pass the time during the anti-rabies treatment I have been undergoing and am just finishing at the Pasteur Institute in Paris.

Yours sincerely,

E. E. Evans-Pritchard

After a further exchange of letters in September 1934 discussing the possibility of meeting in London, Evans-Pritchard writes to Thesiger again in October:

that 'in pre-war days his hobby was anthropology', as well as the fact that 'his [Anuak] men wore black shirts so as to nonplus the enemy and satisfy his own sense of humour', a reference to the Italian 'blackshirts' or Milizia Volontaria per la Sicurezza Nazionale, a paramilitary wing of the Fascist Party.

---

[15] I am grateful to Alexander Maitland who alerted me to the existence of Evans-Pritchard's letters to Sir Wilfred Thesiger, for his help in copying them for me, and for his permission to quote from them here.

Oct 2, 1934 from Royal Societies Club, London

Dear Thesiger,

Very many apologies for not having long ago answered your letter. I have no excuse save that I was hoping to have something definite from the Foreign Office to tell you.

I will write tomorrow to Walker & find out all about Walega from him. Thanks so much for writing to him.

I think you misunderstand me about the question of servants. I have no objection to any number of Galla servants once I am in Ethiopia but the difficulty is about starting off with servants from the Sudan. Even if the Sudan Government permitted me to take Sudanese boys with me they would probably exact £50 a head as a guarantee. Also my experience with natives has been that however eager they are at the start they very soon become miserable & get sick out of their own country. The 'one boy' I mentioned was to be the single boy I took with me from the Sudan. Elliot Smith and Corfield who have just made the journey from the Sudan to Addis Ababa advise strongly against this route so I shall probably enter via the Sudan (Kurmuk I expect).

The Ethiopian Government have at last agreed to my work 'in principle' (whatever that means) but want further details.

I saw Hamilton, the Sudan Agent at Cairo, the other day & he mentioned that he was going to meet you.

When things are more fixed up I will drop you a line as I would like further advice. I assure you that I was most grateful for your assistance.

Yours,

E. E. Evans-Pritchard

The Walker mentioned in Evans-Pritchard's letter was Craven Howell Walker, who published *The Abyssinian At Home* in 1933 and who was British Consul at Gore in the 1920s. Unable to attend Thesiger's lecture at the Royal Geographical Society in November, Evans-Pritchard writes to him to apologize, but also to say that he was 'still in "conversation" with Addis Ababa. Probably I shall go back to the Sudan & work there till the Sobat River is navigable & then go & see H.M. Consul at Gore & make arrangements to work in Abyssinia in 1936.' Although known as His Britannic Majesty's Consul at Gore, the consul's salary and the expenses of the consulate were paid by the Sudan government.

We can only speculate about the reasons Evans-Pritchard gave in his application for funding to the Leverhulme Trust to go and study the Oromo people, but it is clear that there had been some interest in them among colonial travellers and anthropologists for some time due to their traditional religious beliefs. It is likely that Evans-Pritchard had in mind investigating this aspect of

Oromo culture, but also expanding the scope of what he later termed 'Nilotic studies'. In 1936, for instance, he undertook a six-week tour of western Kenya to survey the Luo people in order to make comparisons about social and political organization with groups in South Sudan (see chapter 8). So it is likely that Evans-Pritchard's interest in the Oromo just over the border in Ethiopia was also part of gaining a better understanding of the historical relations between, and migrations of, neighbouring peoples in the region. In his Presidential Address on the subject of Nilotic studies to the Royal Anthropological Institute in 1950, Evans-Pritchard argued that 'the different Nilotic peoples have been, and in some cases quite considerably, diversified culturally and racially by both varying ecological circumstances and contacts with their non-Nilotic neighbours. Nevertheless, when all these considerations are given due weight, we can still without hesitation place all the Nilotic peoples together.'

The Consul in Gore that Evans-Pritchard mentions to Thesiger in his letter was Captain Esme Nourse Erskine, who had succeeded C. H. Walker as Consul in 1928. Erskine set about building an impressive residency on a hill overlooking Gore, with outbuildings, barracks, and stables for ten special constables, and a pack of hounds.[16] We know that Evans-Pritchard visited Erskine at Gore briefly since a small number of photographs from the visit exist (see Figures 6.1 and 6.2), and he notes in his study of the Anuak that, while he was considering settling down to an intensive study of the Anuak in a village near Akobo, he suddenly received the permission he had been waiting for to enter the country and discuss the feasibility of Galla fieldwork for which he had been awarded the Leverhulme Fellowship. The visit to Ethiopia was abortive, however, since the Italian invasion 'compelled me to leave the country'.[17] Evans-Pritchard arrived back at Akobo Post from Gore on 15 May 1935, some months before the Italian invasion in October, so there must have been additional factors at play that denied Evans-Pritchard his fieldwork goal in Ethiopia.

In fact it was a time of turmoil in the region in terms of relations between the administration in Sudan and the Ethiopian government, and also between the administration and the peoples either side of a poorly conceived border. After Haile Selassie came to power in 1930, there was an attempt to exert greater control over the entirety of the country, supported by the British who also wanted a strong government in Addis Ababa for strategic reasons. This inevitably led to tension in the borderland with South Sudan since the area had been effectively managed by the British either side of the border since the early 1920s. With the British

---

[16] R. O. Collins. 1983. *Shadows in the Grass: Britain in the Southern Sudan, 1918–1956.* New Haven, CT: Yale University Press, 373.

[17] E. E. Evans-Pritchard. 1940. *The Political System of the Anuak of the Anglo-Egyptian Sudan.* London: The London School of Economics and Political Science, 5.

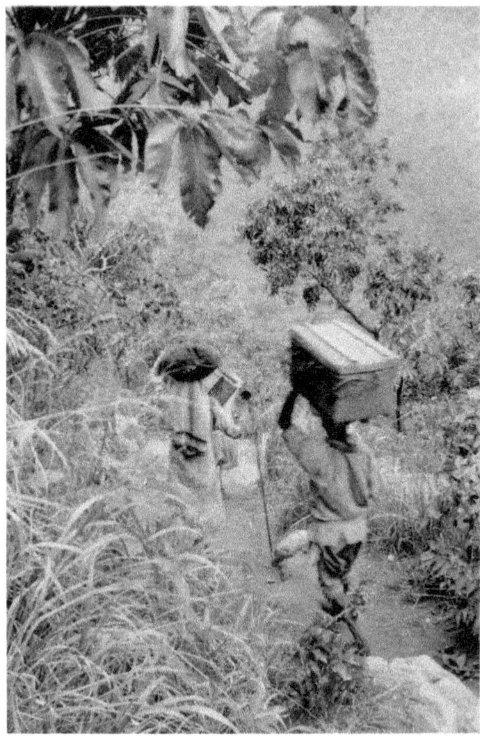

Figure 6.1 Porters carrying baggage in Ethiopia. Photograph by E. E. Evans-Pritchard, 1935.

confined to their side of the border, the poor decision to draw the border along rivers, rather than highland escarpment, became painfully clear, since dispersed groups such as the Anuak lived either side of rivers and could play colonial agents off against each other. In 1932 for instance, Anuak on both sides of the border joined forces to raid the Murle near Akobo Post, returning to Ethiopia with cattle to sell for firearms. The Ethiopian government had to pay compensation, and captives taken on the raid were eventually returned. As a result of events such as this, and Erskine's requests for action, a frontier agent, Kanyazmatch Majid Abud, was appointed shortly after to assert control over the region. Erskine's hopes were high that Majid Abud would settle frontier disputes, yet he quickly fell out with British administrators the other side of the border, such as Corfield among the Nuer, and the situation did not improve. Majid Abud was badly injured in May 1934 during an attack by the Baro Anuak while trying to collect taxes, and had to return to Addis Ababa. Sixty of his men also died in the attack. This was a major disappointment to Erskine who had hoped for effective Ethiopian administration of the Baro salient, and in October 1935 the British Foreign Office agreed to let Sudan district commissioners cross the border when required for the purposes of

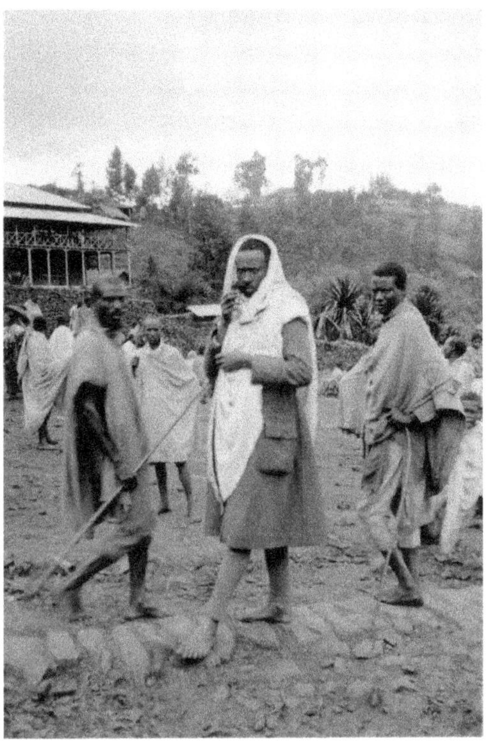

Figure 6.2 Ethiopian men outside the British Consulate at Gore, Ethiopia. Photograph by E. E. Evans-Pritchard, 1935.

order and security.[18] So at the time of Evans-Pritchard's attempt to begin field-work in western Ethiopia, there were significant additional tensions to the threat of an Italian invasion (some of them ending violently) that may well have influenced the delays Evans-Pritchard experienced in getting permission to go to Gore; it may have even influenced Erskine's decision, or their joint decision, to abort the proposed fieldwork altogether.

Erskine himself may well have been supportive of Evans-Pritchard's proposed study of the Oromo people. According to one historian, Erskine was prejudiced against the Amhara, extremely pro-Galla, and had dreams of extending a British mandate over the south-west of Ethiopia.[19] Apparently Erskine had been encour-aged in this by the British Intelligence services who had asked him to help create a 'Galla confederation' that might ask Britain to intervene and extend such a mandate. After the Italian invasion in June 1937, Erskine obliged, sending a

<hr>

[18] Collins, *Shadows in the Grass*, 375–81.
[19] A. Mockler. 1984. *Haile Selassie's War*. Oxford: Oxford University Press, 163.

telegraph to London that read: 'A Galla delegation of chiefs would like to transmit via Khartoum to the League of Nations the request for a British mandate in Ethiopia to the west of the 36th meridian. All the Galla chiefs refuse to be represented by their enemies and oppressors—that is, the Amhara delegation now present in London.'[20] Despite an obviously shared interest in the Oromo, in May 1935 Erskine obviously felt that the presence in south-western Ethiopia of a British anthropologist known for his connections to the Sudan administration was not something the Ethiopian government would have tolerated, and may even have made difficult or unsafe. The British feared the return of a vengeful Majid Abud to the region trying to reassert Ethiopian control in the borderlands, and the presence of a Sudan government anthropologist working among a people known to be seeking an alliance with the British was obviously a proposition that Erskine may well have found politically untenable. No doubt the storm clouds of Italian invasion, with provocative statements and the massing of Italian troops on the Ethiopian border, may have contributed to this decision. But given that the Italian invasion did not happen until October 1935, Evans-Pritchard's published claim that 'the Italian invasion of Ethiopia compelled me to leave the country'[21] should now be seen as a much more complex decision, involving just as much local as international politics. Evans-Pritchard's simplification of the fieldwork narrative is another instance of Akobo Realism; the contract between author and reader is such that we take it on trust that a no doubt difficult and complex experience is being glossed over, but we are encouraged not to worry since it is hardly worth more than a passing mention. As Geertz notes, 'the tale has clearly been through too many pub recitals to be the offhand account it so industriously pretends to be'.[22]

One king or many?

In 1939, as war with Germany beckoned, Evans-Pritchard produced, somewhat hastily, a volume based on his Anuak fieldwork. Presumably due to problems with publishing at the outbreak of war, this was done by the Replika process, in which a typescript was reproduced directly rather than typeset. He later noted that it seemed unlikely at that time that he would return to his Anuak research, presumably because the impact of war on the course of academic research in the region was so uncertain. Yet surely he also felt, as did many young men likely to enlist, that the personal outcome of war was also unknown, and that it would be better in this case to disseminate the results of research while the opportunity was there to do so. The account is particularly revealing of the way Evans-Pritchard as an anthropologist reconciled his relationship to Sudan government sponsorship and

---

[20] M. B. Lentakis. 2005. *Ethiopia: A View From Within*. London: Janus Publishing, 67.
[21] Evans-Pritchard, *Political System of the Anuak*, 5.   [22] Geertz, *Works and Lives*, 57.

influence. Although his own agenda was to widen the scope of Nilotic studies by studying a neighbouring people to the Nuer, the study was shaped significantly by administrative need:

> The investigations were made at the request of the Government of the Anglo-Egyptian Sudan, which had encountered some difficulties in its dealings with the Anuak nobility, and may, therefore, be considered as a piece of 'applied anthropology' in the only reputable sense this expression can denote at the present stage of the anthropological sciences: the discovery of facts so that a government can organize its administration in the light of them. I hope that it may prove of use to administrators.[23]

The colonial 'difficulties' that Evans-Pritchard refers to, and which had precipitated his work, were mostly of the government's making, and act as a crucial backdrop to his ethnography. Although formal administrative control of the Anuak began in 1921, the British had asserted themselves militarily on them since 1911 when the government decided to try and stop Akwei-wa-Cam from raiding the Nuer, sending a gunboat to shell villages on the right bank of the Pibor River, killing people, capturing livestock, and burning villages.[24] The government established a post at Akobo and continued to influence control over Akwei-wa-Cam's raiding of the Nuer. So by the time of Evans-Pritchard's fieldwork, the Ciro Anuak had been subject to British military control and influence for some twenty-four years. The effects of this become apparent in the published account, especially when government actions impede the anthropologist's work: 'It is difficult to estimate the number of cattle kept by the Anuak today', he wrote, with restrained frustration, 'as in 1932–34 the Governments of the Anglo-Egyptian Sudan and Ethiopia removed most of the animals in the Ciro and Nyikaani districts as a penalty for a raid carried out on the Beir.'[25]

The first ethnographic notes about the Anuak written for a British colonial audience were published in 1921, 1922, and 1924 in *Sudan Notes & Records*, a diverse journal for those involved in the Sudan administration or otherwise having a scholarly interest in the region, and were penned by Colonel C. R. K. Bacon. These accounts detail Bacon's first visit as British government representative to the village of the Anuak King, Cam-war-Akwei (who he calls Sham Akwei), the 12 year-old son of Akwei-wa-Cam, who had died in 1920. In keeping with British policy elsewhere in Africa, the object of the exercise was to recognize the authority of the king, through which British colonial power might be exerted and negotiated. But how to make a suitable impression? Bacon took a nineteenth-century

---

[23] Evans-Pritchard, *Political System of the Anuak*, 5.
[24] Evans-Pritchard, *Political System of the Anuak*, 13.
[25] Evans-Pritchard, *Political System of the Anuak*, 20.

approach: 'As these Anuak had never seen a camel', he relates, 'I decided at the cost of some discomfort to make my entrance to the village on one of these baggage animals, seated on empty sacks covered by a red blanket.' He also presented Cam with a military sword by way of symbolically recognizing him as king.[26] Among the existing Anuak emblems of authority that Bacon noticed was a four-legged stool, 'the emblem of Sultanic authority' that Cam-war-Akwei was jealously guarding from rival claimants among the Ethiopian Anuak. Clearly fascinated by a society with a very English approach to emblems of traditional authority, Bacon published a note the following year listing more of these emblems, including a small drum containing noble children's teeth, and certain bead necklaces. Two years later Bacon wrote a further note clarifying the emblems and their relative importance, but he was also clearly struggling to understand the role they played in Anuak politics and what the colonial government's response should be to competing rivalries for the kingship. After his colourful and symbolic recognition of Cam-war-Akwei in 1921, it quickly became clear to Bacon that there were a number of Anuak families that claimed descent from the originating ancestor and that they were all considered to share the right to sit upon the throne and wear or handle the regalia. Having experienced a few years of internal Anuak political strife he concluded that most of this was down to these competing rivalries for the throne and possession of the emblems of authority. The blame for this strife he laid at the door of Cam's father, Akwei, in whose 'despotic reign it was not too easy to obtain his consent to sit upon the throne. The result was that a number of feuds existed when he died and these are gradually being settled by enabling claimants to obtain their right.' In 1924 therefore, Bacon allowed Ujulu-war-Udiel, a claimant to the throne who had been cut off in Ethiopia when Akobo became the frontier, to come and sit on the throne and handle the emblems.[27]

It is clear that these first few years of British administration of the Anuak were riddled with colonial confusion as to how this society regulated its seemingly perplexing political systems of village headmanship, nobility, and kingship. What Bacon was at a loss to see was just what a devastating new influence colonial control was for the Anuak, not just in the way it imposed a completely arbitrary international frontier across Anuak territory, but also in its military interferences, punitive raids, and strategic support of particular figures irrespective of local wishes. Evans-Pritchard was the first to recognize this, pointing out that from 1921, when administration began, to 1935, when his survey was made, 'the Government was a

---

[26] C. R. K. Bacon. 1921. 'Kingship among the Anuak', *Sudan Notes and Records*, 4(3), 163. Evans-Pritchard later noted that the sword presented to Cam-war-Akwei by Bacon had been added to the royal emblems of the Anuak, but that it was not regarded as a genuine emblem and in fact had been so badly burned when hidden in the grass that only the non-inflammable parts remained intact (Evans-Pritchard, *Political System of the Anuak*, 58). Bacon published a further note in 1922: 'The Anuak', *Sudan Notes and Records*, 5(3), 113–29.

[27] C. R. K. Bacon. 1924. 'The investiture of an Anuak nyeta or sultan', *Sudan Notes and Records*, 7(2), 115.

new political factor of even greater influence than the introduction of firearms in the preceding period.'[28] Having invested Cam-war-Akwei with his regimental sword and sash, by 1927 the government were frustrated enough by Anuak noble rivalries to try another approach, especially after a group of nobles approached the civil administrator to complain that their traditional right of access to the emblems was being denied. The decision was taken, implemented by Major G. W. Tunnicliffe, that from then onwards the emblems should be held by one of the leading nobles for a year at a time, with the next custodian being elected by a council of nobles. The government was evidently persuaded by the disgruntled nobles that such a system might be more in accordance with Anuak custom. At the first such election the noble Nyang-war-Agaanya was elected, but he carried off the emblems to Pinyghuudu in Ethiopia and didn't return until 1929 when Akwei-wa-Alal was elected custodian. In 1930 it was Cam-wa-Medho's turn, but after some hostilities Cam fled with the emblems to Ethiopia in 1931; the authorities there later forced him to return to the Sudan. The noble Aguaa-war-Akuon was elected custodian of the emblems for 1932, but political difficulties continued which led to the death of the holder Cam-war-Akwei in 1933 while in captivity, and Cam-wa-Medho was deported from the country in 1934. During the time Evans-Pritchard was in Anuak country in 1935, the noble Aguaa-war-Akwon was elected to hold the emblems again, but many influential nobles were openly against this decision, not considering that Aguaa would have enough backing to hold onto them without government support.[29] Evans-Pritchard was evidently a participant in the meeting at which Aguaa was reappointed as the holder of the emblems in 1935, since there is a photograph in his collection briefly captioned 'Aguaa being selected' (Figure 6.3). This image doesn't just give us a brief glimpse of one of the selection meetings of nobles, presided over by the district commissioner; it places Evans-Pritchard within the meeting itself, seated among the Anuak nobles, and so at the heart of colonial politics for the Anuak. The photograph ostensibly shows Aguaa-war-Akwon, but it is more importantly one of the most fascinating documents on the intertwining nature of colonial politics and anthropology I can think of.

Government policy of rotating the emblems among the nobles after 1927 had therefore not had the hoped-for effect of defusing rivalries and smoothing the path of indirect colonial rule through native power structures. In practice it appears that the rotation of the royal emblems was under the direct control of the district commissioner, since each noble would usually vote for themselves to receive them. The need for an anthropologist to understand Anuak social and political organization was therefore great, and who better than the man who had done something similar already among the neighbouring Nuer?

---

[28] Evans-Pritchard, *Political System of the Anuak*, 95.
[29] Evans-Pritchard, *Political System of the Anuak*, 97.

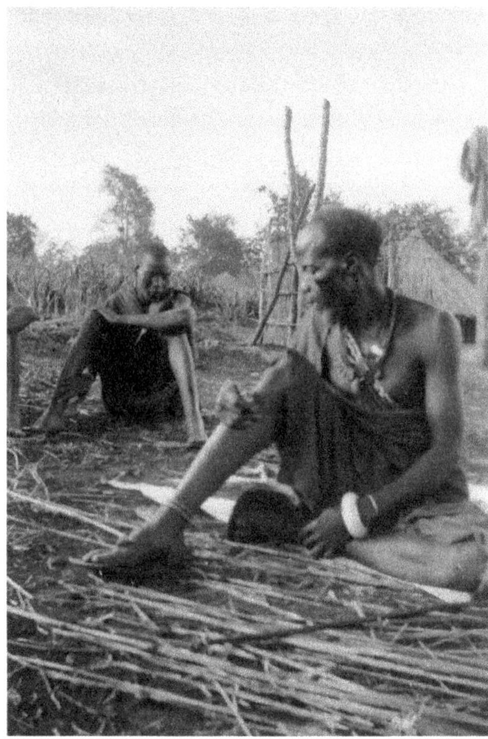

Figure 6.3 Aguaa-war-Akuon being selected as king at a meeting of nobles and government officials. Photograph by E. E. Evans-Pritchard, 1935.

Evans-Pritchard immediately recognized that the government had mistakenly taken Anuak politics for something it was not. Assuming that it was similar to Shilluk kingship they had unquestioningly used words such as 'sultan', 'king', 'royal', etc., which had obscured a much more complex reality. Evans-Pritchard found instead a society in which rule by nobles was restricted to only one part of the country (east), and that over the generations the emblems had passed between nobles who were then forced to relinquish them to another, sometimes by force. But even more importantly, nobility itself was tied up with access to the emblems since one's investiture into nobility was done through them. This was a system quite different from that of the Shilluk *reth*, or for that matter any other encountered in the Sudan. However, Evans-Pritchard summed it up with characteristic simplicity and brilliance, suggesting that as long as used in a qualified way:

> there is little objection to speaking of the noble who at any time is in possession of the emblems as the king and of the emblems as the royal emblems. However, it must be emphasized that a man becomes a noble with the full status of nobility by

being invested with the royal emblems, that is by becoming king, even if only for a few hours. Consequently all nobles are ex-kings and the king is only primus inter pares, a noble among his fellow nobles, and distinguished from them only by his temporary possession of the royal emblems.[30]

One can imagine the frustration of the colonial official hoping for some certainty from Evans-Pritchard's report. Kings for just a few hours? All nobles ex-kings? But this is all part of the challenging task that Evans-Pritchard was set, to research and write, at least in part, for a colonial administrative audience, and yet also for an academic one, for whom critiquing oversimplified assumptions was of vital importance. In light of this, one could almost paraphrase Evans-Pritchard's paragraph above as 'carry on calling them "kings" and "royal emblems" if you wish, but to do so is probably meaningless'. As if to underline this point he also points out that the four-legged stool was not a throne, and that it was in fact a particular set of *ucuok* beads that conferred nobility/kingship. He also pointed out that government control of the circulation of emblems had led to nobles charging other nobles to allow their children to be invested with the emblems and thereby join the nobility. Since they knew they would not retain them for long, they sought to maximize their return in the context of an altered economic and social context. Not all anthropologists have agreed with Evans-Pritchard's view of Anuak nobility however, with one going so far as to argue that his downplaying of the political power of the Nuer prophets, the Shilluk *reth* and the Anuak king, 'contradicted prevailing interpretations of their political significance, with little regard for the value of historical documentation and ethnographic factors to the contrary'.[31] It is a critique that Evans-Pritchard would no doubt have robustly challenged, given his particular regard for both historiographical and ethnographical evidence.

Although G. W. Tunnicliffe and the Sudan government thought they were returning to some established custom by electing a new holder of the emblems each year, the research and recommendations of both Evans-Pritchard and the District Commissioner G. L. Elliot-Smith, who took over in 1932, confirmed Bacon's original recognition of a single custodian on an ongoing basis. As a result, the last elected holder at the time of Evans-Pritchard's visit, Aguaa-war-Akuon, was given more permanent custody, a salary, and the strong support of the government, in the hope that administration might run more smoothly. But much damage had been done, lamented Evans-Pritchard, since government interference had meant that many young nobles had been invested with the emblems and thus held royal rank, reducing the significance and stability that it almost certainly had in the past.[32]

---

[30] Evans-Pritchard, *Political System of the Anuak*, 53.

[31] W. Arens. 1983. 'Evans-Pritchard and the prophets: comments on an ethnographic enigma', *Anthropos*, 78, 5.

[32] Evans Pritchard notes that Antonio's 1855 account suggests that the emblems were held for very many years, or for life (Evans-Pritchard, *Political System of the Anuak*, 63).

Trekking the Akobo

In March 1935, with colonial knowledge of turbulent Anuak politics significantly lacking, and constant trouble between rivals on either side of the Sudan–Ethiopia border leading to friction between both governments, Evans-Pritchard arrived at Akobo. Having made all necessary arrangements with the District Commissioner, G. L. Elliot-Smith, he set off with his porters along the Akobo River to the village of Pochalla, where he arrived seven days later. From Pochalla, Evans-Pritchard spent the next ten weeks travelling westwards and eastwards along the river visiting villages on both banks, covering an estimated 400–500 miles, camping each night in the centre of a village. Usually Evans-Pritchard and his porters would spend only one day in any village, not wanting to impose too much on the scarce resources of their hosts, who had to feed them. In exchange for this food, Evans-Pritchard gave his hosts cloth, spears, hoes, or other objects. There was another reason for the brevity of each village visit, and that was the fact that this was ostensibly a survey of environmental conditions, political relations, and the distribution of clans, all of which was vital information for the colonial administration.

Although, as I have already described, the main objective of Evans-Pritchard's survey was the political organization of the Anuak nobility, he spent only three weeks in the area inhabited and controlled by nobles. Yet Evans-Pritchard wasn't to know this at the outset of his fieldwork, and indeed the speed and scope of the survey was intended to try and establish the range of influence of the noble clan across Anuak territory. It turned out to be much less in extent than previously thought, with most Anuak village leaders being headmen who were not nobles. In general, Evans-Pritchard seems to have been tolerated by the Anuak he met, a consequence, he felt, of British administrative influence. This meant that he was able to trek throughout Anuak country with just local porters and, for the first time he believed as a European, no police escort. Not having time to learn any Anuak, an interpreter was provided named Omot, the senior interpreter at Akobo. He didn't prove a success, but his servant Oyo was 'a valuable substitute' since he spoke Arabic and Nuer, which Evans-Pritchard used as a lingua franca since he was proficient in both.

As he trekked, Evans-Pritchard photographed. His porters, the path ahead, bush and general vegetation, tree burials, fenced graves away from villages, waterways, groups of people on the river banks. They are photographs of survey and chance encounter, but although not categorized, and infrequently and briefly annotated, they reflect the nature of the fieldwork closely. There are no physical type portraits; he was never interested in this type of anthropological enquiry. Instead, the camera frame is laid carefully over the anthropological question and in answer to the curious anthropologist's visual query. As Geertz noted, Evans-Pritchard's writing style was all about visualization—a 'magic lantern ethnography'. Take, for instance, the following, simple, and beguiling imagery:

One of the first sights that strike a visitor to Anuak country is the crouching of the people when they approach or walk across the line of vision of their village headmen and the formal respect paid them is likely to mislead him about their real powers. People bow lower to a village headman than to a noble. It is truly remarkable to observe the ceremonious respect paid to a mere stripling like Aguaa-wa-Medho, the headman of Uwelo.[33]

Evans-Pritchard captured this show of respect in a photograph of a woman crawling on her knees past his tent (tent peg visible in the foreground) as he sat talking to a headman (Figure 6.4). It is of course an ambiguous image on its own, one that shows little of the social context in which the woman's posture finds its meaning. It is an opportunistic picture; the woman has already crawled past Evans-Pritchard, and he has the time as she slowly makes her way past the tent to reach for his camera and frame an exposure. A number of Evans-Pritchard's images of people are taken in this space of cultural encounter around the edges of the tent, something that features also in his Nuer images. The ethnographer's tent is an important zone of engagement between the outsider and the host society, and it is clear from the regularity of images taken in this zone that Evans-Pritchard felt at liberty to photograph people as they sat and talked or approached. These images show how important the tent was as a social space in which information was sought, offered, exchanged, translated, and negotiated. Here among the Anuak, Evans-Pritchard pitched his tent alongside the houses of his host, joining the community, briefly. In a number of photographs he looks back at the homestead, having wandered away from it, taking a photograph of the scene, the tent blending into the village surroundings. But around the tent there are no carefully posed portraits, only fleeting moments of engagement captured in a spontaneous man-ner, with little evident concern with the pictorial. A group meeting of men at one village is so poorly framed that one is led to wonder whether Evans-Pritchard took the image accidentally, or whether he had taken it furtively; given this is the only exposure of this meeting we might be led towards the latter interpretation. Another image of a meeting of men is more squarely framed, but the heavy intrusion of Evans-Pritchard's pith helmet in the foreground suggests that again the photograph was taken quickly, with little attempt to compose a studied scene (Figure 6.5). The men look back at him intently, quizzically. This photograph, taken at Kinha village, includes three nobles seated on an animal skin, identified from the left as Abula-wa-Gilo (smoking a water pipe), Anyoonya-wa-Thomo, and Por-wa-Ngeenyo.

These images are better understood as records of moments of social encounter, rather than ethnographic description. They include, rather than attempt to

---

[33] Evans-Pritchard, *Political System of the Anuak*, 39.

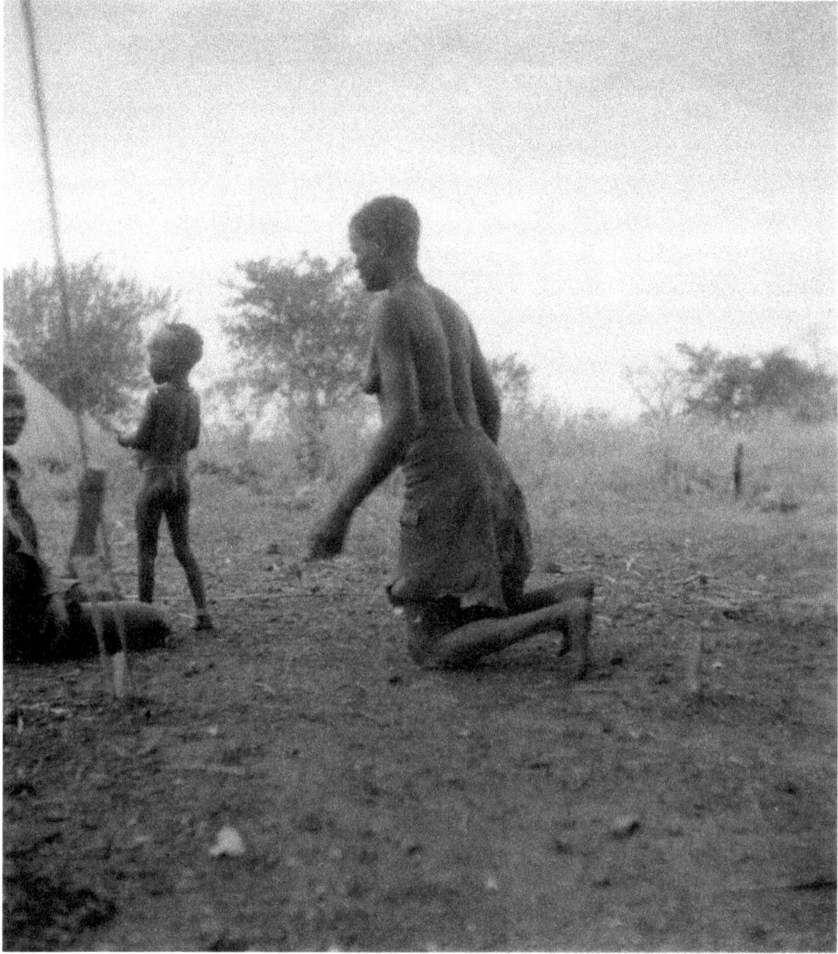

Figure 6.4 Woman crawling past Evans-Pritchard's tent, showing respect to headman, Pochalla village, Jonglei, South Sudan. Photograph by E. E. Evans-Pritchard, 1935.

exclude, history, in the way that ethnographic field imagery often sought to. The tent flaps, tent pegs, pith helmet, items of luggage, camera case, and porters are often evident as unintentional props that ground and historicize the social encounter in time, and place rather than exclude it. This is nowhere more evident than in the images taken of groups of Anuak people taken from the deck of the river steamer along the Baro River, which Evans-Pritchard relates was his only means of observing these communities (Figure 6.6). In these images, large groups gather on the bank gazing back at the Europeans on board, and the camera looks

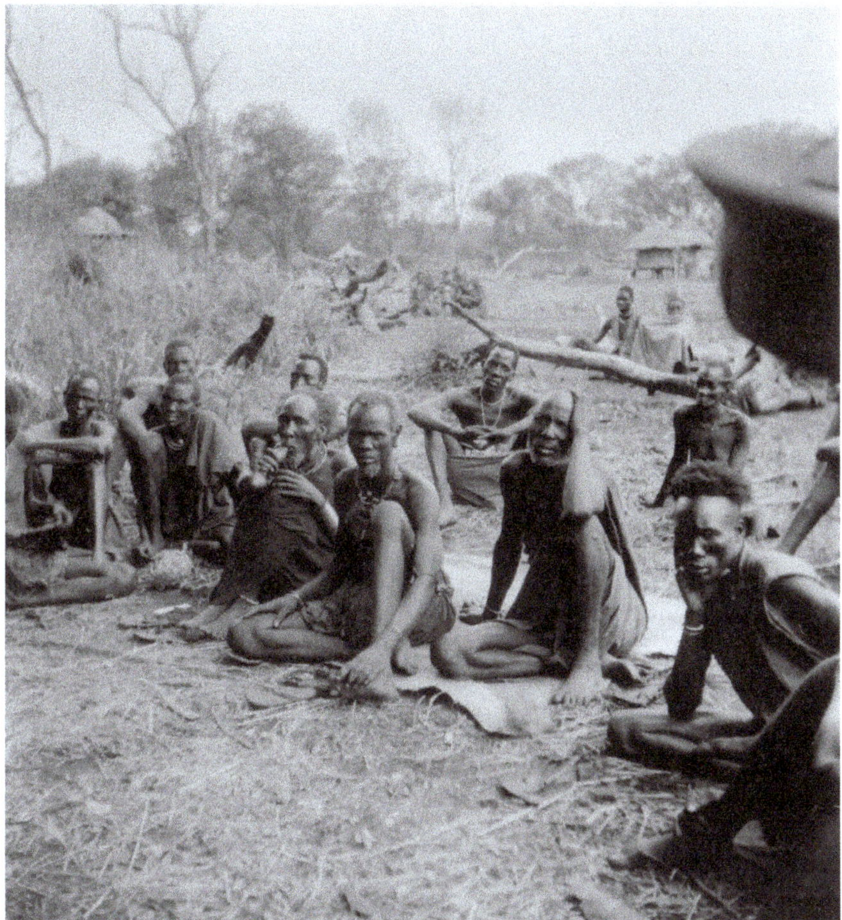

Figure 6.5 A group of men, including three nobles, at Kinha village, Jonglei, South Sudan. Photograph by E. E. Evans-Pritchard, 1935.

back. The resulting images frame the Anuak group with the canvas-covered shelter of the deck, and bundles of firewood for the steamer engine in the foreground. These images are almost entirely lacking in ethnographic information beyond showing the people in the most general terms possible, and at a distance. They are again records of encounter that intentionally historicize the social space of engagement, rather than seek to deny it.

As I discussed in chapter 5 in the case of the tent flap in Evans-Pritchard's Nuer photograph 'August shower', the canvas deck cover here acts as the mise en scène within the theatre of cultural encounter between Evans-Pritchard and the Anuak. There is no attempt to exclude the historical context of encounter; it forms part of

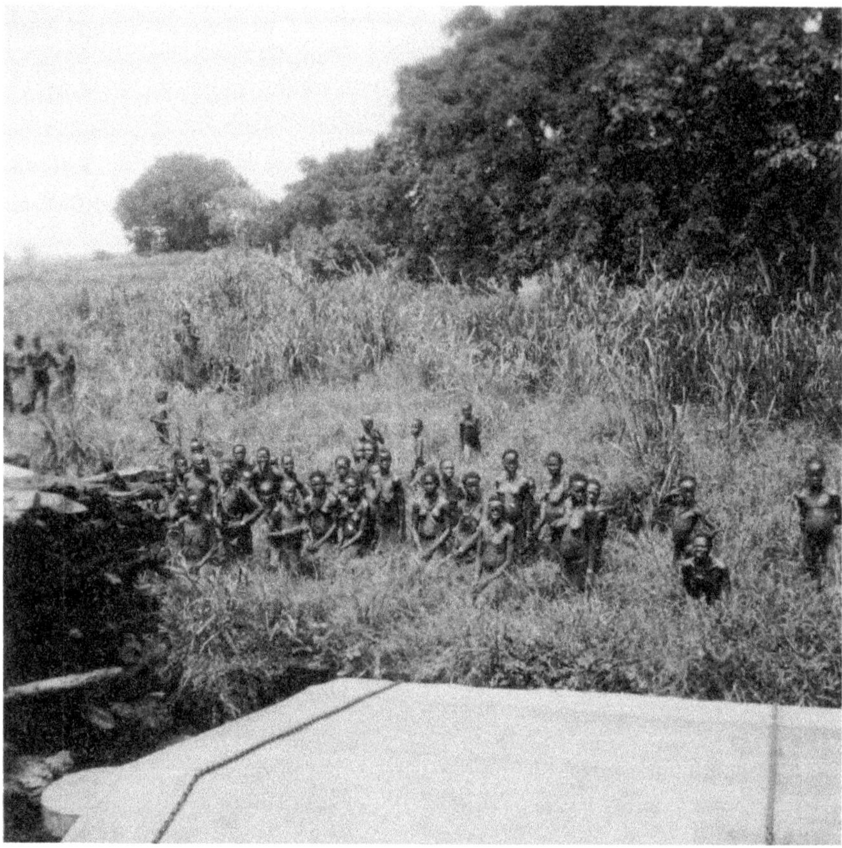

Figure 6.6 Group of Anuak gathered on the bank of the Baro River in South Sudan, the deck of a steamer in the foreground. Photograph by E. E. Evans-Pritchard, 1935.

the situation in which the work of anthropology takes place. I would argue that Evans-Pritchard's Anuak images are particularly good examples of the way in which historical context in both his ethnography and photography is intentionally included, rather than excluded. Although in all of his ethnography there is an attempt to weave generalizable theory, whether it be about kinship and social organization, concepts of time and space, or rationality, there is no explicit attempt to understand communities as living in a timeless or ahistorical situation, or even exclude the way in which ethnographic knowledge was formed through fieldwork. A good example of this occurs in his Anuak monograph in his discussion of the royal emblems: 'Though I had ample opportunity', he wrote, 'to note the character of the emblems and to photograph them I considered it inadvisable to handle them. However, for a time they were in the custody of the Government at Akobo Post and Mr Elliot Smith took the opportunity to record exact measurements.'[34] This historically loaded statement is revealing in a number of different ways. Firstly, it is clear that Elliot-Smith showed Evans-Pritchard his photographs of the royal emblems before he set off on his long trek around Anuak country. If he did not know of Elliot-Smith's photographs, why would he not have taken the opportunity to photograph them in detail when visiting Aguaa-war-Akuon (the holder of the emblems) at Obuodhi village?

He did photograph Aguaa-war-Akuon (Figure 6.7), seated on one of the royal stools (*wal Adhapa*), while to the side stand the royal spear-rest (*dikweri*) and

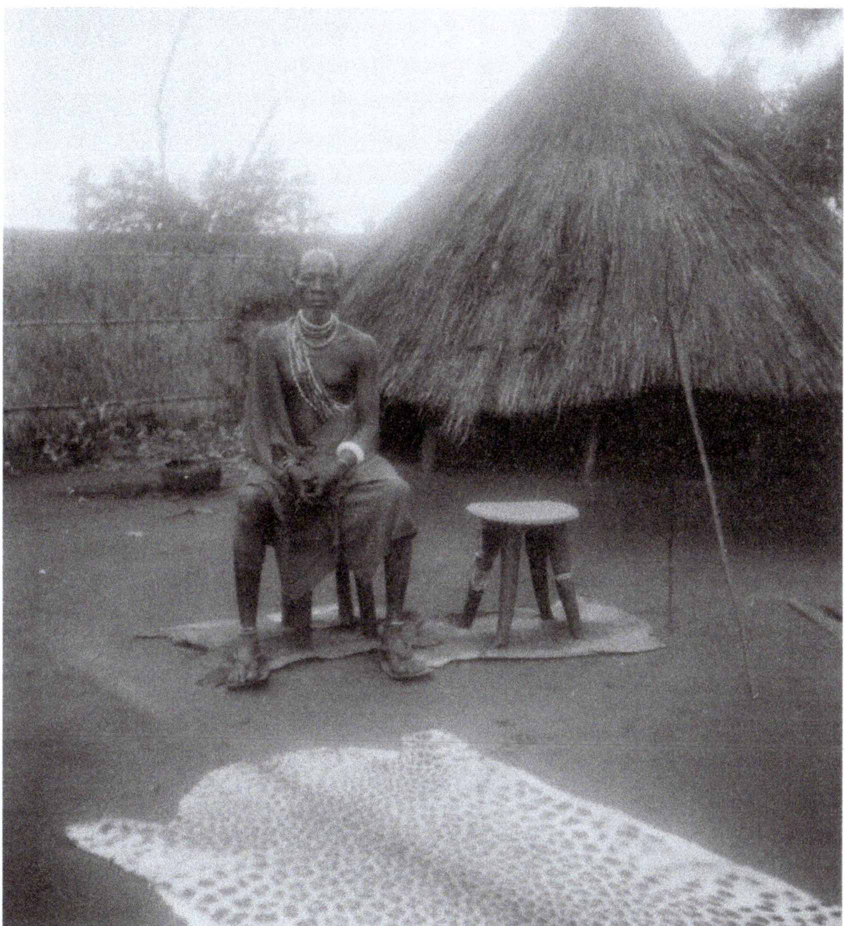

Figure 6.7 Aguaa-war-Akuon (the holder of the Anuak royal emblems) at Obuodhi village, Jonglei, South Sudan. Photograph by E. E. Evans-Pritchard, 1935.

---

[34] Evans-Pritchard, *Political System of the Anuak*, 54.

spear (*ucula*). Turning the camera a few degrees to the right, Evans-Pritchard took another photograph, of one of the royal stools, the spear-rest (now without spear), and a group of royal spears lying on the ground. He took another photograph shortly after this one, from slightly further back, but in the same direction. This image seems to have been prompted by the arrival of a young man who has come to sit near the leopard skin that Evans-Pritchard was evidently sitting on in front of the king. At his feet are a side-blown horn and small drum (*Udola*). The man has evidently been asked by Aguaa-war-Akuon to bring out these two special items and show them to the anthropologist. At the bottom of the frame (Figure 6.8) can be seen Evans-Pritchard's camera case, a reminder of the anthropologist's presence, suggestive of his movement from being seated on the leopard-skin rug, to standing position as the man brings out the *Udola* drum and horn so that he might photograph them. The camera case and sequence of images is another instance in the archive of the embodied presence of the anthropologist in the production of ethnographic knowledge, as I explored in detail in chapter 3 in relation to the initiation of Kamanga. Evans-Pritchard describes the drum, horn, and scene briefly in his list of the royal emblems:

> Udola...is a small wooden drum containing the six central teeth of the lower jaw of children of nobles...the drum is kept in a special hut (kodo) at the rear of the king's homestead and it is there beaten every morning before sunrise and every evening after sunset. After sunset a horn is blown at the front entrance to the quarters of the royal wives while a few raps are beaten on the drum at the back entrance. As soon as those in court hear the drum they shout their ox-names, the ox-names of their fathers and grandfathers, and the king's ox-name. I have witnessed this scene at the home of Aguaa-war-Akuon.[35]

Although Evans-Pritchard photographed some of the royal emblems during his visit to Aguaa-war-Akuon, the five exposures taken were little more than recording their setting in the very particular context of his being received by the king. They obviously spoke for some time about the issue of the emblems and the history of the Anuak nobility since references to remarks made by Aguaa-war-Akuon are scattered throughout his text. It is worth comparing Evans-Pritchard's images with those taken of the emblems by Elliot-Smith when they were in his possession—or 'custody', as Evans-Pritchard rightly phrases it—presumably at a moment when he was brokering a handover between nobles. Elliot-Smith's images of the emblems are like physical anthropology portraits; the spears and necklaces are photographed against a white surface to enable close scrutiny of their form, and the necklaces are even numbered in the image to enable their identification, a

---

[35] Evans-Pritchard, *Political System of the Anuak*, 57.

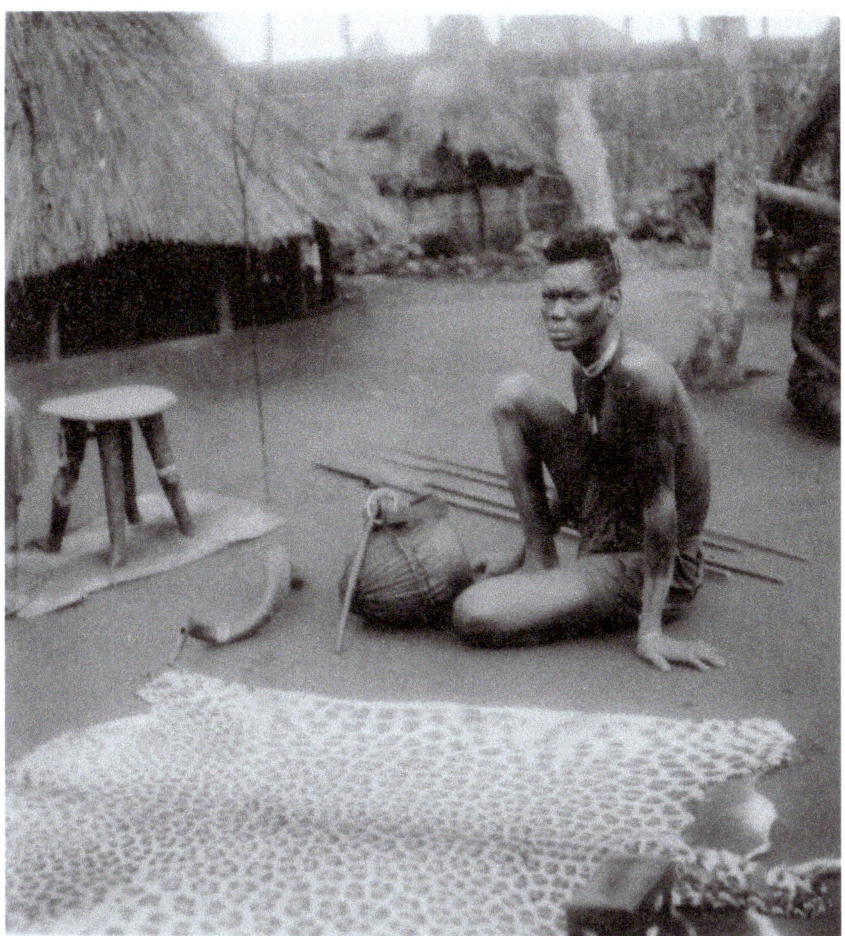

Figure 6.8 Attendant with the royal drum (Udola) at the home of the Anuak king
Aguaa-war-Akuon at Obuodhi village, Jonglei, South Sudan. Photograph by
E. E. Evans-Pritchard, 1935.

further resonance with racial type imagery. Evans-Pritchard reproduces these
images in his Anuak monograph, presumably to better help administrators
recognize the objects in the future. Elliot-Smith himself penned a short article
about the royal emblems, and particularly the royal spear-rest, at the time of
Evans-Pritchard's visit, in which he states that the spear-rest had been lost for
some years 'but was recovered in 1934 and delivered to the custodian. The
photograph shows to what use he put it'.[36] The article in fact reproduces two

---

[36] G. L. Elliot-Smith. 1935. '106. Spear-rest and other tribal heirlooms', *Man*, 35, 96.

images of the spear-rest—the one used by Evans-Pritchard of the spear-rest with spear leaning against it, the roof of a nearby hut in the background, and alongside it a further image of just the spear-rest, with a sheet as a backdrop to delineate its features even better, in classic physical anthropology fashion.

Although, after sunset at Aguaa-war-Akuon's homestead, Evans-Pritchard saw and heard the drum *Udola* being beaten, the horn being blown, and the people living there calling their ox-names, he did not take any photographs of this interesting usage of the emblems in their social context. One is left to wonder—why not? There is, perhaps, a simple explanation, and that is that the activity took place after sunset when sufficient light was unavailable for photography. I think this is likely to be a large part of the explanation for why a number of important social or ritual activities across all of Evans-Pritchard's writings are nowhere found recorded in his photographic archive, taking place in the dim light after sunset or at night when the cooler air brought people together for dances, feasting, and rituals. A particular example of this contrast in visibility, both in terms of action in daylight or night-time, as well as thereby the subsequent photographic record of fieldwork, can be found in Evans-Pritchard's photographs of the work of diviners and healers.

In a short article published in 1953, Evans-Pritchard describes how he witnessed Anuak diviners or 'magicians' (*ajua*) at work. The first type he describes, who may be either men or women, are the *ajuan wäri*, diviners who divine by throwing strips of leather (*wäri*) decorated with brass rings into the air, and seeing how they fall onto a goat's skin in front of them (Figure 6.9). Evans-Pritchard takes several photographs of this activity, one from a standing position in front of the diviner, with a small group of women around her, and two more of the divining activity itself taken with the camera placed on the ground right in front of the diviner, showing that he was seated immediately in front of her. There are two important inferences to be made from these photographs. Firstly, the images are taken with the camera placed on the ground, Evans-Pritchard having first framed the view by peering over into the ground-glass viewer on the top of his Rolleiflex (or more likely, Rolleicord) camera. The Rolleicord was introduced in 1933 as a less expensive version of the Rolleiflex, and Evans-Pritchard first used the 120-size film format used in this type of camera in his 1935 fieldwork. The fact that he placed the camera on the ground to take two exposures of the *ajuan wäri* at work suggests that he was wary of holding the camera as he sat in front of her. Perhaps he felt (or was told?) that photography was not appropriate during a divination session, and so took a couple of images surreptitiously? The second point is that his position shows that he played a central role in the divination session, and was in fact likely to have been the sponsor of the diviner, sitting with her as she divined for him. We know that Evans-Pritchard did this occasionally throughout his fieldwork in order to observe activity that he might not ordinarily get the opportunity to see during a brief visit.

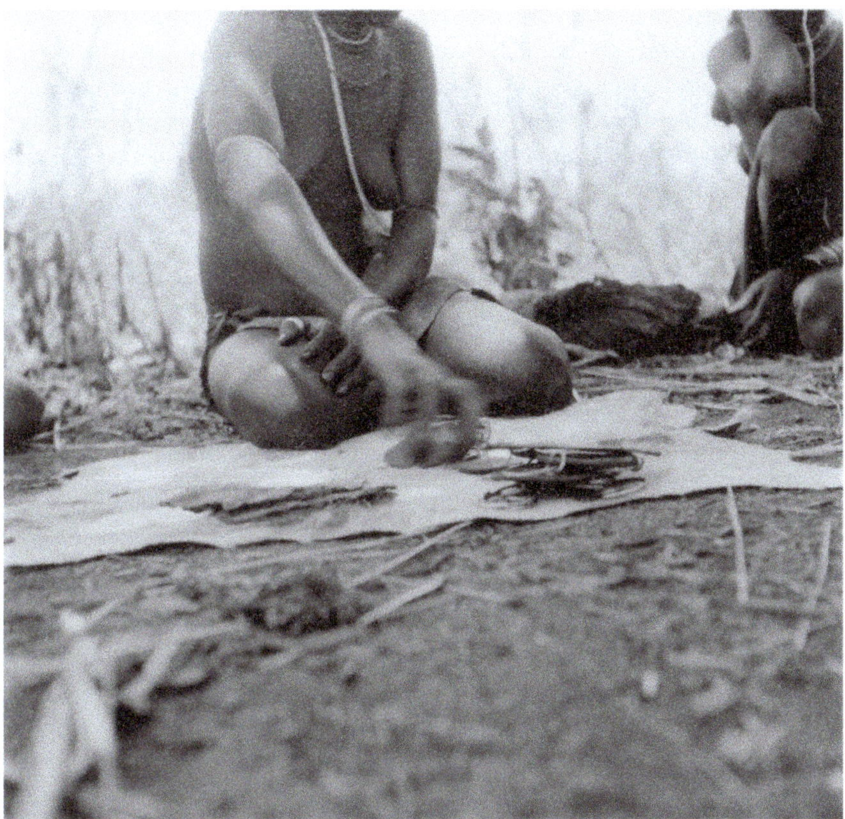

Figure 6.9 Anuak diviner (*ajuan wäri*) throwing strips of leather to observe how they fall. Photograph by E. E. Evans-Pritchard, 1935.

Note, for instance, the fact that Godfrey Lienhardt, who spent more than a year with the Anuak between 1952–4, never saw a séance involving an *ajua* removing *acyeni* (the haunting vengeance of the dead, leading to pains) from a victim, and yet Evans-Pritchard did during his extremely brief visit to Pochalla.[37]

In his account of this séance, Evans-Pritchard first sketches some background to it, stating that when someone falls sick they are treated by an *ajua* to find out the cause and to remove the *acyeni* items from the victim. 'I was told in 1935', he relates, 'that the reason why many people had recently died of sickness in the village of Pocala was that there had been much fighting there in the years before, connected with struggles for power between various nobles, and that many of the

---

[37] G. Lienhardt. 1962. 'The situation of death: an aspect of Anuak philosophy', *Anthropological Quarterly*, 35(2), 85; E. E. Evans-Pritchard. 1953. 'A note on ghostly vengeance among the Anuak of the Anglo-Egyptian Sudan', *Man*, 53, 7.

men who took part in attacks on the village had been slain in it and their ghosts were taking vengeance.' The homestead of a man called Abula, next to which Evans-Pritchard had pitched his tent, was afflicted with *acyeni* sickness, and young women were suffering and collapsing. Returning a few days later, he saw that the family were now consulting a Nuer diviner, who told them to sacrifice a goat. Abula said he did not have a goat, and so the Nuer diviner told Abula to treat the patients in the usual Anuak way. Evans-Pritchard goes on to describe an extraordinary sequence of ritual activities that then took place throughout the hours of darkness, with around 200 people gathered near Abula's homestead in a wide circle, clapping and singing, with the diviners performing at the centre. Now and then the diviners would rush up to the women, grab *acyeni* from their bodies,

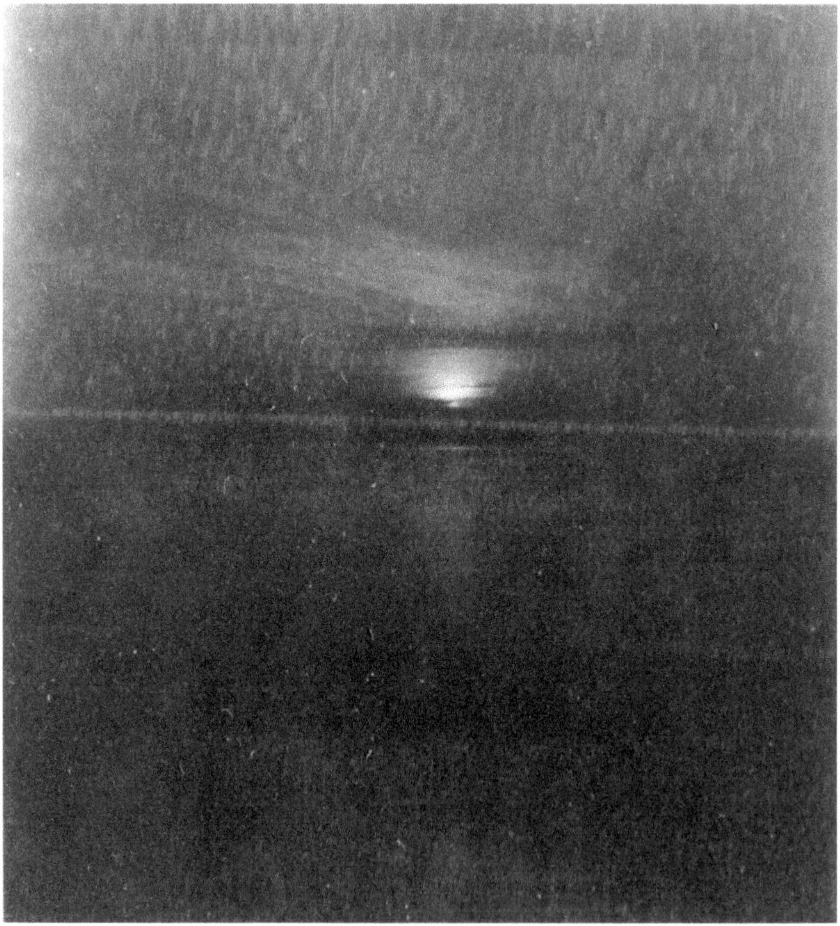

Figure 6.10 The sun setting over Nuerland. Photograph by E. E. Evans-Pritchard, 1935–6.

and throw it into the embers of a fire, dancing into a frenzy. Evans-Pritchard concludes the description with the following account:

> As night lengthened the singing and dancing and clapping of hands grew wilder and the men in the audience stood up. The doctors were now so uncontrollable when dancing that their escorts gave up the attempt to hold them ... [e]xcitement was caused from time to time by the doctors dashing to the fire and either scattering its embers or swinging one of the blazing logs among the spectators, who ran for safety till men were able to pin the doctors' arms from behind. On several occasions the doctors fell prostrate to the ground. The séance continued until close on midnight.[38]

It is one of the most dramatic descriptions of ritual activity in all of Evans-Pritchard's ethnographies, but it did not make it into the 1940 monograph due to its focus on political matters for an administrative audience. It also didn't make it into his photographic archive since all of the activity took place at night. This serves to remind us that the relationship between anthropology and photography, albeit sharing a close relationship and parallel histories, is also, by and large, a daytime relationship, with a curfew of visualization that ends with the setting of the sun (Figure 6.10).

As the Anuak séance reminds us, however, much important social and ritual activity takes place at night, beyond the camera's reach. Evans-Pritchard never used a flash, and few anthropologists ever have. Instead of relying on the photographic image to relay the complexity or nuance of a social scene, as he occasionally did, here Evans-Pritchard conjures up one of his most memorable 'anthropological transparencies', a moment of magic lantern ethnography that brilliantly connects the visual aspects of fieldwork observation and experience with the visualizable as a literary device in his project of translating cultural phenomena.

---

[38] Evans-Pritchard, 'Ghostly vengeance among the Anuak', 7.

7

The participant-photographer

Encountering Nuer ritual

Photography and participant-observation

This chapter examines Evans-Pritchard's Nuer fieldwork photography in the context of the emerging methodology of social anthropology in the early twentieth century—participant-observation. In doing so I also seek to understand the photographs within a more general history of the relationship between anthropological fieldwork and visual methods. I use as a case study Evans-Pritchard's photographs of the Nuer rite of *gorot*, taken during his last fieldwork trip among the Nuer, a period of six weeks in 1936 soon after his visit to the Luo in Kenya (see chapter 8). In thinking through this set of images it will be necessary to keep open two streams of evidential awareness—that of the indexical image (what the photographs show happening before the camera) and that of the archival object (what has happened to them as objects since their original exposure). This dual awareness is essential if we are to understand the notion of photographic evidence as an essentially historical construction, and to see the accrual of meaning around Evans-Pritchard's fieldwork images as reaching beyond the photographic frame towards both archival and situational relationships. Photography's intrinsic relationship to notions of evidence, particularly in anthropology, has often been just as much about the evidential power of the archive as what the image shows; photographs have complex forms of relatedness to other photographs and other ways we make visual assumptions about the world, embodying complex visual and technological relations both within the archive and beyond. Although attention to the relational and material nature of the photograph is evident in some of the best writing on the history of anthropology's visual methods (especially in the work of Elizabeth Edwards), elsewhere analysis has too often been restricted to the evidential possibilities of isolated and decontextualized image content, something that I unpick and problematize in this chapter.

Most analytical work on anthropology's visual projects over the last thirty years or so has focused on the categorization, dissemination, and collection of visual imagery in the nineteenth century, especially in relation to questions of race.[1]

---

[1] See for instance E. Edwards. 1990. 'Photographic "types": the pursuit of method', *Visual Anthropology*, 3(2–3): 235–58.

Most of the essays published in the 1992 volume *Anthropology and Photography*, edited by Elizabeth Edwards—a turning point in the research, interpretation, and publishing on the visual cultures of anthropology—are informed to some extent by theoretical models that had been developed in relation to text (as discussed in chapter 5), which provided a stringent critique of the processes through which anthropology had traditionally made its object and articulated its disciplinary authority. In relation to photography, the methodological and analytical focus engaged with, on the one hand, a broadly Foucaultian configuration of surveillance, gaze, and objectification,[2] and on the other, the influence of semiotics in the reading of images.[3] Photography, because of its analogue and indexical nature—a trace of light reflected off the colonized land and subject person—and given the manner in which it had been objectified, categorized, and controlled in the scientific archive, constituted a potent and fertile field for such analyses. More recent work, certainly in the last ten years or so, has demonstrated how such overly deterministic ways of approaching colonial photography and its archive privileged colonial power relationships at the expense of other minority and alternative histories and glimpses of local stories. Furthermore, such approaches denied the agency of those represented in the photographs, seeing them as distinctly two-dimensional subjects rather than as having the potential for subversion and critique, even in the full face of colonial oppression. It has even been suggested recently that we should see colonial photographs as 'creative actors within, not merely representations of, the development of "anthropological" ideas'.[4]

This noticeable shift in current research directions has had an important influence upon recent writing on the historical relationship between photography and anthropological fieldwork. Photography has been used as evidence to question the legitimacy of long-held assumptions about the existence of a sudden methodological shift towards a more participatory form of fieldwork, as instilled by Malinowski in students at the London School of Economics from the 1920s. The fieldwork of John Layard (1891–1974) on Malakula, for instance, which he began in 1914, the same year as Malinowski, was also influenced by the older A. C. Haddon, whose guidance can be seen to have shaped the photographic activities of both anthropologists. Haddon had written a long appendix on fieldwork photography in the 1912 edition of the British Association's *Notes and*

---

[2] For instance in M. Foucault. 1979. *Discipline and Punish: The Birth of the Prison*, trans. Alan Sheridan. New York: Pantheon; D. Green. 1984. 'Classified subjects—photography and anthropology: the technology of power', *Ten8*, 14, 30–7; J. Tagg. 1988. *The Burden of Representation: Essays on Photographies and Histories*. Basingstoke and New York: Palgrave Macmillan. Geismar expense of other ways of reading the archive, minority and alternative histories and glimpses of local stories.man is le.

[3] In particular the work of R. Barthes. 1977. *Image-Music-Text*, trans. Stephen Heath. New York: Hill and Wang, as elaborated in B. Street. 1992. 'British popular anthropology: exhibiting and photographing the other'. In *Anthropology and Photography 1860–1920*, edited by E. Edwards (New Haven, CT, and London: Yale University Press).

[4] H. Geismar. 2006. 'Malakula: a photographic collection', *Comparative Studies in Society and History*, 48, 524.

Queries on Anthropology: for the use Travellers and Residents in Uncivilized Lands, and we know of the influence of this text on Malinowski's fieldwork from diary entries such as '[t]hen I wrote my diary and tried to synthesize my results, reviewing Notes and Queries... Read some more N&Q and loaded my camera. Then I went into the village.'[5] The text of the 1912 edition of *Notes and Queries* makes it clear that photography was seen as a crucial tool in a more responsive and participatory method of fieldwork, arguing that 'for anthropological work a snap-shot camera is quite indispensable; many incidents must be seized as they occur. Some people will not consent to be photographed and must be taken instantaneously, without their knowledge.'[6] The suitability of a mobile snapshot camera for the seizure or capture of 'incidents' can be compared to the concern with more 'scientific' photography (physical types, artefacts), for which a stand camera was considered more appropriate: 'a certain number of typical individuals should always be taken as large as possible, full face and exact side view; the lens should be on a level with the face'.[7] It is perhaps surprising, given the influence of both Haddon and *Notes and Queries* on Layard's fieldwork, that an attention to such 'scientific'-reference photography is absent from his archive. One reason for this may be the influence on Layard's theoretical interests of W. H. R. Rivers, whose emphasis upon the genealogical method of investigation had less use for physical type imagery. Layard's archive, Herle argues, thereby already suggests a transition from a more typological to a more sociological mode of enquiry, in which 'the developing observational style at times breaks through to a much more participatory and experiential mode'.[8] This process is also shown to a certain extent in the archive of another early fieldworker, Diamond Jenness, in the D'Entrecasteaux Islands in 1911–12, whose albums show 'an evident tension between personal impression and scientific expression' and whose photographs demonstrate 'a nascent observational model' and 'non-interventionist quality' that 'challenge the stereotype of pre-Malinowskian fieldwork as distanced and non-participatory'.[9]

Ironically, despite our greater knowledge of Malinowski's photographic output, thanks largely to scholars such as Michael Young, the relationship between his photography and fieldwork methodology remains largely unanalysed. One interesting observation that Young makes is that, in his emerging functionalism, Malinowski was subconsciously anxious to photograph the context of social activity, rather than the detail, which resulted in a methodology that privileged

---

[5] B. Malinowski. 1967. *A Diary in the Strict Sense of the Term.* London: Routledge and Kegan Paul, 30.

[6] B. Freire-Marreco and J. L. Myres (eds). 1912. *Notes and Queries on Anthropology.* London: Royal Anthropological Institute (4th edition), 268.

[7] Freire-Marreco and Myres, *Notes and Queries,* 269.

[8] A. Herle. 2008. 'John Layard's photographs on Malakula: from observational to participant field research'. In *Moving Images: John Layard, Fieldwork and Photography in Malakula since 1914,* edited by H. Geismar and A. Herle. Adelaide: Crawford House Press and University of Hawaii, 95.

[9] E. Edwards. 2001. *Raw Histories: Photographs, Anthropology and Museums.* Oxford: Berg, 89.

the middle distance.[10] This is a tempting hypothesis but it doesn't really stand much scrutiny; Malinowski's pictorial interests have been shown to have largely determined his approach rather than his interests in visually recording social context, as he himself makes clear in his lament about his fieldwork photography in the Appendix to *Coral Gardens and Their Magic*, where he admits that his lack of interest in photographing social context was 'a deadly sin against the functional method, the main point of which is that form matters less than function'.[11] Although his diaries show an ongoing concern with photography throughout his fieldwork, there is little sense of a nascent participatory style of photography in his archive. So in the end, as Elizabeth Edwards concludes, Malinowski's photography 'does not appear to use photography as a site of interaction with his indigenous subjects in a way many anthropologists of the period did. That is, photography served as a crucial tool of his observation but not of his participation.'[12]

This serves to remind us of the importance of reading photographs in the context of the whole archive as well as historical developments in the discipline, using it to reinterpret previously assumed fieldwork relationships. As Edwards argues, the intention that directed Jenness's image-making created a specific form of anthropological gaze, and this 'intention, meshed with the evidential, articulates a meaning to be communicated. However, inscription outlives intention by the very nature of the photograph, and thus we have the beginning of a refiguration.'[13] In other words, a photographer may have intended one thing, but photographs have their own trajectories once they are sent out into the world. The content of a photograph can transcend both the ethnographer's original intention and their subsequent communication of ideas, and can be recoded many times, legitimizing its subsequent use as evidence in often radically altered cultural contexts. For me, the usefulness of this approach is only tempered by an awareness that the 'recodability' argument often in fact just seeks to substitute one set of evidential readings (reinterpretation) for another (ethnographic intention), reconsolidating rather than questioning anthropology's relationship to the indexical nature of the image. Are Layard's photographs evidence of a more sociological and participatory approach to anthropological fieldwork? What is the evidential basis for the assertion that Jenness's photographs do not show the 'tension of intrusion' by a fieldworker?[14] The value of any archival reinterpretation is of course limited

---

[10] M. Young. 1998. *Malinowski's Kiriwina: Fieldwork Photography 1915–1918*. Chicago and London: Chicago University Press, 19.

[11] B. Malinowski. 1935. *Coral Gardens and Their Magic: A Study of the Methods of Tilling the Soil and of Agricultural Rites in the Trobriand Islands. Vol. 1: The Description of Gardening*. London: Allen & Unwin, 462.

[12] E. Edwards. 2000. Review of *Malinowski's Kiriwina: Fieldwork Photography 1915–1918* by M. Young, *American Anthropologist*, New Series, 102(3), 600.

[13] Edwards, *Raw Histories*, 89.   [14] Edwards, *Raw Histories*, 89.

by its ability to offer a nuanced and reflexive critique of the evidential basis upon which it rests.

The problems surrounding evidential value and archival reinterpretation are particularly acute in the case of an archive such as Evans-Pritchard's. During the process of cataloguing the some 4,000 photographic objects in the collection it became clear that the photography of his first period of fieldwork in late 1926, among the Ingessana of Blue Nile Province in Sudan, was sometimes markedly different from that of his subsequent Zande fieldwork. Among the Ingessana, Evans-Pritchard took a number of physical type photographs, usually both profile and full-face, occasionally using his coat for a backdrop (see chapter 2), whereas such scientific-reference imagery is entirely absent from his Zande photographs, although they were taken on the same expedition to the Sudan. Although Evans-Pritchard took a large number of Zande portraits, they are all characterized by a less scrutinizing style and more distanced position, and although often repetitive (such as the series of portraits of the sons of Prince Rikita) each image allows for significant personal and cultural inflection. On the surface, a cross-section through such an archive could be taken as evidence for a shift in Evans-Pritchard's fieldwork methodology—a development represented in the retreating focal depth of the images—from scientific scrutiny to relaxed portraiture, from an approach where context is intentionally excluded to one where context crowds in. Following Edwards's formulation just cited that 'intention, meshed with the evidential, articulates a meaning', we might interpret a progression in Evans-Pritchard's photographic intentions as well as communication of meaning, suggesting that the Ingessana photographs demonstrate the characteristic concerns of a more limited survey-style ethnography, whereas his Zande portraits show social relationships established over time, and thereby an indirect product of the longer-term fieldwork method. Tracing our development from the surface of the image, it could be argued that Evans-Pritchard's archive demonstrates vividly the identity crisis of British anthropology in the 1920s, with radically different notions of what constituted a 'scientific' approach laid bare in the photographic record.

The evidence for this interpretation is complicated by the written record, which in fact indicates not a linear progression in Evans-Pritchard's methodology, nor any identity crisis, but the coexistence of parallel ethnographic investigations with differing methodological concerns, one of which was being undertaken on behalf of his supervisor C. G. Seligman. The written record for instance states that Evans-Pritchard did in fact carry out physical measurements during his Zande fieldwork,[15] and that although not taken according to accepted methods, six of his Zande portraits were cropped and enlarged to provide a comparison of 'Zande types' in Seligman's survey of the Sudan.[16] Evans-Pritchard later wrote that

---

[15] C. G. Seligman and B. Z. Seligman. 1932. *Pagan Tribes of the Nilotic Sudan*. London: Routledge, 496.
[16] Seligman and Seligman, *Pagan Tribes*, Plate LVI.

on his first expeditions to the Sudan he had 'taken around…callipers and a height-measuring rod…to please my teacher Professor Seligman. I have always regarded, and still regard, such measurements as lacking scientific value, even being almost meaningless; but so it was at that time.'[17] Evans-Pritchard's Ingessana photographs can in one sense be understood as those of a research assistant, operating according to the needs of Seligman's project. This example demonstrates the inherent problem of using photographic content alone to reinterpret the archive, since there is a tendency simply to replace one set of naive assumptions about the evidential value of photographic inscription with another. The interpretation of retreating focal depth in Evans-Pritchard's Ingessana and Zande portraits shows how a metaphor can heavily influence our reading of intention, evidence, and meaning, as I mentioned earlier in relation to Young's metaphorical reading of Malinowski's use of the middle distance. Further, it excludes other possibilities, such as the agency of Azande in shaping the photographic record, an idea I explore in chapter 4, as well as the apparently contradictory existence of parallel and contrasting fieldwork methodologies (such as survey and participant-observation) rather than a smooth, or even abrupt, Malinowskian revolution.

Photographing ritual

I now consider further the question of evidence and interpretation in the photographic archive in relation to two further abstractions: those of seriality and partiality, by which I mean the relational situation of a photograph to others in a series, as well as the often fragmentary nature of the series or archive itself. The most obvious example of the relationship between photographic seriality and the methodology of participant-observation in Evans-Pritchard's entire collection, or for that matter any that I am aware of, is the series of twelve images devoted to the initiation of Kamanga as a *binza* (witch doctor) that I discussed in chapter 3, where Evans-Pritchard embodies the role of the participant-photographer in a dramatic fashion, standing on the edge of the ritual 'grave' where he ritually acts as sponsor of the initiate, throwing offerings into the hole, while at the same time taking images of the ritual.

Around 1934 Evans-Pritchard purchased a Rolleiflex or Rolleicord camera and with this his photography changed, becoming more prolific and creating photographic sequences in a more systematic way. Without doubt, the most extensive of these sequences relates to his record of the Nuer rite of *gorot* which he witnessed in 1936. After carrying out a brief survey of the Luo of western Kenya, Evans-Pritchard spent seven weeks in western Nuerland, his fourth and final piece of

---

[17] E. E. Evans-Pritchard. 1973. 'Some recollections on fieldwork in the twenties', *Anthropological Quarterly*, 46(4), 242.

fieldwork among this Nilotic group. Most of this time (five weeks) was spent in Nyueny, the home village of a youth called Nhial, whom Evans-Pritchard had employed on both his first and second expeditions to Nuerland in 1930 and 1931. This long-term connection with Nhial meant that, as in 1935 when he visited the home village of another former servant Tiop (at Mancom at the mouth of the Nyanding River), he was able to conduct fieldwork 'as a friend of the family'.[18] This binding of the ethnographer into Nuer social relations had been something entirely lacking in Evans-Pritchard's longer, and yet ultimately frustrating, first two expeditions to Nuerland. This shift in social acceptance also had a dramatic impact upon his photography. Whereas the political situation in 1930 meant that he had 'abstained from photographing a single cow',[19] as a result of the mistrust caused by punitive strikes against Nuer herds by the colonial administration, his photographs from both 1935 and 1936 show that he was at liberty to photograph within the cattle camps of his hosts. Although relatively brief, the improved access to Nuer social and ritual activities that Evans-Pritchard enjoyed in 1936 meant that the information he gathered then came to dominate his subsequent analysis published in *Nuer Religion*.[20]

According to Evans-Pritchard's published account, the Nuer rite of *gorot* was carried out by female diviners (*tiet*) to ensure the fertility of a couple married at an unusually early age.[21] It involved the suffocation of an ox by blocking its orifices with grass, the cooking and feeding of some of its meat to the young couple, the circling of the couple's hut by the wife's young brother with the boiled hump of the ox on the end of a spear, and the smearing of blood and butter on the body. When cataloguing these photographs, it became apparent to me that, although subsequently jumbled and disconnected within the archive, Evans-Pritchard had taken three films (thirty photographs) at the time of this ceremony, of which one image was published in *Nuer Religion* as Plate 3. According to his account, *gorot* is very different to most Nuer sacrifices since the ox was not stabbed through the heart but suffocated, no invocation to God was made before it was carried out, and since female diviners (*tiet*) were involved when senior male family members were more usual. Although it bore similarities to sacrifices to the python-spirit in which she-goats were sometimes suffocated after the manner of a python, and also probably having been borrowed from the neighbouring Dinka, Evans-Pritchard was unsure

---

[18] E. E. Evans-Pritchard. 1974 [1956]. *Nuer Religion*. New York and Oxford: Oxford University Press, 35.

[19] E. E. Evans-Pritchard. 1937. 'The economic life of the Nuer: cattle (part 1)', *Sudan Notes and Records*, 20(3), 242.

[20] Evans-Pritchard's Nuer fieldwork comprised four expeditions: 1930 (three and a half months at Yoinyang, Pakur, and Muot Dit); 1931 (five months at Nyanding River, Yakwach and Kurmayom); 1935 (approximately six weeks at Yakwach and Mancom); 1936 (seven weeks in western Nuerland among the Leek (Lek) Nuer, five of them in Nyueny). For a detailed account of Evans-Pritchard's relationship with the Sudanese administration see D. H. Johnson. 1982. 'Evans-Pritchard, the Nuer, and the Sudan Political Service', *African Affairs*, 81(323), 231–46.

[21] Evans-Pritchard, *Nuer Religion*, 217–18.

of how to consider it aside from it being a notable aberration, admitting that 'I cannot explain the symbolism, if it has any'.[22]

Just what the *gorot* rite might symbolize within Nuer ritual practice formed the basis of a later heated debate between anthropologists T. O. Beidelman, John Burton, and William Arens in the correspondence pages of the journal *Man* between 1969 and 1976, in which Evans-Pritchard's description and published photograph of the *gorot* rite were drawn on as evidence on both sides.[23] Beidelman's original comment was a brief suggestion that the symbolism of *gorot* was 'to contain the taint transferred within the animal...that the sacrificial animal absorbs the polluting aspects of the couple who were married somewhat irregularly, and that this taint is then mastered by being consumed as flesh'.[24] In reply, Arens and Burton objected to this, arguing that *gorot* should not be understood as a sacrifice at all, and that indeed Evans-Pritchard makes this point himself. Although Evans-Pritchard does claim that 'what I witnessed should not be regarded as a sacrifice at all',[25] he titles the published illustration of *gorot* as 'Sacrifice of ox by suffocation'.[26] His use of the word sacrifice in the image caption was probably a convenient shorthand, but it also adds to the ambiguity of his interpretation. Arens and Burton further argue that Beidelman's proposition— that the taint of an unusual marital union is being mastered through the consumption of the ox's flesh—is not in accord with existing evidence about Nuer ritual practice, which usually privileges the position of sacrificial blood in the removal of taint or evil. They then appeal to the evidence of Evans-Pritchard's published photographs of Nuer ritual to argue that it is 'typical of sacrifices...for the participants to shave their heads and affect special bodily ornaments. However, a glance at a photograph of the ritual in question indicates that here this is not the case'[27] (Figure 7.1). In formulating their own interpretation, Arens and Burton again turn to the published image: 'The photograph of the *gorot* ritual... depicts forcing grass into the orifices of the ox. Unlike Nuer sacrifices, in which there is a preference as to which side the animal should fall, in this instance it is actually positioned on its left side.'[28] According to Arens and Burton, the ox's death by suffocation and the spitting-out of the ox meat were symbolic of a marriage that, although consummated, had not produced offspring. Other elements of the rite symbolized the desired state—the production of a child.

---

[22] Evans-Pritchard, *Nuer Religion*, 218.

[23] T. O. Beidelman. 1969. 'The ox and Nuer sacrifice', *Man*, New Series, 4(2), 290–1; 1976. 'Death by suffocation', *Man*, New Series, 11(1), 119–21; 1976. 'Death by suffocation', *Man*, New Series, 11(4), 591; W. Arens and J. W. Burton. 1975. 'Death by suffocation', *Man*, New Series, 10(2), 313–15; J. W. Burton. 1976. 'Death by suffocation', *Man*, New Series, 11(4), 588–91.

[24] Beidelman, 'The ox and Nuer sacrifice', 290.

[25] Evans-Pritchard, *Nuer Religion*, 217.   [26] Evans-Pritchard, *Nuer Religion*, 68.

[27] Arens and Burton, 'Death by suffocation', 314.

[28] Arens and Burton, 'Death by suffocation', 314.

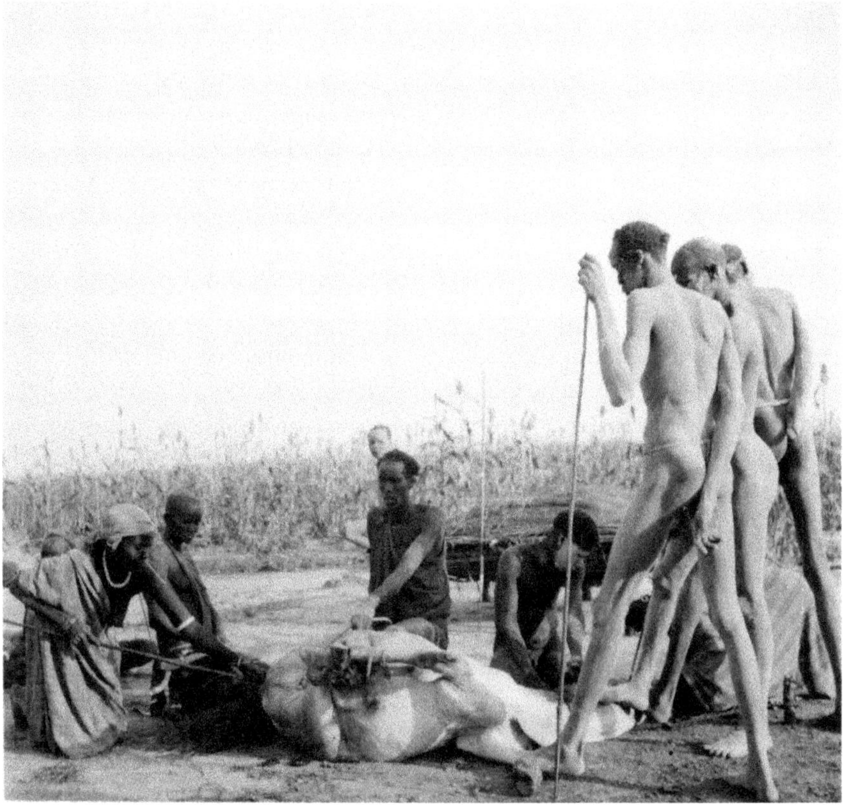

Figure 7.1 'Sacrifice of ox by suffocation', published as Plate III in *Nuer Religion*, Nyueny village, Unity State, South Sudan. Photograph by E. E. Evans-Pritchard, 1936.

Beidelman's defence focuses upon the definition of sacrifice within Nuer religious practice as well as the distinction between magic and religion, but he also returns to Arens and Burton's point about the ritual preparedness of people depicted in Evans-Pritchard's photographs:

> A. & B. observe that Nuer shave their heads and wear special ornaments when involved in sacrifice and note that this is not the case in a photo of *gorot*, arguing that this demonstrates that *gorot* is not a form of sacrifice (1956: plate 3). Photographs are sometimes deceptive, yet in all the other photos of sacrifice in this same book, most of the protagonists appear unshaved and adorned in no special manner   (plates 8, 9, 10, 11)[29]

[29] Beidelman, 'Death by suffocation', 11(1), 120.

The question of context hangs over not only the published image of *gorot* but over all the other images in *Nuer Religion*, and yet the appeal to the veracity of this image as an unmediated window onto Evans-Pritchard's witnessing of Nuer ritual continues. This particular debate about the significance of the *gorot* rite certainly demonstrates an ongoing ambivalence in anthropology's relationship to the archival image, in which both truth and deception are equally possible outcomes of the interpretive process.

It appears that Evans-Pritchard took three films of photographs at the time of the *gorot* rite at Nyueny village. In the fullest account Evans-Pritchard gives of his five-week stay there, he also suggests that the success of this fieldwork came as a result of a gradual build-up of trust with the community:

> It [Nyueny] was not selected at random but was chosen because it is the home of my servant Nhial whose family already knew me. Though his father resides there it is the village of his maternal kin and they had known for some years about my work. I was therefore sure of a friendly welcome and consequently it was possible to make a rapid survey. Had I been a complete stranger the enquiry could not have been accomplished in the short time I had to give it, because Nuer oppose any investigation till they have seasoned one and, even then, are stubborn informants.[30]

Sometime during his stay at Nyueny, he hears of a ritual about to take place, and is evidently allowed by the community to witness it at close quarters. Spending his time surveying the kinship connections of each and every one of the 130 inhabitants of the village, Evans-Pritchard and his camera were no doubt familiar to all. One of the films he shoots during the ceremony focuses upon the suffocation of the ox (Figure 7.2), another the young boy circling the hut of the young couple with the ox's boiled hump (Figure 7.5), and a third film contains portraits of seated participants and onlookers as well as possibly the distribution of cooked meat (Figure 7.6). The textual description of the *gorot* ritual in *Nuer Religion*, however, includes additional elements such as the distribution of cooked ox meat to the married couple and other kin, as well as ritual activity inside the hut by the female diviner.

Evans-Pritchard's photographic record of *gorot*, then, is marked by an attention to the seriality of two elements of the rite, and yet partiality in its record of the overall event. One reason for the partiality of the record may lie in the proxemics of Evans-Pritchard's involvement with events; certain areas or elements of the rite were not judged appropriate to photograph, or some events took place inside the hut of the young couple, which Evans-Pritchard does not seem to have entered.

---

[30] E. E. Evans-Pritchard. 1945. *Some Aspects of Marriage and Family Among the Nuer*. Rhodes Livingstone Paper No. 11. Livingstone: The Rhodes Livingstone Institute, 29.

However, most other elements not photographed, such as the smearing of butter on the participants, happened outside and presumably for all to witness. It is noticeable both here and elsewhere in the archive that anthropological photography rarely takes place inside the African hut. There are a few examples of Evans-Pritchard having attempted it, with failed results due to low light levels. I return to the issue of anthropology, photography, and the dark in chapter 6 in relation to ritual activity that takes place after sunset. Here however I just note the dangers of metaphorical readings of inside/outside when technical restrictions are probably the main constraint, making the creation of photographic images inside small dark spaces impossible. We know that Evans-Pritchard frequently sat inside Nuer huts, but he normally photographed outwards towards the light, as anyone would if they hoped for a successful exposure.

Evans-Pritchard's record of the *gorot* event is marked then by intense photographic engagement with two elements of the ritual activity, and complete non-engagement with other elements. Just why he was so careful to visually record two aspects of the rite but not to build up a representative series of the overall rite is a question that has no definitive answer, and raises interesting questions, as well as providing important evidence, about the role of photography within his Nuer fieldwork.

Film 7

The group of eleven prints in Evans-Pritchard's archive identified as from film 7 (Figure 7.2) show the suffocation of the ox as part of the *gorot* rite. It is probably the most ethnographically distinctive aspect of this particular rite since it differs from the more usual Nuer sacrificial method of sacrificing an ox by piercing its heart with a spear. Evans-Pritchard describes it in this way:

> An ox was thrown and its forelegs and back legs tied in pairs. It was then slowly suffocated, grass being first pushed up its anus with a stick, and then into its mouth and nostrils (Plate III). During its sufferings the husband and a youth of his age-set, the wife and a maiden of about her age, and a small boy and a small girl sat on its flank. After a while they rose and the ox's throat was slit.[31]

As discussed earlier, the abnormality of this method of killing the ox, in addition to the lack of any consecration of the beast or invocation to God before killing it, is central to the interpretation of the rite within Nuer religious practice. Evans-

---

[31] Evans-Pritchard, *Nuer Religion*, 217–18.

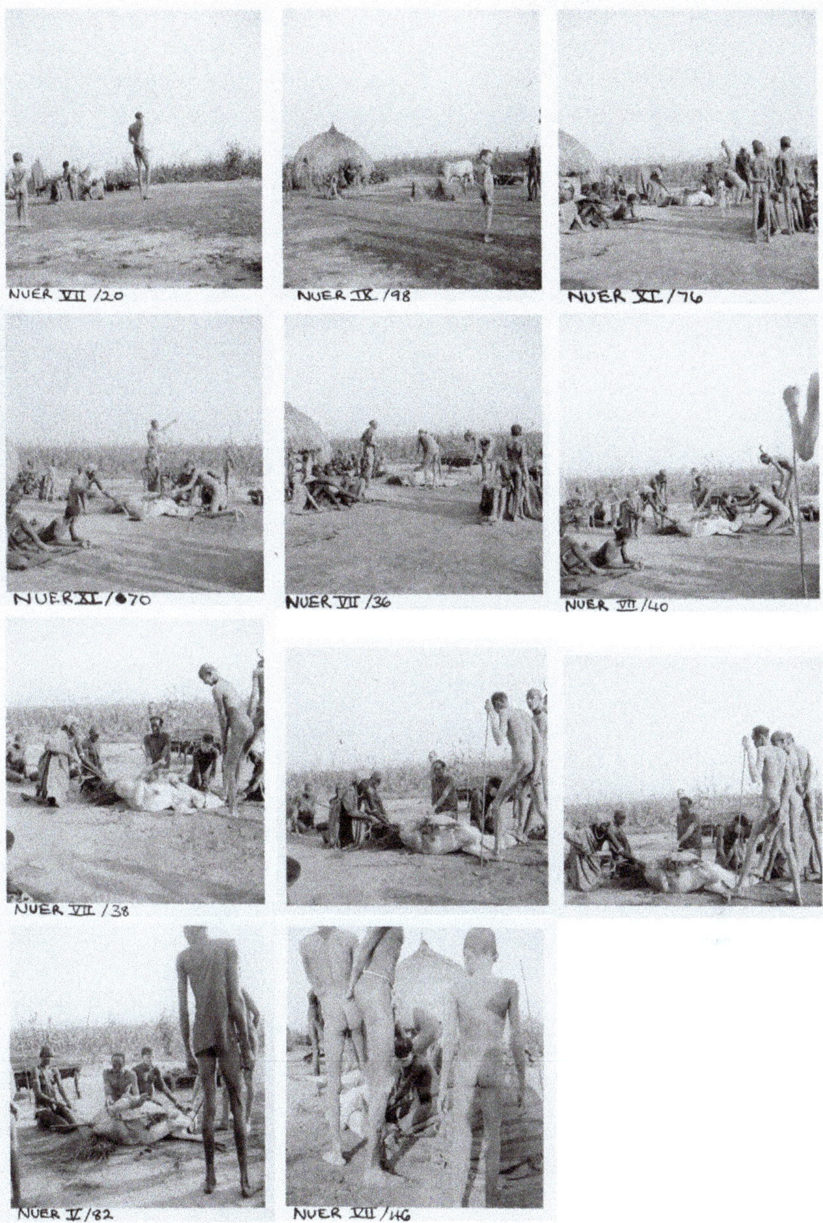

Figure 7.2 Eleven prints identified as film 7, showing the suffocation of an ox as part of the Nuer rite of *gorot*, Nyueny village, Unity State, South Sudan. Photographs by E. E. Evans-Pritchard, 1936.

Pritchard's repetition of views of the killing method in this sequence indicate a desire to record something of ethnographic interest, perhaps rarity. An especial awareness of Nuer sacrificial method in the form of the presentation, consecration, invocation, and immolation of a beast was later to be central to Evans-Pritchard's analysis of Nuer religious thought.[32] Although frame numbers are not recorded, the photographs demonstrate Evans-Pritchard's movement within the ritual arena; he begins to photograph from where onlookers are gathered (Figure 7.3), getting gradually closer in his desire to record the technique of suffocation, until he is

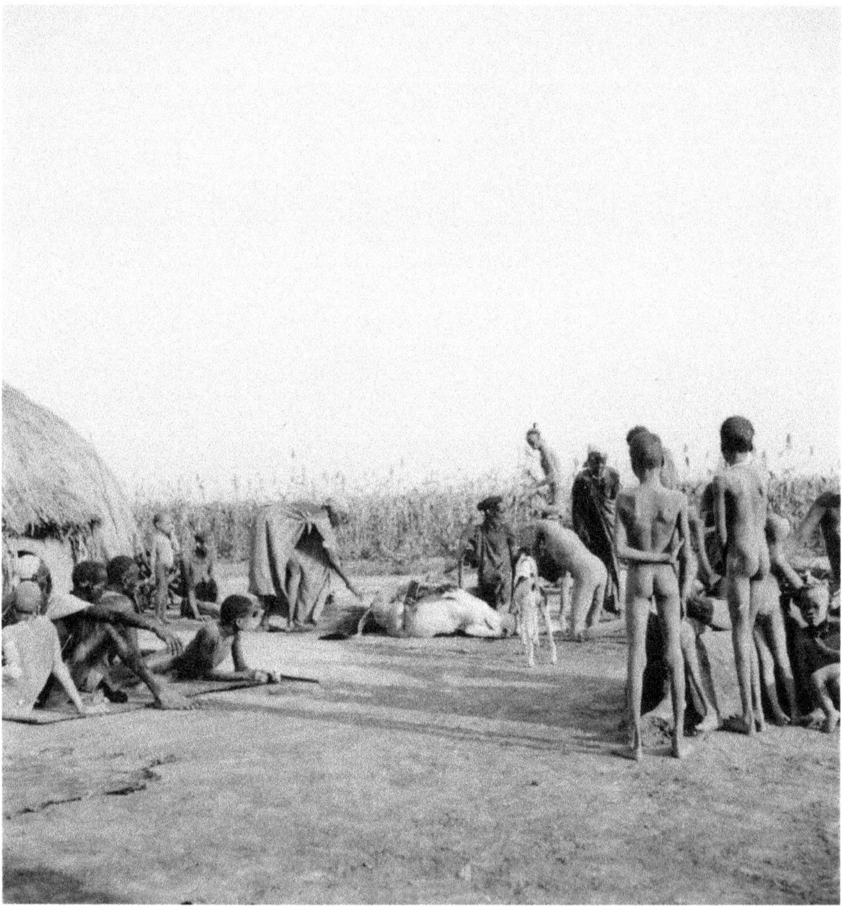

Figure 7.3 Suffocation of an ox, part of the Nuer rite of *gorot*, Nyueny village, Unity State, South Sudan. Photograph by E. E. Evans-Pritchard, 1936.

[32] Evans-Pritchard, *Nuer Religion*, 215.

finally standing next to the female diviner (*tiet*) and is able to record the stuffing of grass into the ox's anus. He then moves round the assisting senior male family members to record the insertion of grass into the ox's nostrils (Figure 7.4).

Although the ox suffocation forms a series within this film, there are no images recording the sitting on the ox by the husband or other ritual participants, an element which forms an important part of not only Evans-Pritchard's description but also subsequent interpretation of the rite.[33] The proxemics of Evans-Pritchard's movement within the ritual arena are of interest here since the

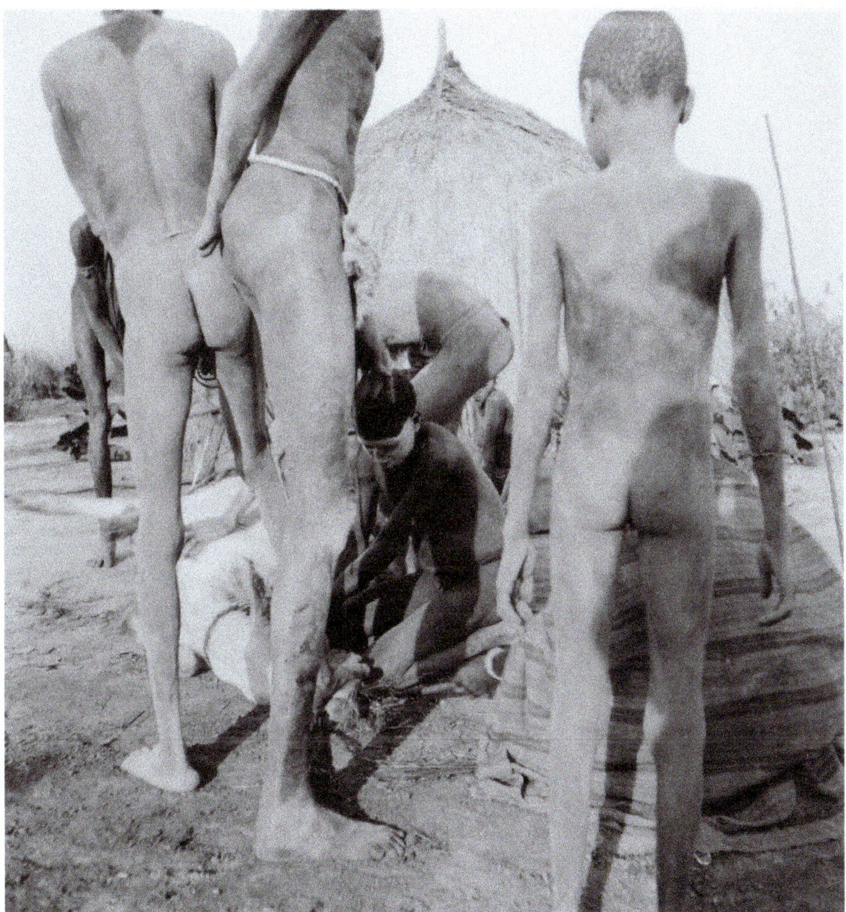

Figure 7.4 Inserting grass into the ox's nostrils, part of the Nuer rite of *gorot*, Nyueny village, Unity State, South Sudan. Photograph by E. E. Evans-Pritchard, 1936.

[33] Beidelman, 'The ox and Nuer sacrifice', 290; Arens and Burton, 'Death by suffocation', 314.

sequence demonstrates his movement from a more distanced position (of lower social status or relevance to the couple involved) to one very close to the activity itself (highest social status or connection to the couple). This movement through social and ritual space was of course occasioned by Evans-Pritchard's desire to record close detail of the suffocation, but it also demonstrates a tolerance or acceptance by the Nyueny community of his movement into the heart of the ritual arena—perhaps something only possible due to having known Nhial for five years, whose own standing within the community had no doubt increased also.

Both the immediacy and performative flow of the suffocation event is perhaps why Evans-Pritchard takes so many similar images of the suffocation, revealing a

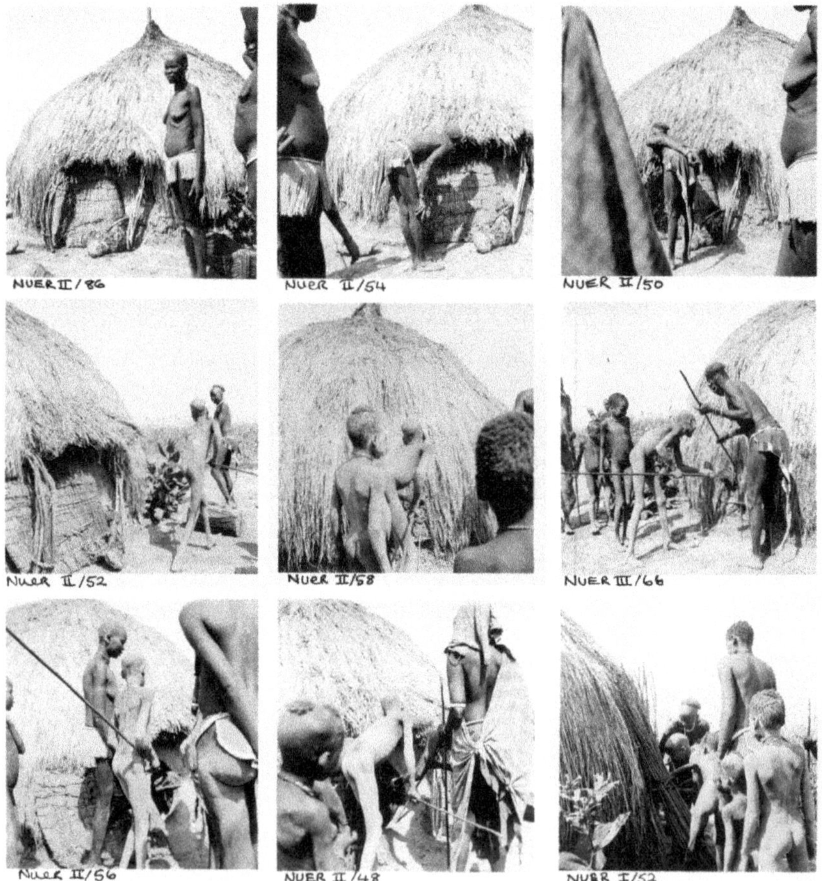

Figure 7.5 Nine prints identified as film 9, showing the circling of the young couple's hut as part of the Nuer rite of *gorot*, Nyueny village, Unity State, South Sudan. Photograph by E. E. Evans-Pritchard, 1936.

heightened concern with capturing in a cinematographic manner the temporal flow of events. Most fieldworkers have probably also experienced this repetitious element in their own fieldwork photography, with some significant situations leading to numerous exposures in an attempt to circumscribe the experience, or perhaps rather to capture it from the all too rapid flow of experience. And there is also the added anxiety of not knowing how close one might get, and closer usually means better images. As he gets gradually closer he is able to get a better view, leading to another exposure. The question then is, why gradually closer? Was it something to do with the social expectations of those attending the rite, as I explored also in the context of Kamanga's initiation ritual in chapter 3? By considering the seriality of the archive, the temporal relationships between images, we get an insight into Evans-Pritchard's engagement with the medium during key moments of fieldwork, and how that engagement was shaped and influenced by local social and cultural factors.

Film 9

The series of nine prints identified as belonging to film 9 (Figure 7.5) relate to the circling of the young couple's hut with the boiled hump of the suffocated ox. Evans-Pritchard describes what he saw:

> The door of the hut was then closed and the butter was placed on the fire. While it was melting, a boy, the wife's brother, circled the hut outside with the boiled hump of the ox on the point of a fishing-spear. When he stuck the hump through the first window of the hut the diviner asked 'what will you give me?' and someone in the hut answered that she would give a brown calf. The action was repeated at the other windows of the hut, the answer referring to either a brown or black calf. Then the door was opened and the diviner hung round the wife's neck the stomach lining of the ox and the skin of its umbilicus to which brass rings and part of its tail had been attached.[34]

In comparison to the ritual elements surrounding the suffocation aspect of the ritual, in this series of photographs Evans-Pritchard seems to attempt to construct a visual sequence, beginning with the female diviner standing outside the hut, leading the boy around the windows, and finally the opening of the door and the feeding of pieces of meat to the couple. In several of the images Evans-Pritchard does not have a direct view, but instead we gain a vivid impression of his position within a gathered group of onlookers, with family members all around him. All of the images are taken from a position adjacent to the door of the hut, suggesting that he did not follow the boy as

---

[34] Evans-Pritchard, *Nuer Religion*, 218.

he was led around the hut by the female diviner. Although he states in his account that the door of the hut was closed and then butter was placed on the fire, we must assume that he was told this information, since the photographs show that he remained on the outside to witness the circling of the hut. Although he records the female diviner offering meat to the couple, there is no photograph of the *tiet* placing the ritually important parts of the ox around the wife's neck, possibly suggesting that his view of this stage was impeded by other onlookers who were evidently beginning to gather closely around the doorway at this point to witness.

Film 4

The series of ten images identified as film 4 in the archive (Figure 7.6) are a mixed group of mostly portraits taken at the time of the *gorot* event. They may have been taken during the wait for the rite to begin, but one of the images shows a group of youths and others gathered on the spot where the ox was killed, with what may be the indistinct form of the ox on the ground visible between them, suggesting that these images were perhaps taken at some point after the suffocation. Three of them were taken with the camera resting on the ground, which Evans-Pritchard props up and turns slightly to the left in order to take a portrait of a youth sitting nearby. In only one of the other portraits is the subject seemingly aware of the photographer's attention—that of a smiling youth. This print has been marked by a printer for cropping on the right side, but evidently was not used since it does not seem to appear in any of Evans-Pritchard's publications. These images vividly demonstrate the use made of the twin lens reflex camera to take photographs in an inconspicuous manner by lining up the portrait by looking down into the top-viewer and taking the image from chest-height, angling the camera upwards for the portrait of the man with the ivory arm-ring, and downwards towards a seated man with an ornament tied at the back of his head. All of the images in this film are of people seated or standing in the homestead, and the series is revealing of the embodied ethnographer moving around Nuer social space in a peripatetic manner. Evans-Pritchard described Nuer ritual as:

> a rather lengthy affair, and for a European rather tedious to assist at. He has to sit in the sun for several hours listening to addresses that are difficult for him to follow. Some of the sentences may be inaudible, the speaker speaking too low or having his back turned to the audience, who may also be talking among themselves.[35]

It would be easy to over-interpret film 4 in the context of its connection with the *gorot* event. It seems clear that Evans-Pritchard did not use film 4 to document Nuer

---

[35] Evans-Pritchard, *Nuer Religion*, 209.

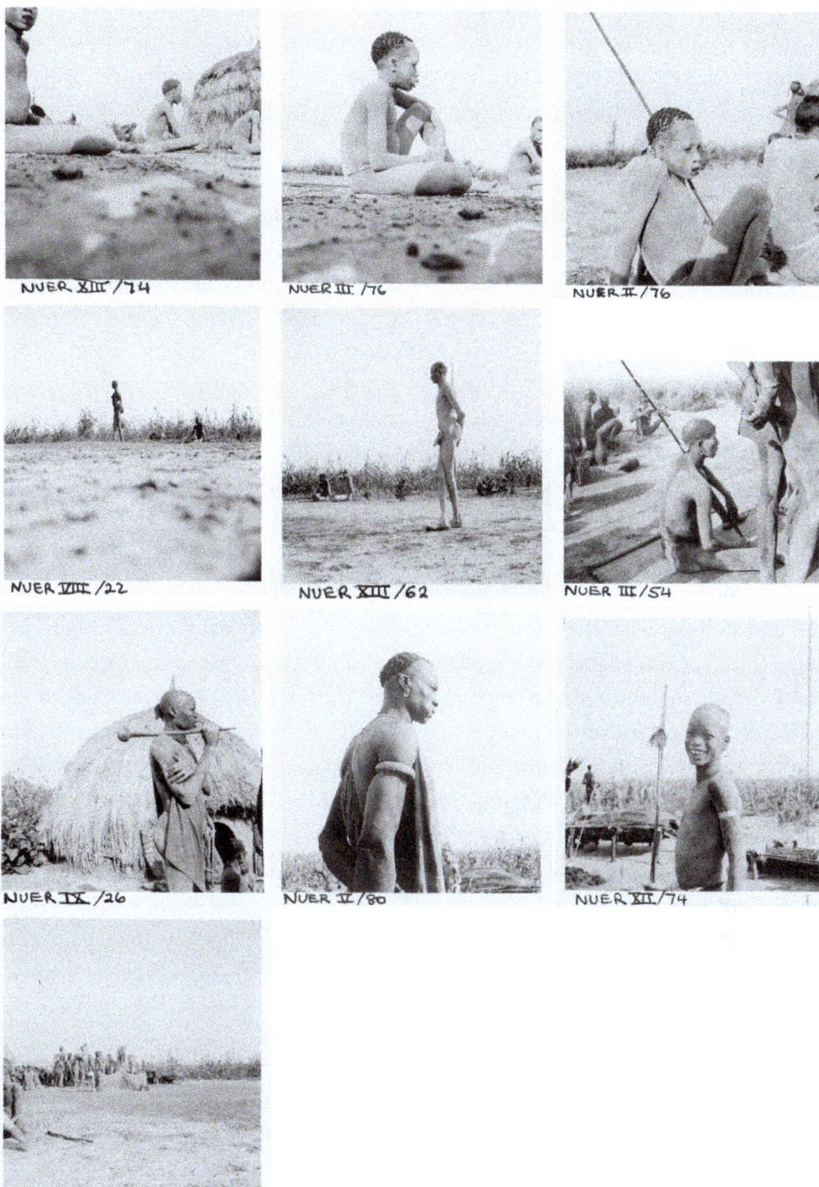

Figure 7.6 Ten prints identified as from film 4, taken at the time of the Nuer rite of *gorot*, Nyueny village, Unity State, South Sudan. Photographs by E. E. Evans-Pritchard, 1936.

social activity preceding or proceeding from a rite, but for taking portraits that were often difficult to obtain during his earlier periods of Nuer fieldwork. Given that scenes of ritual action entirely fill the other two films, there is the possibility that these portrait images were actually taken in the long build-up to the *gorot* event, and that he took these portraits in order to finish one film and have a new one ready for the rite to come, which might require quick repeated exposures. Although there are dangers in over-interpreting film 4's meandering and opportunistic portraits, it does allow us to witness far more than Evans-Pritchard intended, especially those onlookers less central to the rite itself, sitting on its edges, waiting, talking to each other, perhaps about the European in their midst. They are glimpses, fragments, condensed narratives about an event that we can now attach them to in the ethnography, opening up a space around it to allow new contexts to emerge.

Seriality and partiality in the archive

The notion of seriality in still photography is one that stresses the dynamic relationships between images, a dynamic that retains 'the fetishistic power of the still and the argumentative capacity of the moving'.[36] One of the most interesting explorations of the relationship between the evocative power of the still photograph and its relational and filmic potential is Chris Marker's *La Jetée* (1962), a film that invites consideration of the still photograph and the construction of a cinematographic narrative and meaning. Two of the most interesting published examples of seriality in anthropology or documentary are Mead and Bateson's *Balinese Character* (1942) and Agee and Evans's *Let Us Now Praise Famous Men* (1941),[37] two works that have their roots in projects carried out in 1936, the same year as Evans-Pritchard photographed the rite of *gorot*; 1936 was the year of Mead and Bateson's first visit to Bali as well as Agee and Evans's original assignment for *Fortune* magazine. Both these projects involved collaboration in order that both textual and visual narratives could be developed alongside each other, something only possible to a partial extent for the sole fieldworker. Bateson and Mead, for instance, wrote that:

> We usually worked together, Margaret Mead keeping verbal notes on the behaviour and Gregory Bateson moving around in and out of the scene with the two cameras... For work of this sort it is essential to have at least two workers in close cooperation. The photographic sequence is almost valueless without a verbal account of what occurred, and it is not possible to take full notes while

---

[36] C. Pinney. 1990. 'Colonial anthropology and "the laboratory of mankind"'. In *The Raj: India and the British 1600–1942*, edited by C. Bayley. London: National Portrait Gallery, 42.

[37] J. Agee and W. Evans. 1941. *Let Us Now Praise Famous Men*. Boston, MA: Houghton Mifflin Company.

manipulating cameras. The photographer, with his eye glued to a viewfinder and moving about, gets a very imperfect view of what is actually happening, and Margaret Mead...had a much fuller view of the scene than Gregory Bateson.[38]

Bateson's model of ethnographic collaboration involving a bilateral approach to the visual and textual record of events leaves the sole fieldworker in a precarious position, unable to be both photographically engaged as well as an overall observer in a position to take full and meaningful notes. The existence of partial series in Evans-Pritchard's record of *gorot* could then be understood in the context of the ethnographer either being photographically engaged or taking notes, leading to some sequences and some gaps. This model would suggest Evans-Pritchard's sequence of photographs of the ox suffocation (film 7) and the circling of the hut (film 9) as two periods during which he was photographically engaged, with the intent of recording a sequence of events, and during other elements of the rite he was engaged with observing and note-taking. Since none of Evans-Pritchard's Nuer field notes have survived it is not possible to trace the pattern of his observational activity from this source.

So far I have discussed two explanations for the coexistence of partiality and seriality in Evans-Pritchard's record of *gorot*, both of which emerge from a close reading of the archive itself. The first suggests that since the photograph is a product of a camera operated by a fieldworker, the archive is necessarily shaped by the proxemics and movement within the fieldwork encounter; for instance, images of the *gorot* rite that took place inside the hut interior don't exist since Evans-Pritchard's entry would not have been considered appropriate, or because photographing the couple eating meat together would have been to record something considered humiliating, since married couples did not eat in each other's presence, or simply because the low light levels inside the hut mitigated against it. The second explanation considers that photographic engagement on the one hand and note-taking and observation on the other are essentially different modes of fieldwork that the lone fieldworker cannot hope to combine effectively at once. This explanation would see the partiality of Evans-Pritchard's record of *gorot* as the inevitable result of his successive attempts to combine photographic engagement alongside detailed note-taking and observation. I want now to briefly consider a third approach to understanding the partiality of the *gorot* series, one that pays more attention to the agency of the group involved in shaping the archive, since it directly relates Evans-Pritchard's photographic engagement to the engagement of the social group gathered to witness the ceremony.

Taking another look at films 7 and 9, what seems to emerge is a strong sense of the collective nature of the *gorot* ceremony, with family members gathered closely

---

[38] G. Bateson and M. Mead. 1942. *Balinese Character: A Photographic Analysis*. New York: New York Academy of Sciences, 49–50.

around, some assisting at points, others watching. The importance of collective witness and group involvement is a common feature in Nuer religious practice, especially sacrifice, which often involves numerous relatives who travel considerable distances to attend, and which ends with the distribution of meat among them. The group witnesses that a sacrifice has been carried out as part of the collective's obligation to spirits, they witness which direction the beast falls after sacrifice, and they gather to hear the lengthy invocations that precede it. Evans-Pritchard as participant-photographer is also part of this dynamic of collective witness, moving with onlookers as they witness different aspects of the ceremony. In these two films the nature of his photographic engagement seems to sway with the collective witness of the group, shown by the presence of other onlookers on either side of the frame. The images of the circling of the hut by the youth with the boiled ox hump in particular demonstrate that the socio-spatial dynamic of the earlier suffocation element of the rite, where onlookers sat patiently nearby to watch, had transformed into a more participatory and informal rite, in which Evans-Pritchard had to jostle for position to gain a view of the scene (Figure 7.7).

The importance of the active witness of kin is often an intrinsic part of the efficaciousness of ritual, and it is during these periods of concentrated and focused, almost structured, participation and witness by the wider group that Evans-Pritchard seems to become photographically engaged, rather than a more detached observer. The model of the participant-photographer forming part of the collective witness of the group is also evident in other published ethnographic series of ritual, such as Victor Turner's photographs of the Ndembu ritual of *isoma*, where the couple being treated stand in a ritual hole, while the ethnographer takes his place alongside the officiants and other kin members gathered to witness and sing the *kupunjila* or 'swaying' song.[39] From this perspective, the agency of the collective group in shaping the activity of the participant-photographer and the resulting archival record is key. The ethnographer's engagement with events is often guided by the engagement of the witnessing group, and his or her photographic engagement forms part of the way in which the collective witness of the group is dynamically involved with events as they unfold.

The sight of the field in the archive

We know that Evans-Pritchard used his Nuer photographs as a source of ethnographic data when re-examining his Nuer notes some twenty years later when preparing *Nuer Religion*. In his chapter 'Spear Symbolism', an examination of the

---

[39] V. Turner. 1969. *The Ritual Process: Structure and Anti-Structure*. London: Routledge and Kegan Paul, Figs. 1–7.

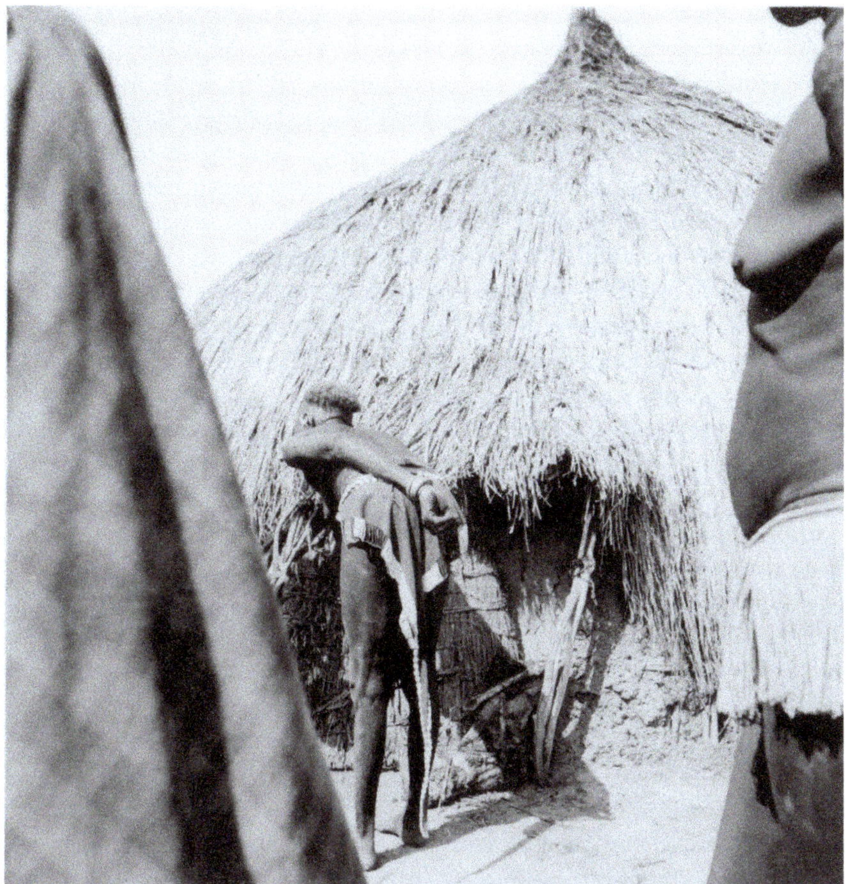

Figure 7.7 Print from film 9: Evans-Pritchard photographing between those witnessing the rite of *gorot*, Nyueny village, Unity State, South Sudan.

importance of left/right symbolism in Nuer religious thought and culture, he argues that the Nuer invariably train the left horns of their favourite oxen, whereas they erect sacred poles to the right of their shelters. His turn to the archive for confirmation however proved less than helpful:

All deformed horns in the photographs are left horns. Some branches in them, however, are to the left of the windscreens, but Nuer erect branches for practical purposes as well as for religious reasons, and I do not think it is possible to distinguish between them by sight.[40]

[40] Evans-Pritchard, *Nuer Religion*, 235n.

But the sight of the field in the archive, although related to the notion of sight-as-witness, has remained an ambiguous source of evidential value in the reinterpretation of anthropological data gathered through note-taking. The reinterrogation of the field archive, premised upon photography's indexicality as a store of cultural data, is also understood here, to use Christopher Pinney's phrase, as both 'cure' and 'poison'—both the potential source for reinterpretive evidence and yet unable to record the contextual transformation of a practical object (a pole for hanging personal items) into a ritual one (the 'sacred pole, associated with God, the spirits of their lineages and also with its ghosts') (Figure 7.8).[41]

Yet sight alone is here an essentially limited sense, distanced from visual experience—a scrutiny imposed upon the image as source of data, which needs qualification and context. As a reinterpretive sense, it becomes separated from the notion of witness as a key ethnographic method. The importance of sight-as-witness to the method of participant-observation was the subject of one of Malinowski's letters from the field to Layard, urging him that 'I find the first rule: <u>see it yourself</u>. Don't be satisfied with what the missionary and settler, nor even what the native tells you. <u>See it</u>; live through it. I find this is the main thing.'[42] Throughout his published writing Evans-Pritchard also compares the authority of his having witnessed an event directly to that of earlier writers whose information was mediated by another—'[w]hat I record', he wrote in the Preface to *Nuer Religion*, 'I witnessed myself or is information given spontaneously'.[43] Yet he elsewhere writes that the notion of witness, the passive 'being-there' of the ethnographer, is only the prerequisite to the more scientific activity of anthropological observation, since 'one has to learn what to look for and how to observe'.[44] The discrimination of the trained ethnographer's eye, he wrote, cannot be compared to the indiscriminate viewfinder of the camera:

> The work of the anthropologist is not photographic. He has to decide what is significant in what he observes and by his subsequent relation of his experiences to bring what is significant into relief. For this he must have, in addition to a wide knowledge of anthropology, a feeling for form and pattern, and a touch of genius.[45]

There is of course an inherent irony in this statement since both a 'feeling for form and pattern' and 'a touch of genius' are qualities more usually applied to

<hr>

[41] Evans-Pritchard, *Nuer Religion*, 234.

[42] Letter from Malinowski to Layard dated 9 June 1915 from Samarai, Papua New Guinea. University of California San Diego, Mandeville Special Collections Library, John Willoughby Layard Papers, Box 10, Folder 6.

[43] Evans-Pritchard, *Nuer Religion*, v.

[44] E. E. Evans-Pritchard. 1952. *Social Anthropology*. Glencoe, IL: Free Press, 81.

[45] Evans-Pritchard, *Social Anthropology*, 82.

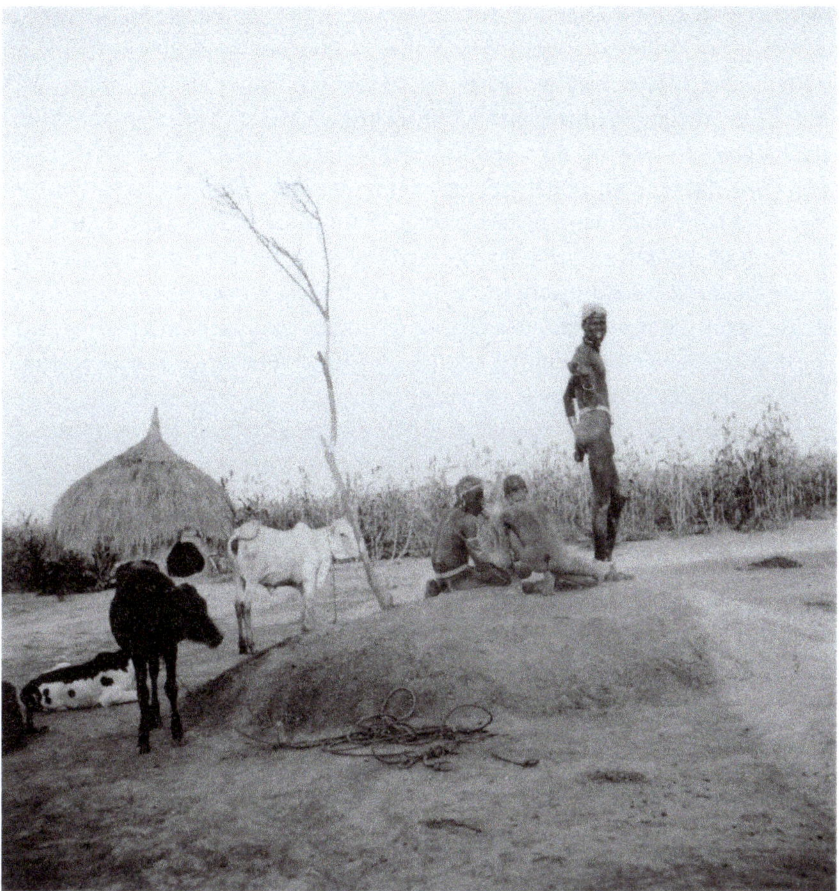

Figure 7.8 A sacred post-shrine (*riek*) and mound (*gol*) in a Nuer homestead, Unity State, South Sudan. Photograph by E. E. Evans-Pritchard, 1936.

photographers than anthropologists. Although his employment of the term photographic to mean the indiscriminate capture of information negates the discriminatory processes involved in field photography, as well as the nature of photographic objectivity, we take his point. What it also raises is the question of the relationship between the direct observation and witness of the ethnographer, photographic engagement with events at the time, and the subsequent usage of the field archive in his later writing.

Evans-Pritchard's textual description of *gorot* occupies less than two pages in *Nuer Religion*, and, as with much ethnographic writing about ritual, there is a very linear progression of meaningful elements in the description. Within this linear description, each stage is given equal weight in a this-happened-then-this-happened manner; there is no sense of greater and lesser ritualized activity, gaps or secondary social events or contexts. It is a structured procedure, but nonetheless not abstracted from the particularity of the event witnessed. This is heightened by retrospective inserts such as 'the husband told me afterwards that this was the most humiliating part of the rite', which introduces a participant's reflection and judgement into the flow of ethnographic description.[46] There is an effortless and constant shift of the balance of ethnographic authority between Evans-Pritchard and informant in the text. The authority of the anthropologist in determining the structured linear sequence of ritual has been much discussed in anthropology. The anthropologist Howard Morphy, for instance, discusses the filming of ritual events, where a false concreteness can easily creep in, as well as the retrospective interpretation of ritual which is then presented as experientially a priori.[47] The process of building up observational notes, subsequent commentary, and cross-commentary, all characteristic of Evans-Pritchard's ethnographic method, can then be contrasted with the immediacy of his photographic engagement with ritual events, and the subsequent textual evocation of the immediacy of participation in the published account. Given Geertz's description of Evans-Pritchard's writing technique as one of creating 'anthropological transparencies',[48] in which the visualizable is given prominence in the way in which social and cultural life is translated to the reader, we can see how a retrospective order can easily be established in such a visual manner. Other writers have also pointed out the way in which Evans-Pritchard accords a central role to vision, not just in seeing another society but in how anthropology communicates its message, thus indicating a certain conception of scientific knowledge. 'The anthropology of Evans-Pritchard', argues Grimshaw, 'is built upon the idea of illumination. The world is ultimately knowable. It is rendered transparent through the exercise of the light of reason.'[49] As Grimshaw also argues, it was perhaps the Malinowskian attention to sight and vision in ethnographic enquiry that ultimately led to the idea that the camera and other scientific instrumentation were tools associated, ironically, with an inability to 'see' social function and therefore only record the surface of appearance.[50]

In rethinking Evans-Pritchard's field photographs of *gorot*, I asked the question why the archival record seemed to be characterized by a sustained engagement with two distinct stages of the ceremony, and why other aspects of the ceremony were not represented. In order to explore this question I was led to think of the

[46] Evans-Pritchard, *Nuer Religion*, 218.

[47] H. Morphy. 1994. 'The interpretation of ritual: reflections from film on anthropological practice', *Man*, 29(1), 117–46.

[48] C. Geertz. 1988. *Works and Lives: The Anthropologist as Author*. Oxford: Polity Press, 64.

[49] A. Grimshaw. 2001. *The Ethnographer's Eye: Ways of Seeing in Modern Anthropology*. Cambridge: Cambridge University Press, 66.

[50] Grimshaw, *Ethnographer's Eye*, 54.

ethnographer as 'participant-photographer'—a model that understood his activity during the event as being composed of periods of 'photographic engagement' interposed with observation and note-taking. There are a number of ways in which the episodic nature of this photographic engagement can be understood: from the perspective of a Batesian concern with the incommensurability of visual and textual approaches to fieldwork; as being influenced by technical or other practical considerations, such as the movement from exterior events to those taking place inside the couple's small hut; and finally as being influenced to some extent by the agency of the gathered group, whose role in the active witness and participation in ritual events can be seen to have helped shape the archival record.

The sight of the field in the archive is an ongoing historical process of analytical engagement, and I have explored three instances of it in this chapter: Evans-Pritchard's use of his photographs to cross-check and rethink his textual field notes, the use made by subsequent scholars of his published images when debating and reinterpreting Nuer ritual, and my own use of both published and unpublished photographs to rethink Evans-Pritchard as participant-photographer. The archive suggests that Evans-Pritchard's sight of the field also became confused and partial in the years after his fieldwork. As the numbers written on the fronts of the prints illustrated in this chapter show, his working collection of prints became jumbled over the years. When he received the prints after developing he evidently made a note in pencil on the reverse giving the film number they all came from. But as time went by, no doubt due to rummaging through for potential illustrations and cross-checking notes, the prints ended up scattered throughout his Nuer collection and dissociated from each other. At some point later this jumbled order was set in stone, so to speak, by the systematic numbering of each print in the packets and order in which they were found. It is not known whether this numbering was done by an assistant prior to donation in 1966 or by museum staff after acquisition. By reassociating the photographs as I have done here, the field is brought back into sight to engage with once again, but within an interpretive vision that I have created out of fragments, and imagination.

Yet seeing and imagining the field are both important anthropological processes, as is illustrated by another photograph in the archive (Figure 7.9), which records one of Evans-Pritchard's kinship diagrams from Nyueny village pinned up in a room in Oxford, probably so that the diagram could be converted into a lantern slide for lecturing. It shows the children of a man called Jany by several wives, including one (Nyajal) who was the widow of a man called Kwenwar. While Jany was thereby genitor of Nyajal's children, their pater remained the deceased Kwenwar. One of Jany's other wives in the diagram, Nyamani, was also a 'ghost marriage', since Jany had married her to the name of his dead father Col, since he felt his father should have had a second wife. Therefore, while the diagram's intent is to provide visual clarity to Evans-Pritchard's communication of Nuer marriage practices, it hides the fact that Nyamani was legally married to Col through 'ghost

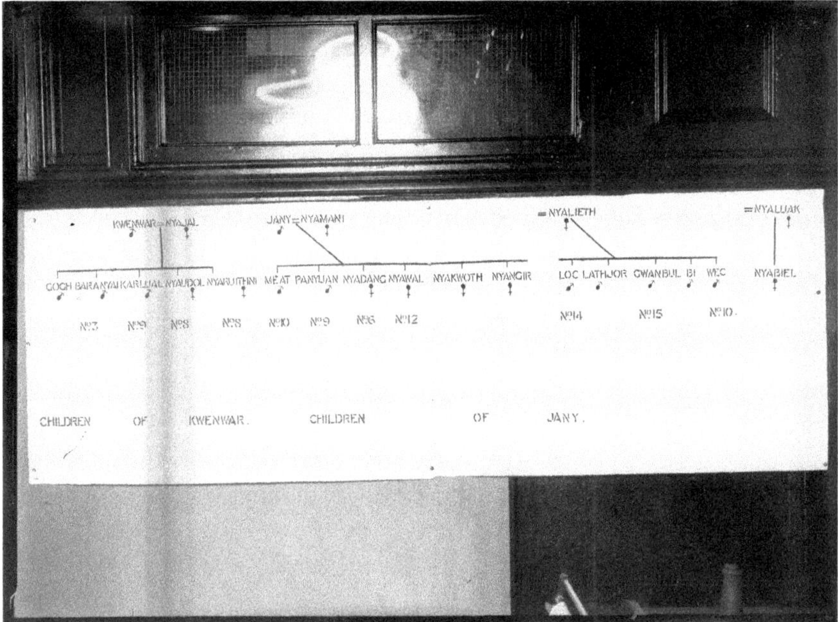

Figure 7.9 Diagram showing the children of Kwenwar and Jany of Nyueny village, pinned up in a teaching room in Oxford, probably late 1930s. Photographer unknown.

marriage' and not to Jany. Evans-Pritchard explains that this is because he is more interested in 'bio-social actualities rather than legal configurations',[51] since the children of Nyamani were always spoken of as the children of Jany and not Col. The principle of agnatic descent that runs through Nuer society, he writes, is thereby something that is paradoxically traced through the mother, since it is through the payment of bride-wealth that children gain a pater. In this way Evans-Pritchard accommodates affinal ties within Nuer society by seeing them as a mechanism for creating agnatic links. However, as Evans-Pritchard acknowledges, social reality is messier than ideal principles of social organization. At Nyueny the actual lived situation was that the community was a confusing mix of cognates and affines, which he assumes held true across Nuerland. Yet despite such messy realities his faith in an underlying agnatic principle in Nuer society held firm, since while 'the actualities are always changing and passing... the principle endures'.[52] The inherent messiness of lived social reality when compared to idealized social rules was certainly a problem for the structural-functional approach of descent theory, and formed the basis of much subsequent critique.

---

[51] Evans-Pritchard, *Marriage and Family Among the Nuer*, 58.
[52] Evans-Pritchard, *Marriage and Family Among the Nuer*, 64.

As I discussed in chapter 3, there is a parallel here between the excess or abundance of ethnographic information in the photographic record and the social excess and abundance of lived social reality in comparison with anthropological social theory. When we look at the photograph of the Nyueny kinship diagram, we do not only process the kinship information, we gradually begin to notice much more—letters stencilled on two sheets, the first sheet pinned to a blank board or sheet perhaps normally used for lantern slide projections, the second extending sheet pinned to the side into the textured wallpaper, the light from the camera flash glaring off the glass partition in the upper part of the wall, while below we notice what might be the leg of an upturned chair and a piece of equipment. All of this visual abundance crowds in, and we are suddenly aware of the institutional space in Oxford in which anthropological knowledge is being created and taught, and that we are witnessing its mediation again in a photograph that will be copied and cropped into a slide for Evans-Pritchard to project into another space, and interpret the children of Jany for another class of students.

8

The poet, the missionary,
and the sacred spears

In 1936, Evans-Pritchard gained a further Leverhulme Grant to continue his comparative studies of Nilotic groups, this time in Kenya. But as with his abortive attempt to study the Oromo in Ethiopia the year before, things did not go to plan. Although he eventually spent some six weeks in western Kenya among the Luo people, he hadn't originally intended to study this society.[1] His original plan was to visit the Masai or Turkana, but the Kenyan government 'considered it unwise', given the difficulties they faced in administering these parts of the country.[2] So Evans-Pritchard decided that a survey of the Luo would be a good alternative, especially since little social anthropological attention had been directed towards them. It isn't clear exactly which month he visited Luo country, but since we know that his subsequent visit to the Nuer in South Sudan took place in October/ November of that year, we can assume that his visit took place before this, possibly around August/September. We know that he visited the (at that time, not formally trained) anthropologist G. W. B. Huntingford near Eldoret during this trip, since a small set of photographs exist of Nandi people in and around the family residence there. Huntingford and Evans-Pritchard were almost certainly known to each other before Evans-Pritchard's visit to Kenya, having been only a year apart at the English public school Winchester College, and both sharing the experience of being sons of Anglican clerics. Unlike Evans-Pritchard however, Huntingford didn't follow the usual route of studies at Oxford, and instead emigrated to Kenya in 1920 with his parents, who had acquired a farm in the Kipkaren valley, west of Eldoret. He was to make this area his base until 1937, when he gave up the family farm (his father had returned to England in 1931) and entered Oxford to read for a BSc in Anthropology, returning to Kenya between 1938 and 1940 to carry out further fieldwork.[3]

Given the timing of Evans-Pritchard's visit to Kenya, and the fact that Huntingford entered Evans-Pritchard's former Oxford college (Exeter), it can be surmised that Evans-Pritchard, who had been a research lecturer in Oxford since

---

[1] E. E. Evans-Pritchard. 1950. 'Marriage customs of the Luo of Kenya', *Africa: Journal of the International African Institute*, 20(2), 132.

[2] E. E. Evans-Pritchard. 1949. 'Luo tribes and clans', *Rhodes-Livingstone Journal*, 7, 1.

[3] J. E. G. Sutton. 2006. 'Denying history in colonial Kenya: the anthropology and archeology of G. W. B. Huntingford and L. S. B. Leakey', *History in Africa*, 33, 296 fn15.

1935, was influential in both Huntingford's decision to write up his researches on Nandi society in Oxford, and also with regards his college choice. We can only surmise whether Evans-Pritchard intended to study the Nandi or one of the other Nandi-speaking groups, but eventually decided that this would deny Huntingford the opportunity to make his own mark academically, writing about a society that he had lived in for some years and whose language he spoke. Evans-Pritchard obviously had an interest in the Kalenjin peoples since he published an article a few years later in 1940 analysing and comparing the existing literature on them, with a view to understanding whether they shared a similar social structure.[4] Noting the recent study by J. G. Peristiany on one of the groups, the Kipsigis, as the first 'scientific account', he is more dismissive of the other available studies, rating them 'sketchy and mediocre', including two published articles by Huntingford in the *Journal of the Royal Anthropological Institute*. No doubt Huntingford himself would have agreed that his published studies to date were partial and not fully informed by academic debates, which fed his desire to study further under Radcliffe-Brown and Evans-Pritchard. One of his major contributions at this time was to suggest that an antecedent culture, which he termed 'Azanian', had been resident in the Kalenjin area some hundreds of years earlier, evidence for which he saw in a variety of earthworks and disused roadways.[5] This culture, he presumed, was most likely to have been 'Hamitic' and spread down from the north, but had been replaced by incoming Kalenjin peoples.

Although later scholars have found no evidence to support Huntingford's Azanian theory, instead seeing a longer time frame for Kalenjin occupation that would explain the archaeological features, he is given some acknowledgment: 'Despite the striking oddity of his deductions, he deserves credit for bringing the regional archaeology . . . to scholarly attention'.[6] The name Azania also still adorns one of the most prominent African archaeology journals, which began publishing in 1966 after Basil Davidson repackaged some of Huntingford's theories as part of his own regional chronology. Although Evans-Pritchard draws frequently on Huntingford's accounts of the Nandi in his survey article, he didn't find the sort of sociological data he required for his own comparison with South Sudanese groups in any of the existing accounts of the Kalenjin group:

> The weakest part of the accounts of the Nandi, Keyu, and Suk is their treatment of the territorial organization of these peoples. After describing that they were divided into sections, what we have called provinces, they tell us that these sections were further divided into sub-sections, but they do not tell us the nature of these sub-sections nor their place in the whole territorial system. We are left to

---

[4] E. E. Evans-Pritchard. 1940. 'The political structure of the Nandi-speaking peoples of Kenya', *Africa: Journal of the International African Institute*, 13(3), 250.

[5] G. W. B. Huntingford. 1933. 'The Azanian civilization of Kenya', *Antiquity*, 7, 153–65.

[6] Sutton, 'Denying history in colonial Kenya', 300–1.

guess what was the organization of a province and how the relations between its parts were regulated.[7]

Given his interest at this time in developing a 'comparative study of Nilotic lineages as a contribution towards that study of lineage systems on a broader African and worldwide basis',[8] the lack of specific and reliable information on this issue was of course the chief reason for his Leverhulme Grant-funded trips to Ethiopia and Kenya in 1935–6. Nonetheless, Evans-Pritchard did conclude that the Kalenjin group, although having a decentralized style of sociopolitical organization, was quite distinct from the 'Nilotic' type where lineage structure and territorial structure were coordinated. And it was here of course in Kenya that he found a society, the Luo, that matched in this respect the Nilotic group he knew best—the Nuer—who he was to visit for the final time on his way home.

Evans-Pritchard's desire to illustrate photographically the correspondence between social and territorial organization had been limited in South Sudan due to the flat terrain, making it almost impossible to see clearly. He therefore relied on an aerial photograph showing the proximity of several villages in Nuong district in his eventual Nuer monograph, supplied by the Royal Air Force, who during his first visit to Nuerland in 1930 had been dropping bombs on their cattle camps. But here in Luo country he was more fortunate in the terrain, and took the opportunity to take a number of landscape images from hilltops to illustrate the point, with fenced homesteads dotted about below (Figure 8.1). Of course, you cannot photographically describe social or political organization directly, and the landscape images themselves only give a general and somewhat indistinct impression of the settlement system. But they do serve also one of the essential aspects of ethnographic photography, if such a term can be used at all, which is to give witness to the focused looking of the ethnographer at a given place and time, an index of a question posed and addressed by direct observation with the camera: what is the nature of territorial organization and settlement here, and how does it connect to sociopolitical organization? In an indirect sense, when we look at this landscape from a hilltop in Nyanza, we are seeing Evans-Pritchard's answer to his own question.

The question of how closely the Luo fitted into Evans-Pritchard's developing theory of a wider Nilotic sociopolitical 'system', and how much he was searching for, and therefore found, corroborating evidence, has been the subject of some critique since. Given that illness kept his visit short, to around six weeks, and that he was restricted to interviewing, in English, mainly Luo mission converts, as well as relying heavily on a missionary to guide him, it is hardly surprising, and fully acknowledged by Evans-Pritchard himself, that his data was 'sketchy'

---

[7] Evans-Pritchard, 'Political structure of the Nandi-speaking peoples', 252.
[8] Evans-Pritchard, 'Luo tribes and clans', 16.

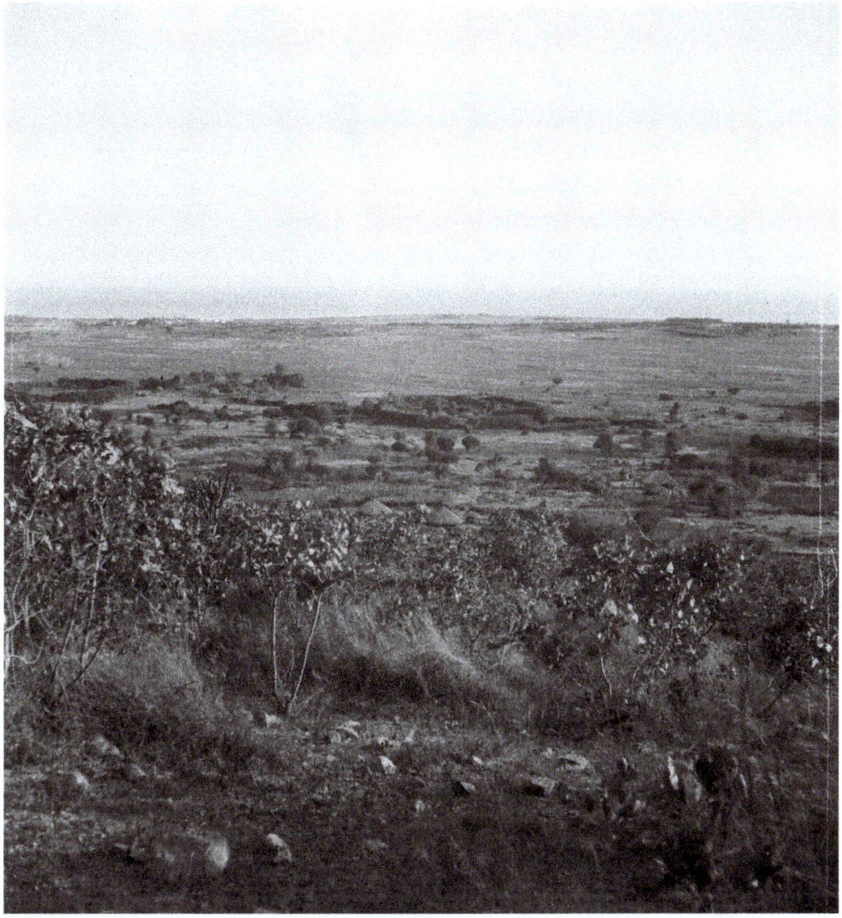

Figure 8.1 View from a hill towards Lake Nyanza, Kenya, showing Luo homesteads below. Photograph by E. E. Evans-Pritchard, 1936.

and 'superficial'.[9] By way of an example, his information on Luo marriage was obtained from just one man of the Alego tribe of Central Kavirondo, Pastor Ezekiel.[10] If Evans-Pritchard's search for a Nilotic lineage-based social 'system', which found its fullest expression in the volume he and Meyer Fortes edited in 1940, *African Political Systems*, represented the vanguard of social anthropological thinking, it was nonetheless unpopular with some of the 'old guard'. Father Pascuale Crazzolara of the Verona Fathers mission for instance, who had

[9] Evans-Pritchard, 'Luo tribes and clans', 16.
[10] Evans-Pritchard, 'Marriage customs of the Luo of Kenya', 132.

been resident in Uganda and South Sudan since 1908, and who wrote a major three-volume work on the wider Luo peoples in the 1950s, wrote:

> I do not agree with the school of ethnology which prefers to use artificial and, in my opinion, meaningless terms such as 'Nilotic', 'Nilo-Hamitic', 'Sudanic' etc as labels for groups of tribes with linguistic and cultural affinities. Here…we are dealing with clearly distinct racial and political communities, and it is both more accurate and more convenient to use the group names by which they have been known to one another for centuries, that is to say 'Lwoo'[11]

As I discussed in chapter 6, the accusation has been levelled at Evans-Pritchard that he downplayed the political power of the Nuer prophets, the Shilluk *reth*, and the Anuak king, and in his account of the Luo a similar criticism has been levelled in his discussion of the status and political significance of Luo chieftainship. In Evans-Pritchard's opinion there were no chiefs among the Luo; the *ruoth* 'was an influential person, but no more'.[12] This suited Evans-Pritchard's developing Nilotic sociopolitical system nicely, but contradicted earlier accounts. Geoffrey Northcote, one of the first British administrators in the area, considered chief-tainship as key to Luo social organization: 'Each chief', he wrote, 'subdivides his territory, placing each portion under a sub-chief.'[13] This was also the view of the missionary Walter E. Owen, who wrote that 'in the tribal organization, the central figure around which all the tribal life revolves, and who embodies the tribal loyalties and welfare, is the *ruoth* or tribal (or clan) head'.[14] This also accords with the view of Bethwell Ogot, the leading Luo historian, who wrote that 'each *oganda* [tribe] was an independent economic, political and ritual unit. Each had its own Ruoth (chief). The Ruoth was the jural-political leader of the "tribe".'[15] The *oganda* itself, of which the Luo in Kenya had around thirteen, was composed of groupings of patrilineal clans or large lineages, which in turn were subdivided into smaller patrilineal segments. This is where Evans-Pritchard found a corres-pondence between lineage segments structuring Luo society, and other Nilotic groups such as the Nuer. Arguably, what muddied the waters considerably in his interpretation was the extent of change and disruption caused to Luo society as a result of around forty years of colonial rule, a set of complex historic circum-stances that his brief study could not hope to unravel.

---

[11] J. P. Crazzolara. 1961. 'Lwoo migrations', *Uganda Journal*, 25(2), 141.

[12] Evans-Pritchard, 'Luo tribes and clans', 28.

[13] G. E. S. Northcote. 1907. 'The Nilotic Kavirondo', *Journal of the Royal Anthropological Institute*, 37, 60.

[14] Owen to Bishop of Mombasa, 3 December 1931. Quoted in M. G. Whisson and J. M. Lonsdale. 1975. 'The case of Jason Gor and fourteen others: a Luo succession dispute in historical perspective', *Africa: Journal of the International African Institute*, 45(1), 52.

[15] B. Ogot. 1963. 'British administration in the Central Nyanza District of Kenya', *Journal of African History*, 4(2), 252.

After the British extended colonial control over the Kavirondo region at the end of the nineteenth century, they decided that administration should follow this segmentary system; the locational boundaries laid out coincided with the former boundaries between *ogendini* (tribes). In each location, there was a government-appointed chief responsible to the district officer, and these men came initially from a dominant (chiefly) lineage. These chiefs, created by the British in 1902, were not like the *ruoth* who was a custodian of tribal law and custom; they were essentially civil servants appointed by the provincial commissioners, and paid by the central administration. As Ogot points out, 'a social and political set-up that had suited a migrating, semi-pastoral, community had now to be converted into an administrative machine for a settled, agricultural population. A centralized system had to be superimposed on a segmentary system with all the weaknesses inherent in the latter.'[16] Given the imposition on the Luo of an alternative system of government-controlled tribal leadership a generation earlier, it is unclear to what extent Evans-Pritchard's downplaying of the political function of the *ruoth* is historically based, or simply reflects the largely symbolic and ritual functions that they occupied by the mid-1930s. When he states, for instance, that 'there was nothing that could be described as political office in a Luo tribe', he is generalizing about a precolonial past for which there was extremely limited evidence available.

It is here where the photographic record acts as a fascinating counterpoint to Evans-Pritchard's ethnography. Besides his portraits of a few elders or ritual experts in more traditional attire, what is most striking about Evans-Pritchard's record of his relatively short six-week visit is his readiness to photograph Luo people as he found them, many of them in Western dress. The fact that he shows little anxiety in his photographs to exclude the acculturation of the Luo is notable, as is the lack of any scientific-reference racial portraiture. Other anthropologists of the period, particularly cultural and museum anthropologists such as Oxford's Henry Balfour, who visited Kenya and Uganda in 1928, tended to lament Western cultural influence (although not colonialism per se) and sought out photographic opportunities to 'salvage' images of native people going about 'traditional' lives.

In some ways it could be argued that Evans-Pritchard's photographic record undermines his written account in *Luo Tribes and Clans*, in that the article pays almost no attention to colonial or mission influences on Luo social life or political organization. The only real mention is his statement that inter-lineage enmity over land 'has certainly been accentuated by European rule and restrictions'.[17] Other than that, a picture is built up in the article of social and political continuity, building towards the conclusion that the Luo have the same type of structure as the Nuer. But as we will see, although Evans-Pritchard's Luo photographs are dominated by individual and group portraits of Luo people in Western dress, this

---

[16] Ogot, 'British administration', 253.   [17] Evans-Pritchard, 'Luo tribes and clans', 15.

isn't necessarily representative of the overall cultural trend in Nyanza in 1936, but reflects the fact that Evans-Pritchard was being guided and introduced to missionized Luo in the direct or indirect network of the missionary Walter E. Owen, Archdeacon of Kavirondo.

The poet and the missionary

Known as 'the Poet' to most administrators in the Sudan in the 1930s due to his liking for English and Persian poetry, as well as Arabic hymns and elegies, Evans-Pritchard's decision to approach the missionary Walter E. Owen (1879–1945) to help introduce him to Kenyan Luo society in 1936 is curious, but entirely in character. It is curious given his well-known dislike for missions and missionaries, despite having dedicated his monograph, *The Nuer*, to the American mission at Nasir. Yet, in actual fact, Evans-Pritchard's attitude towards missions was complex. 'People in the Sudan often say that I am against Christian missions', he once wrote to the American missionary Cora Soule. 'It is largely true that I am against missions, but not against Christian missions, and by that I mean missions which regard it as a privilege to work among Africans and realize that Christianity is a spirit which can permeate any culture and not a body of ready-made and repressive rules of conduct which a native must accept in exchange for a higher social status.'[18] These words show how spiritual a person Evans-Pritchard actually was, with an affinity for the poetic in ritual and religion that would express itself in his conversion to Roman Catholicism in 1944, an experience that would shape some of his later thinking, notably in *Nuer Religion*.

As an intelligent and eloquent critic of the Kenyan administration, and with deep interests in African society and culture, we can only assume that Evans-Pritchard regarded Owen favourably. As he notes, his survey was made possible by the local knowledge and networks already established by Owen, and the cooperation of local Luo people came about 'largely out of regard for the Archdeacon and Mrs Owen'.[19] Thus the photographs taken on his 1936 trip need to be understood not simply as an anthropologist's visual record, but as a record of local responses to an influential and respected missionary, with a European anthropologist in tow. Owen was a controversial figure in the colony, and historians have keenly debated his role in the colonial system. Although an obvious irritant to the colonial administration, arguing vociferously against many policies, and acting as President of the Kavirondo Taxpayers Welfare Association, some historians have come to see his attitudes as 'firmly in the mainstream of Church Missionary Society

---

[18] Letter to Blanche Cora Soule, 24 December 1931. Indiana University Library, African Studies Collection, Nuer Field Notes Project.

[19] Evans-Pritchard, 'Luo tribes and clans', 1.

ideology, and C. M. S. ideology was a vital component of the process of extending and maintaining imperial power'.[20] Yet there was little doubting Owen's influence and reputation locally. 'Judging from oral testimony', writes Murray, 'a more wholehearted admiration – verging on adulation – was extended to the archdeacon by his African protégés and co-workers.'[21] This attitude towards Owen is attested to in Evans-Pritchard's photographs, especially the level of access granted to sacred sites and objects, but also in the more informal and domestic settings of other photographs. Owen's Luo nickname was 'Origre'—someone who pokes their nose into everything—which was possibly earned as a result of his extensive archaeological and palaeontological investigations in the region, which began around 1930, and which led to a number of contributions to academic journals. In fact, shortly before Evans-Pritchard's visit, Owen had been showing local visitors, including the archaeologist Louis Leakey, around an archaeological site at the Kisumu Tennis Club. The combination of an interest in cultural matters, as well as extensive contacts in the region, made Owen an obvious choice for Evans-Pritchard when seeking a local guide—someone 'who knew the Luo better than anyone has known them'.[22]

Evans-Pritchard's Luo photographs are fascinating because they document a sphere of influence around a key person in Luo social and political life in the period, a set of relationships, a series of intensely local and personal colonial connections, varying levels of outsider/insider relations to domestic settings, ritual spaces and secret locations, and the happenstance of photographic opportunities that any rapid tour of a locale might result in, but which nonetheless shows what was deemed worthy to record. So let us start with how the photographs illuminate Owen's presence alongside the ethnographer.

Figure 8.2 shows a group of men, possibly at the Church Missionary Society compound in Maseno where Owen was based. It is one of a number of group portraits that Evans-Pritchard takes, some of which involve schools, the children all lined up in rows for the camera. Here the men sit on a bench with others standing behind, one in a pensive pose holding a book, another with pen poised above a notebook, while another holds a tea pot and cup, as if about to welcome the visitor. It is one of a number of portraits that seem to say so much about the influence of both Christian missions and Owen in particular in the archive, a man whose influence locally in the period, according to Bethwell Ogot, 'it is difficult to exaggerate'.[23] But what were the implications of this influence, both for the Luo themselves as well as the ethnographic record created by Evans-Pritchard about the Luo?

---

[20] N. U. Murray. 1982. 'Archdeacon WE Owen: missionary as propagandist', *The International Journal of African Historical Studies*, 15(4), 654.

[21] Murray, 'Archdeacon WE Owen', 655.   [22] Evans-Pritchard, 'Luo tribes and clans', 1.

[23] Ogot, 'British administration', 263.

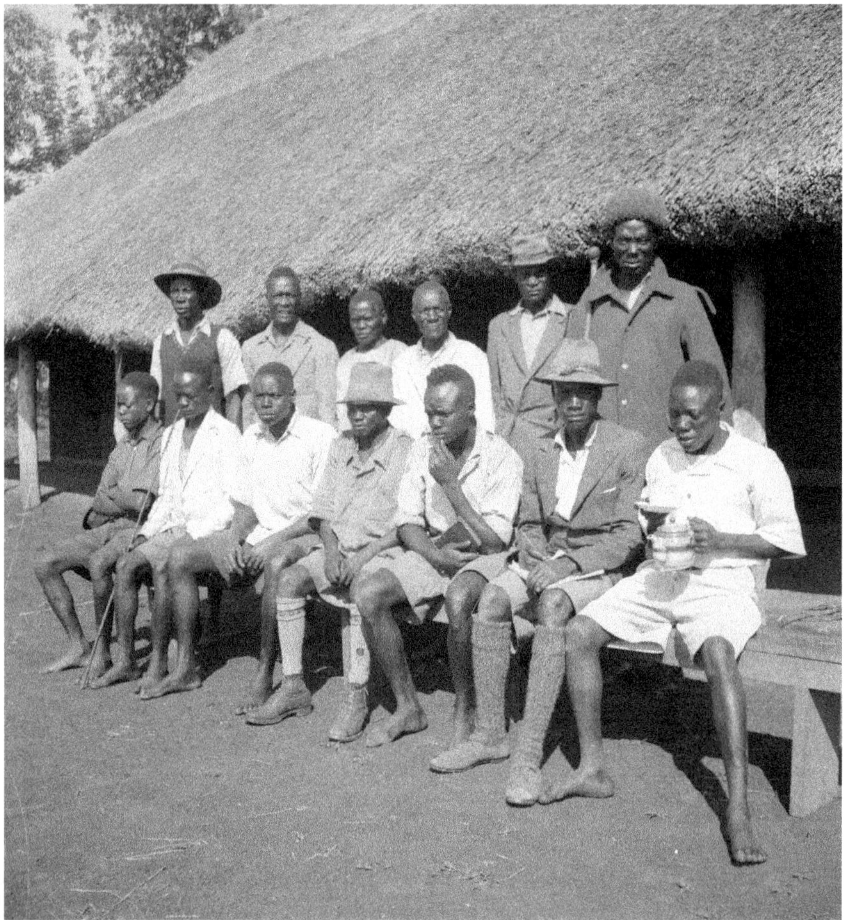

Figure 8.2 Group of Luo men, possibly at Maseno mission, Nyanza, Kenya. Photograph by E. E. Evans-Pritchard, 1936.

Owen was a constant thorn in the side of the colonial administration on a variety of issues, from forced labour to taxation and politics. He was a regular writer to *The Manchester Guardian* about social issues he felt strongly about, a habit that frustrated both the administration and the church equally. One incident in particular that happened just a few years before Evans-Pritchard's visit, known as the Asembo affair, sums up the extent of his political agitation and also why he was held in such regard by the Luo. In 1931, Daniel Odindo the chief of Asembo location had resigned after twelve years in office, following accusations of corruption. The government appointed a man called Ismail Owuor as his successor (Figure 8.3), considered a *janawi* or sorcerer and also a comparatively wealthy

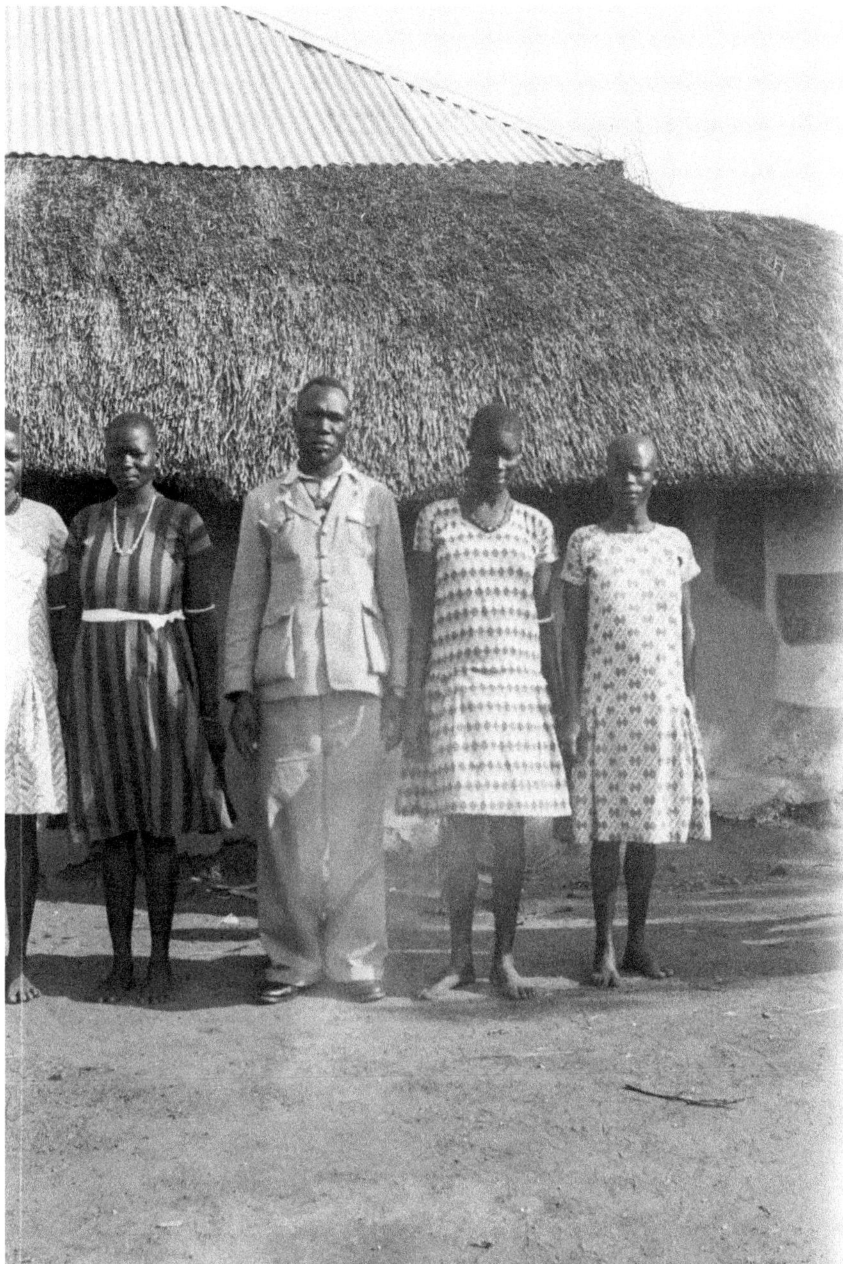

Figure 8.3 Ismail Owuor Molo (1901–86) with four of the eight wives he had married by 1936; the latest, Turfosa Omari, to the right, Asembo, Nyanza, Kenya. Photograph by E. E. Evans-Pritchard, 1936.

trader, and so someone already of political importance. A man called Jason Gor, signing himself Secretary of the Native Anglican Church Council in Asembo, presented the commissioner with a petition against Owuor. He accused him of witchcraft, of selling magic for the seduction of girls, of being a member of religious cults—both traditional and Christian—and called for public meetings to discuss the appointment. The government refused. Owen warned that he would oppose the refusal to allow the people of Asembo to select their own chief, and maintained that 'it was far better to allow the people to suffer injustice and exploitation under one of their own choosing than to be justly and honestly administered by someone whom they did not want'.[24]

Owen was convinced that the government had chosen a new chief too hastily, denying the Asembo people the opportunity of careful deliberation and choice. The district commissioner believed to the contrary that Owuor's appointment served the cause of justice, since someone who supported Odindo would have suppressed evidence against him. Owen disagreed not only with this, but also opposed the suppression of local political meetings, and instigated a commission of enquiry into the whole affair. Plots continued to oust Owuor, but in the end he was removed from office in 1937, a year after Evans-Pritchard met him, convicted for possessing offensive articles under the 1925 Witchcraft Ordinance. Some say that Jason Gor added some incriminating material to Owuor's materials as they were loaded into the district commissioner's vehicle, including a human hand.[25]

To the exasperation of local colonial officers, Owen was very keen to show visitors around the region and raise the profile of issues he was involved in. 'As far as I can gather', wrote the provincial commissioner of Nyanza in 1929, 'he does little or no mission work, but rushes round the country, trying to catch the wretched administrative officers out in some illegal act.'[26] Just occasionally (Figure 8.4) we get a glimpse of Owen as he interacts, cigarette in hand, with a group of Luo people whom he and Evans-Pritchard have met on the path, a joke being shared between them. Owen holds his arm out as if to indicate and include the presence of Evans-Pritchard as photographer, and the young woman raises her arm to her *ligisa* married woman's headdress almost self-consciously. Immediately afterwards, perhaps following a request by Owen, the woman poses for a close-up portrait, pipe in mouth (Figure 8.5). It is from a sequence of several images that document the photographic encounter on a path between two fields of mature sorghum, and that put such ethnographic portraits into their immediate context of production as a chance encounter, but which arguably would have been difficult or impossible to have taken without Owen's influence.

---

[24] Whisson and Lonsdale, 'The case of Jason Gor', 61.
[25] Whisson and Lonsdale, 'The case of Jason Gor', 62.
[26] Quoted in Murray, 'Archdeacon WE Owen', 659.

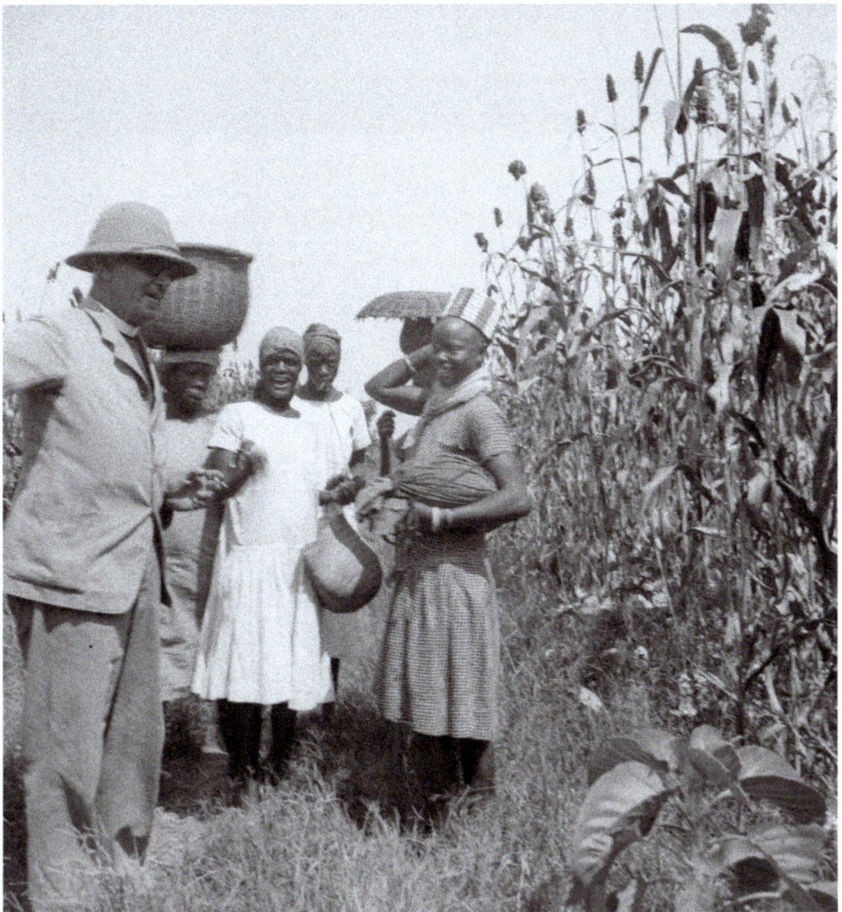

Figure 8.4 W. E. Owen with a group of Luo people near Gangu village, Nyanza, Kenya. Photograph by E. E. Evans-Pritchard, 1936.

In this sense, the Luo people who feature in Evans-Pritchard's portraits are posing for, or rather on account of, the missionary standing beside the ethnographer-photographer, and not for the unknown outsider. Nowhere is this demonstrated more explicitly and clearly than in Evans-Pritchard's extraordinary access to, and photographs of, secret and sacred Luo clan objects, that Owen himself facilitated.

Of sacred spears and their custodians

Owen had become interested in the archaeology of Central Nyanza almost as soon as he took up residence at the mission in Maseno in the 1920s. He began to collect

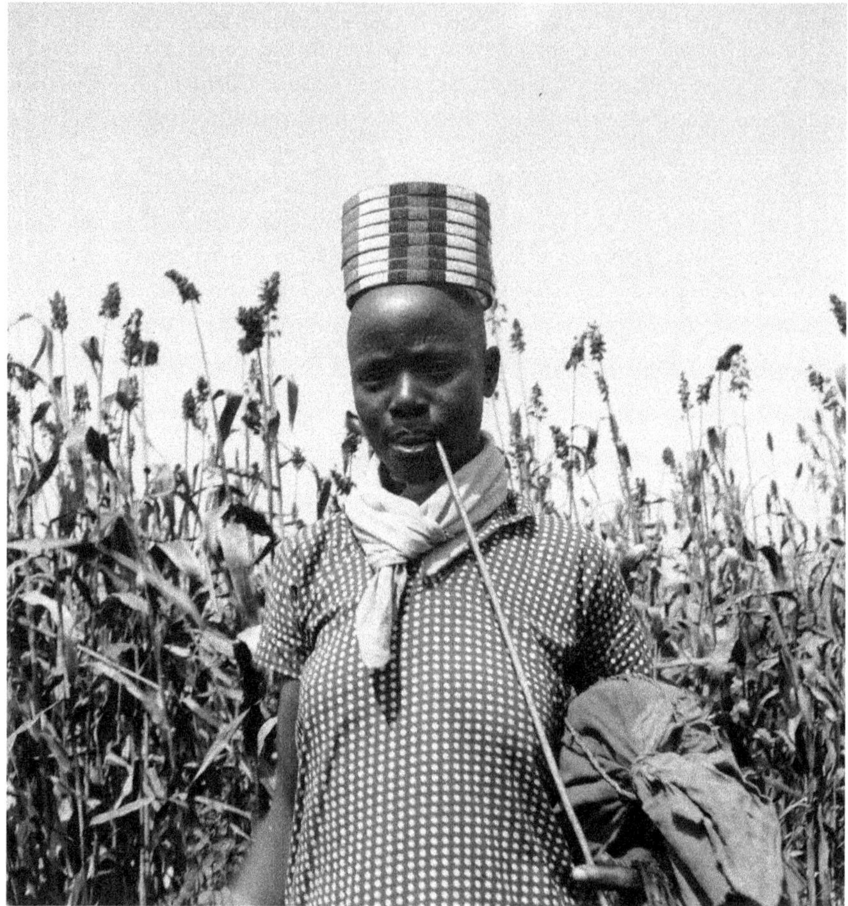

Figure 8.5 Portrait of a Luo woman wearing the *ligisa* married woman's headdress, near Gangu village, Nyanza, Kenya. Photograph by E. E. Evans-Pritchard, 1936.

what he took to be fossils and stone age artefacts on his travels around the region and sought professional opinion on what they might be. In 1930 he found some large fossil limb bones at Kanjera, which set him off collecting palaeontological objects. 'I had, of course, very many contacts with knowledgeable Africans', he later wrote, 'who took an interest in my hobby, and informed me of localities where they had observed bones weathering out of gullies and other places.'[27] He took the opportunity to visit Louis Leakey, working on the Pleistocene deposits at Kanjera in 1932, and in 1934 took D. G. MacInnes and Allan Turner to Kiboko

[27] W. E. Owen. 1939. 'An amateur field collector in Kavirondo. Part 1', *Journal of the Royal African Society*, 38(150), 124.

Island to show them remains he had found. When they left he was so encouraged that he employed a gang of eight men to carry on with the search for fossil remains for another five months, visiting occasionally: 'it is quite ridiculous the thrill one gets from such a find', he wrote.[28] Possibly as a direct result of Owen's sideline in unsupervised excavations, the government began to regulate the activity, stipulating that the gangs should not work unless the collector was with them. 'This has sadly hampered the collection of scientific material', lamented Owen, '[since] the rule is intended to safeguard scientific interests, but has proved to be crippling in action.'[29] Nonetheless, Owen continued to use his local Luo network to collect material. In 1937, for instance, 'a lad brought me during one of my visits to the local school, a few fragments picked up on the surface of the bottom of the gully on the site. He brought them to me on an old enamel plate and among them were some of the unidentified teeth.'[30] He was equally interested in archaeology, and earlier in 1936, shortly before Evans-Pritchard's visit, he was staying in Kisumu when he noticed what appeared to be worked cores and flakes among the disturbed soil during the construction of a new tennis court at the Kisumu Tennis Club. He sent a representative series to the British Museum.[31]

In 1934, Owen used his considerable local influence to gain access to some sacred objects that he had no doubt heard of and been curious about. These were the sacred spears (*tong liswa*) and other items connected with important ancestors, or lineage founders, in the region. Custom held that these items were kept by certain custodians, and sometimes in secret locations. Outsiders would not have ordinarily seen these revered objects, and it is an indication of Owen's influence over certain key Luo individuals that he was taken to see them. A manuscript in the Evans-Pritchard archive in the Pitt Rivers Museum contains a quote, seemingly copied out from Owen's diary, which relays the details of his privileged viewing of *tong* Alego—the spear of Alego—the founder of the Seje clan:

After months of cautiously feeling my way, it has been possible for me today (2nd July 1934) to see the sacred spear, or rather what remains of it. Accompanied by two influential Christians of the Seje clan together with the custodian, Nyaunga, I was taken to bush country bordering on the Yala swamps in Seje country. I was guided to a small clump of bush, from the middle of which rose a tallish thorn tree. At the base of its trunk an ant-hill had formed, its sides harbouring sloes and other bush plants. Protruding from the top of the ant-hill, about three inches from the tree trunk, was an iron object, which closer investigation proved to be the head of a spear. The point of the spear-head was

---

[28] Owen, 'An amateur field collector in Kavirondo. Part 1', 131.
[29] Owen, 'An amateur field collector in Kavirondo. Part 1', 132.
[30] W. E. Owen. 1939. 'An amateur field collector in Kavirondo. Part 2', *Journal of the Royal African Society*, 38(151), 220.
[31] Owen, 'An amateur field collector in Kavirondo. Part 2', 226.

deep in the ant-hill earth, that which protruded being the hollow end into which the wooden shaft formerly fitted. Again proceeding with caution, I was allowed to dig away the earth and lift the head clear. It proved to be twenty inches long, the blade portion being five and three quarter inches, its greatest width, the base, being one and a quarter inches. Down what had been the centre of the blade ran a well-formed rib, or ridge, but the blade was very much corroded, and one side of the blade, is now narrower than the other. The base of the blade was separated from the centre rib for about three quarters of an inch, not apparently by corrosion but by design, and below the base was a strong barb, about an inch long, now out of position and pressed in towards the centre. After I had examined it, it was taken by the three Seje men and reburied in a fresh clump of bush. Apparently after every disturbance in days gone by it was buried in a fresh site to prevent discovery.[32]

The Luo historian Bethwell Ogot reproduced a photograph of Owen holding the spear of Alego in his 1963 book on the history of the Luo, taken by a former district commissioner for Central Nyanza, W. A. Perreau. Given that Owen was taken alone in 1934 by two 'influential Christians', as well as the custodian Nyaunga, to view the sacred spear, he must have taken Perreau on a separate occasion. And as Figure 8.6 shows, he also took visiting academics such as Evans-Pritchard to view the items. Interestingly, Owen poses with the spear in exactly the same manner in both Perreau's and Evans-Pritchard's photographs, with his light shirt being used as a backdrop to help make the spear visible. Although no notebook or journal survives of Evans-Pritchard's Luo field trip, I found two fragments of notes in among his papers, which is extremely unusual given that he habitually destroyed most field notes after he had published them. One of them, handwritten, appears to have been written shortly after Owen had taken him to view the spear of Alego:

These people say that several clans have their ancient spears, but none are of such antiquity as tong Alego which is the father of them all. The keeper of the spear is called won tong. They say that in the days of war the won tong took it down from the tree from which it hung point downwards, and pointed it against the enemy, e.g. Bantu, who would then be driven out of their country with ease. (present keeper of tong Alego is Nyaunga – Ogala of Seje L . . .) (Owen put it at 350–400 years old).

Archdeacon Owen says that if the spear were to be placed point upwards all sorts of calamities would follow. People treat it with great respect and Jakobo and

---

[32] Typed MS on Luo sacred spears in Pitt Rivers Museum Manuscript Collections, Evans-Pritchard Papers, 'Luo Field-Notes', Box 7, item 45.

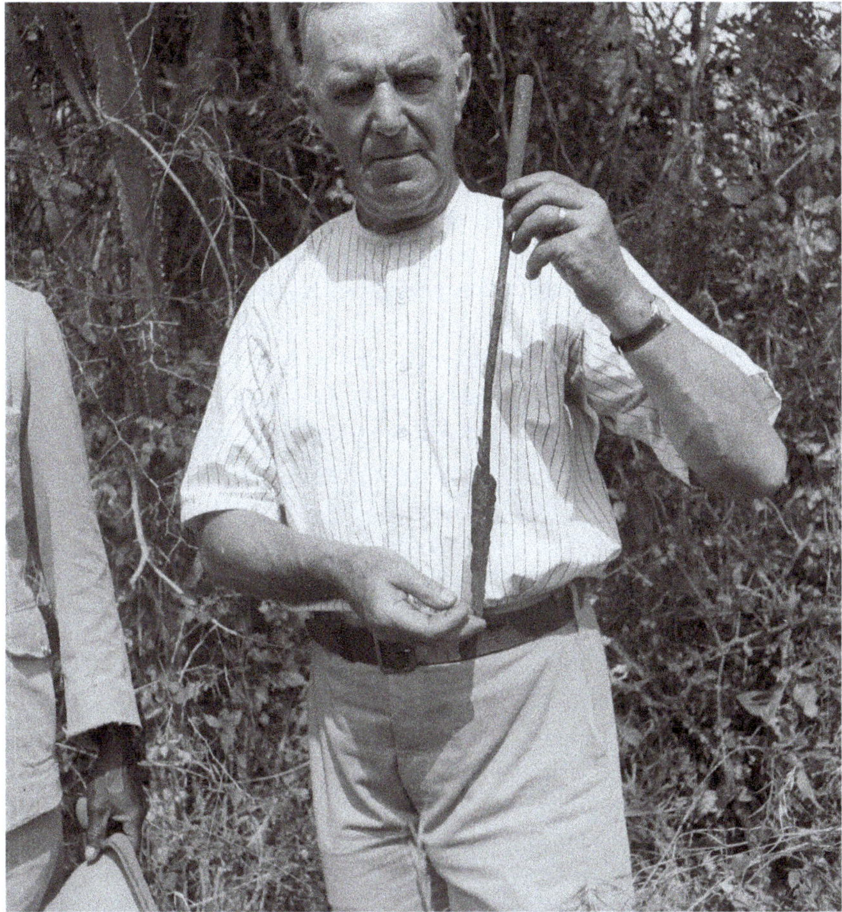

Figure 8.6 W. E. Owen holding the spear of Alego, Nyanza, Kenya. Photograph by E. E. Evans-Pritchard, 1936.

other younger members of the clan with us would not touch it. Owen says that eventually it falls into the earth point downwards. Hence the condition in which he saw it. Government efforts to preserve it useless as all frightened of Jokakar [Jokager?] chief who wants to weaken prestige of Alego's descendants and won't allow them to house it properly. The chief's people came by night the other day to try to find it and throw it away.[33]

---

[33] Handwritten note in Pitt Rivers Museum Manuscript Collections, Evans-Pritchard Papers, 'Luo Field-Notes', Box 7, item 45.

A small section of this note is quoted by Evans-Pritchard in his 1949 article *Luo tribes and clans*, but given that his focus was on political organization it is rather skimmed over. The field note is much more revealing, suggesting not only tension and competition for power between lineages, but that this tension found expression in the potential capture of another lineage's sacred items to try and weaken them. The note also reveals that the colonial government felt unable, or were unwilling for political expediency, to 'house' the spear of Alego, by which is presumably meant in a museum-like repository. The accusation that this was due to the unwillingness of the Jokager chief is presumably an interpretation given to him by his Seje companions, as is the rumour that rival clan members came by night to attempt to steal their sacred relics. This also shows the extent to which

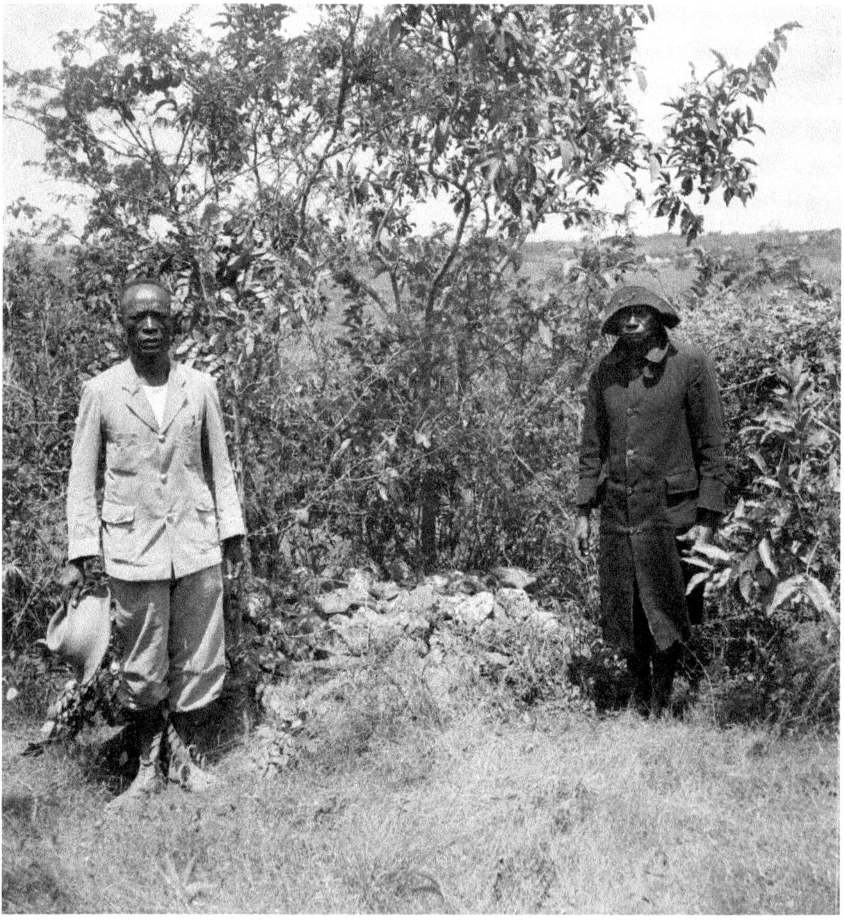

Figure 8.7 Jakobo, a native assessor, and another Seje man at the location where Alego's relics were kept. Photograph by E. E. Evans-Pritchard, 1936.

Owen (and by extension those he took to view and document the sacred objects) was trusted by those influential Seje men that he mentions. Evans-Pritchard also photographed (Figure 8.7) the men that accompanied them to view Alego's spear, including 'Jakobo', the man he mentions in his field note, who has the words native assessor stitched across his jacket, about whom more later.

The spear (and also pot) of Alego were not the only sacred items that Owen took Evans-Pritchard to view and photograph on his tour, no doubt somewhat proud of his unrivalled access to sacred items held by lineage custodians. Owen himself estimated the age of Alego's spear at 350–400 years old, which Ogot concurred with, based on oral history. Given that these sacred spears were only possessed by founders of clans or maximal lineages, Ogot concluded that the Seje clan in Alego 'was founded between 1534 and 1584, which appears to corroborate genealogical evidence'.[34] This should give us pause for thought, when one considers the careful and attentive custodianship that has been involved over many generations to look after these venerated relics, and when some European critics of repatriating objects to Africa consider the continent to have no tradition of curation or stable museum institutions. The Luo custodians would appear to refute such notions entirely. Evans-Pritchard was also clearly impressed by what he saw, and although he barely mentions it in his published account, another document in among his archival papers gives an account of the other Luo sacred objects that he visited, which is worth presenting here in full, illustrated with some of the photographs that he took of them (Figures 8.8 to 8.11):

> The Jokager clan of Ugenya tribe have a number of sacred spears. This clan came into present day Luoland from Buduma (Kadhola) in a migration separate from that of Joalego, who came from Yimbo (Kadimo direction). The three spears I saw were in charge of Ger—Othieno—Ogola—Ger—Omolo—Ger—Ocieng of the Jouhori lineage. There are said to be three other sacred spears, like the ones I saw, in the hands of the Jokowager lineage, though in the past the Joumire lineage owned them. Ger was the won gweng, father of the land, of that part of the country where the Jouhori spears were and was the son of a *ruoth*, a man of substance.

> The local chief had made objections to my seeing the spears but Ger overruled them, saying that the chief was jealous because they did not belong to his lineage. When I arrived at his village he and two men of his lineage went to a hut at the side of which grew tall plants and grasses. They cleared these away with a billhook and Ger stooped down and took out the three spears from under the eaves of the hut. He said that when moving village they buried the spears in the bush; otherwise they were hidden in the thatch of a hut. They had been hafted in the

---

[34] Ogot, 'British administration', 152.

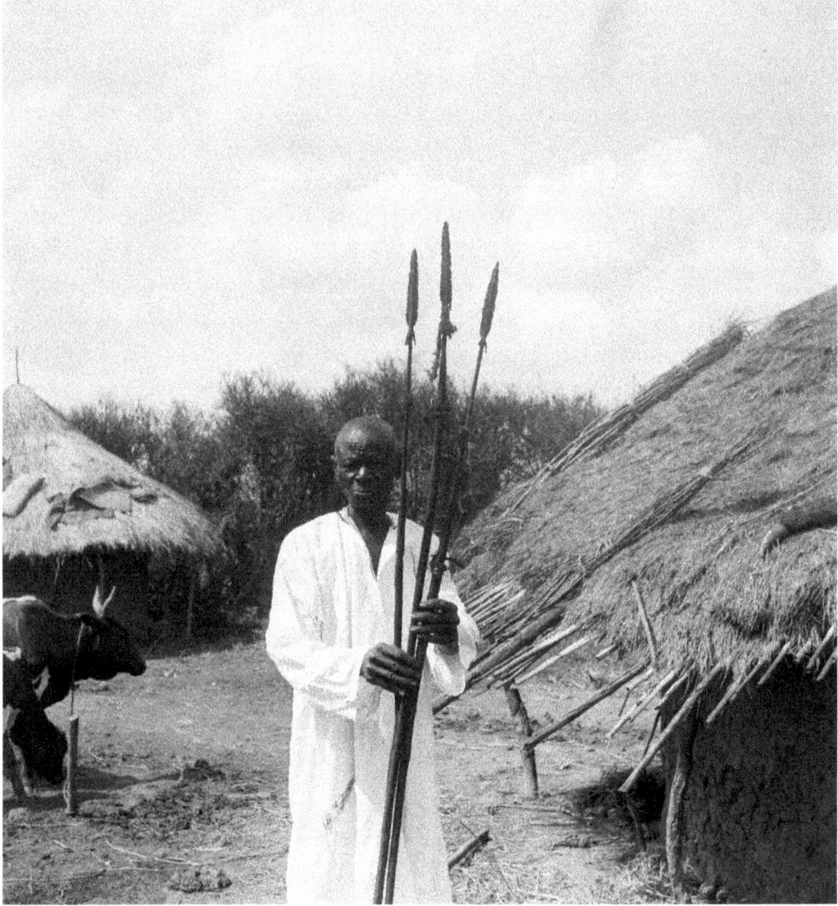

Figure 8.8 The spears of Kager, the founder of the Kager clan, with their custodian, a man called Ger. Photograph by E. E. Evans-Pritchard, 1936.

lifetime of Omolo, a great warrior and leader, and the wood was very worn. The long leaf-shaped blades were corroded with rust. The two on the right in the photograph are said to be males and the one on the left to be female. All three spears had pieces of skin of sacrificial animals tied round them, and one had a coil of iron twisted round the base of the blade. In old days in time of war and other troubles the spears were taken down and a goat sacrificed to the ghost of their ancestors. While I was examining the spears there was talk of sacrificing a goat as the spears were said to be hungry.

I also saw the two sacred spears of the Kaluo clan of the Alego tribe. The 'male' spear was like those of the Jokager clan. The 'female' spear was pear-shaped with

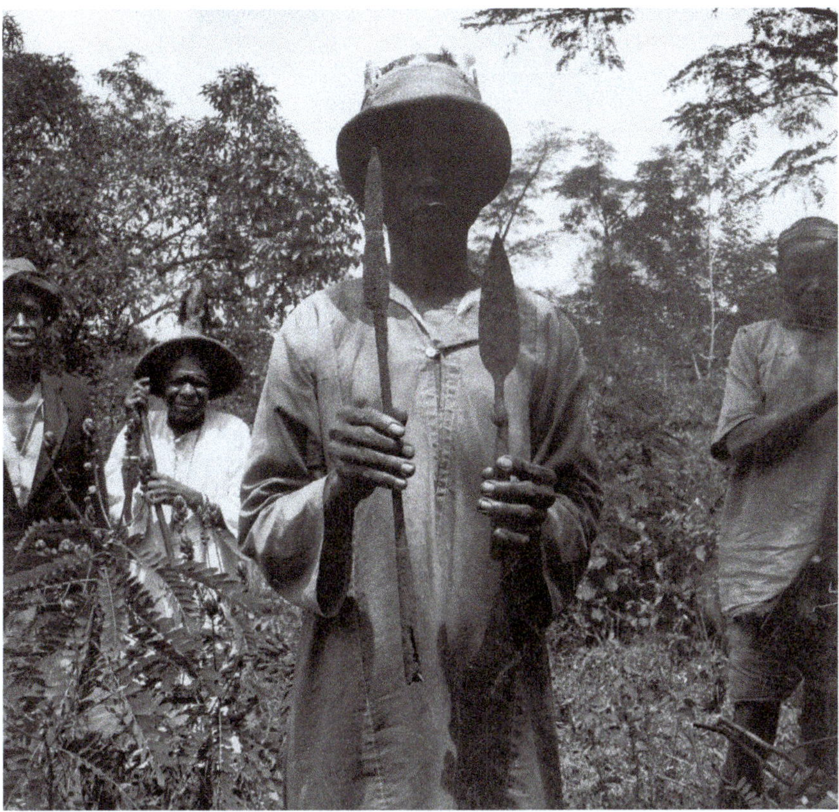

Figure 8.9 The spears of Kaluo, the founder of the Kaluo clan, with their custodian. Photograph by E. E. Evans-Pritchard, 1936.

a peculiar twist in the metal at the base of the blade, as can be seen in the photograph. They were kept at the foot of a tree and some vegetation had to be cleared away before we could get at them. It was noticeable that every time I went to visit clan spears the people cleared away vegetation with spears or bill-hooks and not with their hands. When I had photographed the spears they were replaced horizontally with their points slightly pointing upwards, and branches were cut and placed over them. The elders said that the spears could not be kept in a hut in the village because it would catch on fire, the fire coming from the points of the spears themselves. Even if they were laid flat on the ground they would rise up of themselves and stand on end, and flame would then come from their points and burn the hut.

Another clan of the Alego tribe who have a sacred spear are the Jokogelo. This is tong Owiny, the spear of Owiny, their ancestor. It was different from the other

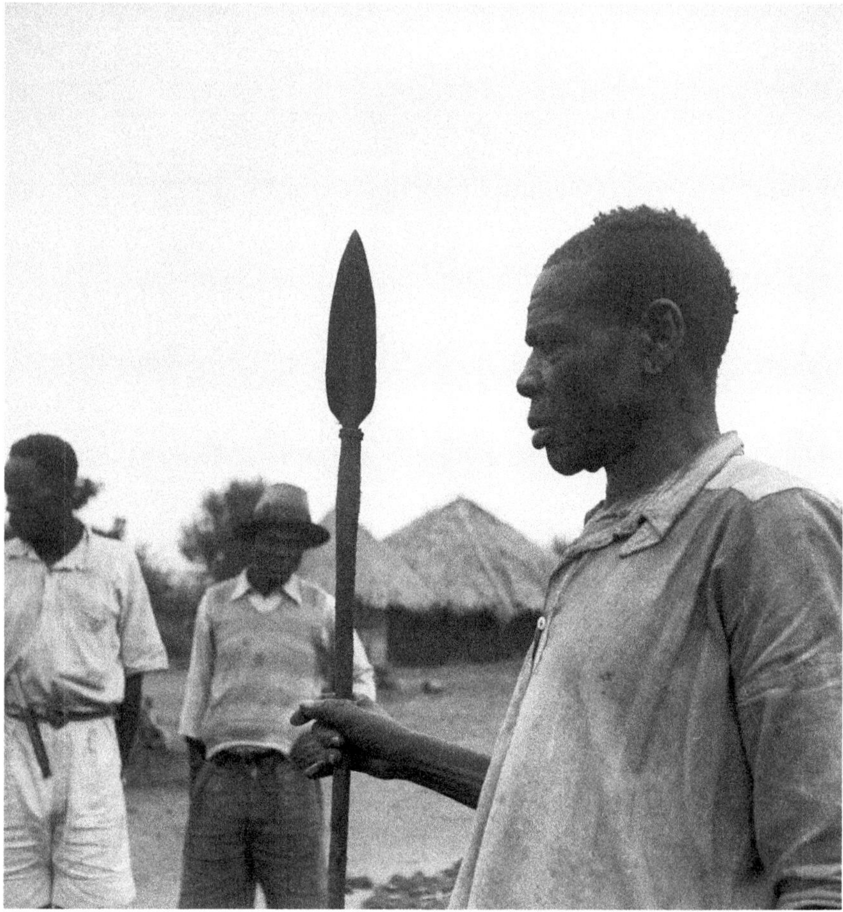

Figure 8.10 The spears of Owiny, the founder of the Kogelo clan, with their custodian. Photograph by E. E. Evans-Pritchard, 1936.

spears I saw in that it was tanged and not socketed; also it was not rusty and appeared to be of no considerable age. A piece of cow's hide had been bound round the spear at the point where it enters the shaft. It was kept in a hut.

The Joagoro clan, also of the Alego tribe, have a sacred stone (rapogi) used for sharpening spears, to which they sacrifice. It is known as rapok Rodi, as it belonged to their ancestor Rodi, who, according to the genealogies, lived between thirteen and nineteen generations ago. It goes together with his pot. On the way to see these emblems we visited an everlasting spring called Baragulu where water is drawn in the pot to take to the stone for sharpening spears. I was then taken to the foot of a tree where, after some clearing away of grass and branches, the stone and pot were

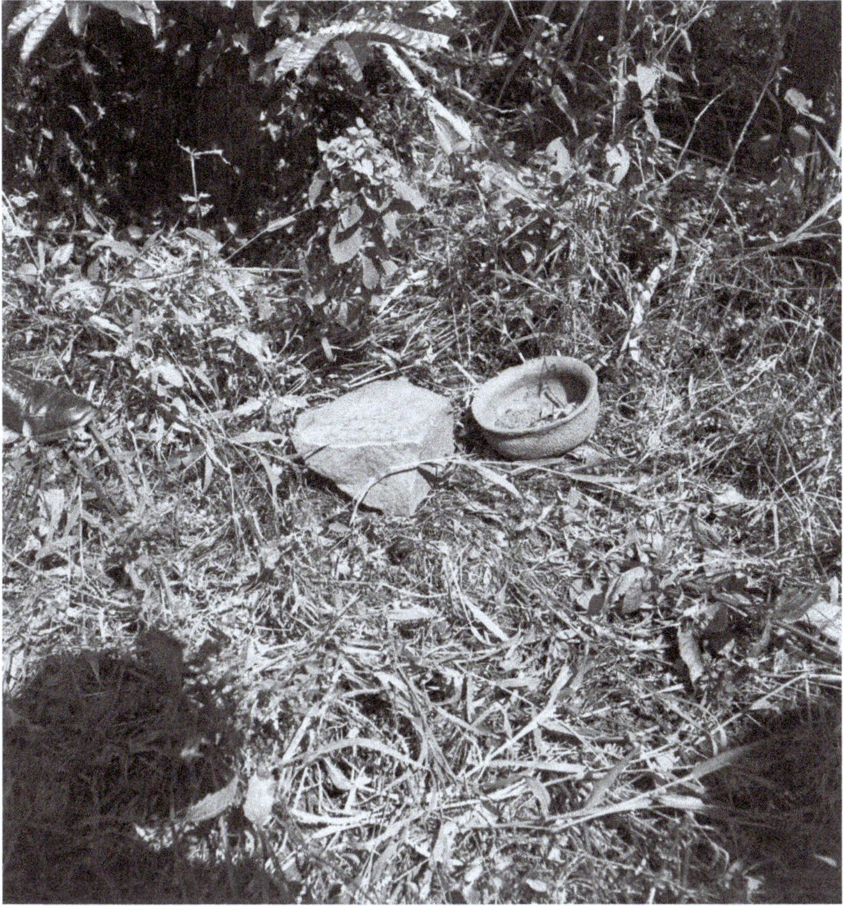

Figure 8.11 The sacred spear-sharpening stone and pot of Rodi, an ancestor of the Joagoro clan. Photograph by E. E. Evans-Pritchard, 1936.

brought forth. The stone was about a foot square, very heavy, and smoothed and shiny black along one edge where spears had been sharpened. The pot was small and of a reddish-earth colour and had been incised round the outside.

There are a number of sacred objects in possession of the dominant clans of Karachuonyo tribe to the south of the Kavirondo gulf: the spear (tong) and drum (bul) of Rachuonyo, the staff (loth) of Owidi, and the spear and arrow (aseri) and stone (rapogi) of Cien, and perhaps others, for I was not able to see any of the objects. I was told that the lineages concerned would first have to be gathered together and a sacrifice performed. I was able, however, to see the ancient pot belonging to the descendants of Ogweno, a lineage in S. Kavirondo and called after his wife Aguch Agola, the pot (agulu) of Agola. It is said to have been brought across the Kavirondo gulf from Asembo Bay when the Luo migrated southwards. Various of the clans and lineages in Luoland have sacred emblems, sacred spears, stones, arrows, staffs, baskets, and pots of which I have heard.[35]

But what was Evans-Pritchard's conclusion about the social function of these sacred clan spears and other objects? For him, these objects were mostly symbolic of lineage unity, and by extension the tribe in which the lineage was dominant, and were mostly used ritually in times of difficulty, such as war or drought. Further, the custodians seemed to Evans-Pritchard to belong to senior lines within the lineage who were called upon to perform sacrifice and provide the sacrificial beast.[36] There are dominant clans, such as the JoAlego (whose sacred spear was considered the most ritually important), and stranger lineages, such as the Kaluo, JoKogelo, and JoAgoro, discussed above. These stranger lineages got grafted onto the main lineage through female links, and so the whole tribe could be considered as a system of cognatic lineages. Evans-Pritchard saw this creating a structured social system in which members of either dominant or stranger lineages found their position, the essential framework being provided by the lineages within a dominant clan, an interpretation that fitted well with his comparative analysis of other Nilotic social groups, as he saw them.

'Jacob wants': returning Luo portraits

In 2007 I organized, with a Luo colleague Gilbert Oteyo, a touring photographic exhibition of Evans-Pritchard's photographs in Nyanza called *Paro Manene* (a Luo phrase that roughly translates as 'reflecting on the past').[37] The exhibition consisted of a number of large printed panels with photographs by Evans-Pritchard and the early colonial administrator Charles Hobley, alongside some explanatory text on Luo culture in the early twentieth century. In part, the project was inspired by Corinne Kratz's (2002) book, *The Ones That Are Wanted*, which examined the political, representational, and ethical issues involved in exhibiting 'ethnographic' photography to audiences in Kenya and in America. However, on reading Kratz's account we were both struck by the unfortunate story of how the Okiek, who were the subject of Kratz's field photographs, never managed themselves to make it to Nairobi to see the exhibition. We resolved that *Paro Manene*

---

[35] Untitled typed manuscript on Luo sacred spears etc., Pitt Rivers Museum Manuscript Collections, Evans-Pritchard Papers, 'Luo Field-Notes', Box 7, item 45.

[36] Evans-Pritchard, 'Luo tribes and clans', 8.

[37] For a fuller account of the Paro Manene project see C. Morton and G. Oteyo. 2015. 'The Paro Manene project: exhibiting and researching photographic histories in western Kenya'. In *International Handbooks of Museum Studies*, edited by S. Macdonald and H. R. Leahy, Vol. 4: *Museum Transformations*, edited by A. E. Coombes and R. B. Phillips. Oxford: Wiley-Blackwell, 311–35.

would move between several village venues in Luo country to ensure that the two least mobile groups of Luo people—the elderly and schoolchildren—would have the most opportunity to see the exhibition. The exhibition venues of Lwak Catholic Church Hall, Bondo Town Hall, and the Siaya Farmers Training Centre Hall were all chosen due to their being the main population centres in the area where Evans-Pritchard took photographs in 1936. The exhibition was also shown, by special request, at Rakombe Primary School. It had already been established some years previously by Oteyo that a number of families connected to the photographs were identifiable in the area, and it was hoped that more would emerge in the process of exhibiting the photographs. Since the area is often poorly served by roads and transport, and since many key informants were elderly, we felt it essential that the exhibition travel to several venues in the locality. Even so, the three days allocated for each exhibition was usually insufficient, given that it took several days for word to spread about the exhibition, a fact that resulted in people arriving to see the displays for several days after they had moved on.

The timing of the exhibitions was important due to a number of considerations. Firstly, in order to enable school groups to visit it was essential that the exhibitions coincide with term dates; secondly, they needed to be in the dry season for ease of transport and travel, both for the public and exhibition staff; thirdly, they needed to be during a period when people were normally free from farming chores, which can be intensive at certain times. Taken together, these local calendrical considerations were considered important so as to maximize the chance that local people would be free to visit something such as a photo exhibition. We also organized for longer than normal opening times to enable as many people as possible to attend, given the distances some people had to travel on foot. This meant that the exhibitions usually opened at eight in the morning and closed after five in the afternoon, or for as long as the respective venues would allow. Prior to the exhibitions, announcements were made on two local vernacular radio stations— Radio Ramogi and Victoria Radio. Adverts were not placed in local newspapers since these are read by only a small minority of Luo people, whereas most families gather to listen to radio broadcasts and spread news about events by word of mouth. Exhibition schedules were also sent to local schools, colleges, and churches, as well as other organizations. A number of flyers were posted in key positions in market villages, hospitals, and public places. As people arrived at the venues, folders of copies of the photographs were available to browse through, and all were encouraged to leave comments in notebooks, either concerning the exhibition itself, or about the imagery or information presented. The decision was made early on to provide the exhibition information and captions in English only, without Dholuo or Kiswahili translations. Few Luo are literate in Dhuluo, and it was felt by Oteyo that additional captions in Kiswahili would be unnecessary, as well as unfeasible, given the restricted space for text on the exhibition panels.

Several families that visited the exhibitions soon emerged as important to follow up, all relations of three key Luo men photographed by Evans-Pritchard in 1936. These families were visited by Gilbert Oteyo for interviews and to make a presentation of framed copies of the photographs. It soon became clear that the presentation of copies of the framed portraits constituted a highly emotional homecoming for the families in question. When Oteyo visited the homestead of the late Chief Owuor of Asembo, he was introduced to his three surviving wives (he had ten in all), one of whom, Turfosa Omari, was photographed by Evans-Pritchard on his 1936 visit, since she had married Owuor earlier that year (see Figure 8.3). Holding the framed portrait of Owuor, Turfosa Omari called his name and touched his image, saying that her husband had returned, and telling everyone that here was the man she had married (Figure 8.12).

The framed photographs were then taken into one of the houses, and one was then placed next to a portrait of one of Owuor's sons, Paul Wariru, so that the family could compare their facial resemblance. The way in which the portraits were emotionally received, and more especially in the way they were treated afterwards, being taken to Owuor's grave where his name was called repeatedly, is in accord with findings in other ethnographic contexts, in which photographs

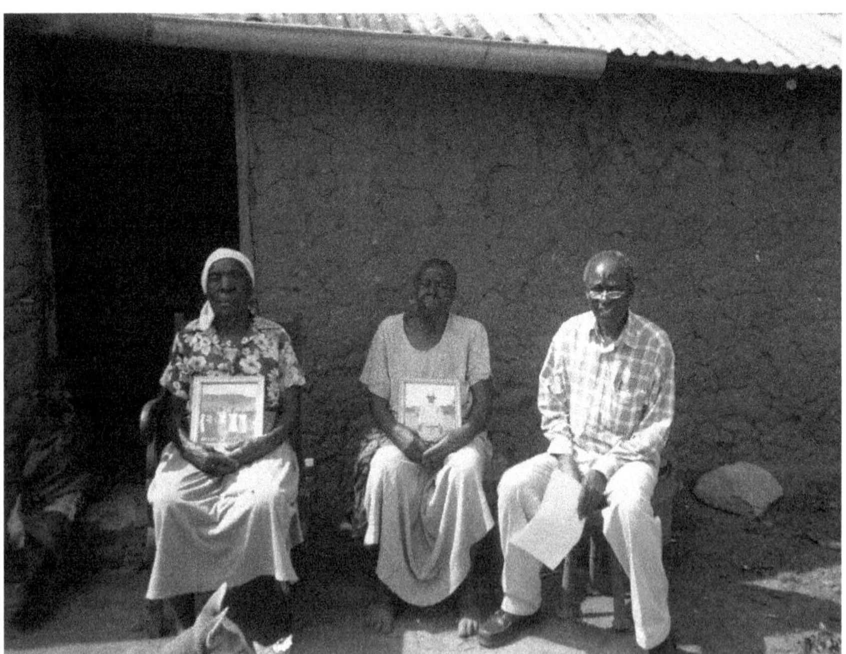

Figure 8.12 Two of Chief Owuor's surviving wives, Dorina Owuor (left) and Turfosa Omari (centre), with Gilbert Oteyo, holding the framed portraits of Owuor. Photograph by Perez Achieng, 2007.

are sometimes 'understood as one way in which the dead or absent kin and places can become (partially) present again'.[38] Other studies have focused on the use of photographs of deceased family members and elites as part of processes of commemoration, in which the mobilization of the photograph effectively extends the social agency of the deceased person beyond death. The anthropologist Charles Gore, for instance, discusses how images of previous Obas of Benin are mobilized to continue their agency into the present, and thereby bolster the hegemony of traditional rulers; and Karen Strassler also discusses the use of ancestor photographs in Chinese Javan domestic and commercial settings, linking it to Chinese rituals of ancestor worship.[39] It may be that the return of Owuor through his portrait constitutes a new extension of his agency or authority locally, problematic as that originally was, as I discussed above.

The next family visited by Oteyo was that of Ezekiel Onyango, who was the subject of a portrait by Evans-Pritchard in 1936 (Figure 8.13), who had married nine wives. The household head who greeted Oteyo was Charles Obewa, son of the third wife, who received a framed copy of the portrait of his grandfather. As with the family of Owuor, the portrait became the only treasured image of their relative, and was the starting point for many recollections. The portrait of Onyango is striking—he stands erect and to attention, with a cane held under his left arm, reflecting his rank as sergeant. The third family visited was that of Jacob Odawo, who is pictured a number of times by Evans-Pritchard, accompanying him and Archdeacon Owen on a number of occasions in his role as a native assessor (court interpreter and advisor on native custom), and who later became an assistant chief (see Figure 8.7, where Jacob stands to the left). Oteyo was able to meet his surviving wife, who, on seeing the portrait of her late husband, related how his involvement with accompanying Evans-Pritchard and Archdeacon Owen, as well as other outsiders, to sacred sites had led to problems for him when he was implicated in the disappearance of the spear of Alego, as well as other sacred objects. The taint of his involvement with this matter apparently never left him, and he lived in poverty later in life. The ongoing suffering of this particular family witnessed by Oteyo during this visit left Oteyo deeply troubled, and placed both Evans-Pritchard's and Owen's research into the Luo in a new historical perspective. The small cash gift that Oteyo made to the family on behalf of our exhibition project could not alter the fact that their situation was serious. As Oteyo wrote shortly afterwards:

It is saddening to say that during my family outreach, I witnessed their stark poverty...In one case, a young school-going boy who is a grandson of

---

[38] B. Smith and R. Vokes (eds). 2008. 'Introduction: haunting images', *Visual Anthropology*, 21(4) (special issue: Haunting Images: The Affective Power of Photography), 284.

[39] C. Gore. 2010. 'Commemoration, memory and ownership: some social contexts of contemporary photography in Benin City, Nigeria', *Visual Anthropology*, 14(3), 321–42; K. Strassler. 2010. *Refracted Visions: Popular Photography and National Modernity in Java*. Durham, NC, and London: Duke University Press.

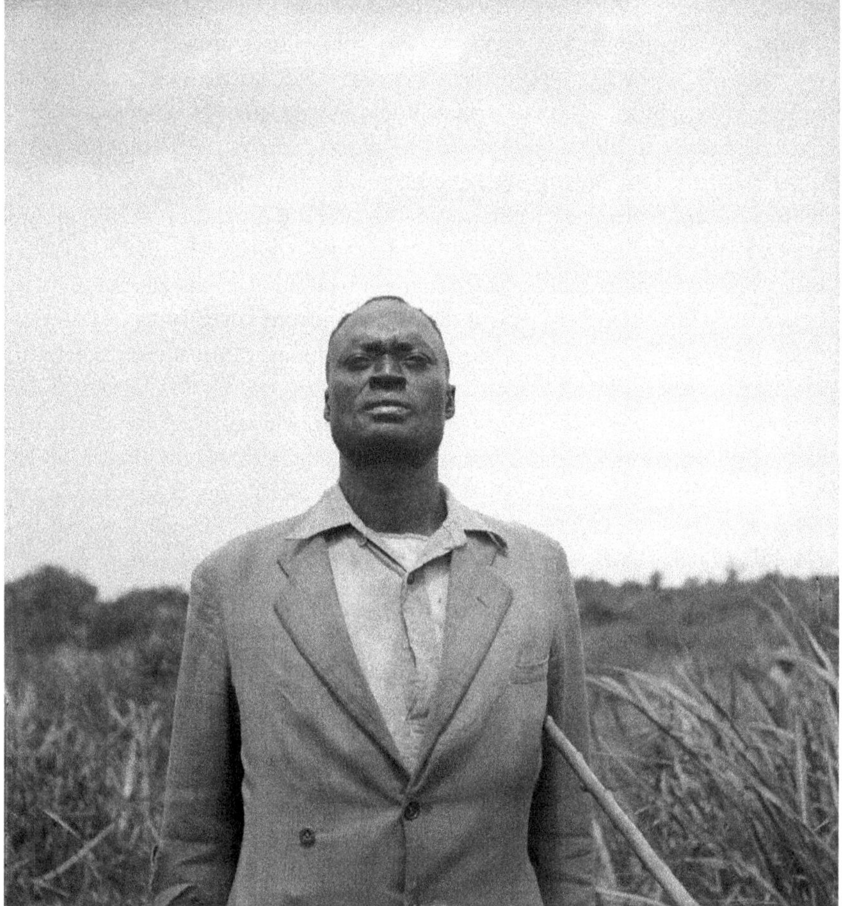

Figure 8.13 Portrait of Ezekiel Onyango. Photograph by E. E. Evans-Pritchard, 1936.

Evans-Pritchard's photographed Chief [Jacob Odawo] pleaded with me to help him buy school uniform. I was even more sympathetic to his jigger-infested feet than his going to school. I really do not know what I can do in such situations. As a Luo and more so as a researcher, I feel subdued when my informers are in this condition.

What the exhibition team were faced with at this point in the project was a conflict between the goals of a research project, in which the presentation of copies of historical photographs were considered integral to the research process, and a completely different set of priorities on the ground. While most people were pleased to receive copies of the photographs—and the emotional homecomings of some portraits attest to this—troubling questions emerged about the nature of the relationship thus formed between the families and the museum that houses the archive, and what its future intentions and obligations were. This situation was compounded by the fact that the family contacts were made by Oteyo and other Kenyan assistants, who did not represent the archive (the Pitt Rivers Museum in Oxford) directly, but who nonetheless were perceived as representatives by the families. What we had not anticipated was the fact that the visual homecoming of an ancestor from a remote Western archive was interpreted as the forging of a special relationship between the ancestor and those involved in the return.

On the back of several of Evans-Pritchard's working prints from his Luo trip in 1936 is the scribbled note 'Jacob wants', indicating that Jacob Odawo had requested copies at the time. Perhaps Evans-Pritchard did send him copies, but none had ever been seen by his surviving wife. The presentation made to her in 2007 went some way to fulfilling this seventy year-old fieldwork promise. But it does not address the expectations raised as a result. On 21 May 2008, more than a year after the exhibitions had ended, Oteyo wrote: 'Jacob's wife died yesterday and [is] to be buried Friday. The poor lady had left a request that I buy her burial material. The family came to see me today.' This experience was a stark reminder for us that this was more than an interesting research project, bringing Evans-Pritchard's photographs back after seventy years to the families of those he met and who informed his research. It was also a historical reminder of the long-term social implications of colonialism and scientific research conducted under its aegis for those families locally who had been involved in different ways. The extraordinary access to sacred sites and objects that Owen facilitated for Evans-Pritchard and other outsiders came at a significant cost to those who were involved.

Index